LIVERPOOL FC 2018/19 SEASON

THE OFFICIAL STORY

BY HARRY HARRIS

WITH ALAN BECK

Harry Harris has twice won the British Sports Journalist of the Year award. Formerly chief football correspondent for the *Daily Mirror*, he has also written for the *Daily Mail*, *Daily* and *Sunday Express* and *Star*, and is author of 80 books, including bestseller *Pelé – His Life And Times* and autobiographies of Steve McMahon, Ruud Gullit, Glenn Hoddle and many more, including George Best's last book *Hard Tackles And Dirty Baths*. Harry has appeared regularly over the years as a football analyst on TV and radio and has directed four football documentaries. He is co-owner and director of H&H Sports Media and lives in Sunningdale, Berkshire.

Alan Beck is a journalist and editor who has worked for BBC Sport, the FA, UEFA, England & Wales Cricket Board and Rugby World Cup, among many other organisations and publishers over a 20-year career in print and digital media. In 2018, he co-wrote *World Cup Motty* with BBC commentary legend John Motson and, at time of going to press, is writing and editing a book commemorating 25 years of Kick It Out, the body dedicated to eliminating discrimination of all kinds in football. He lives in Timperley, Cheshire with wife Kate, children Alfie and Mia and Peggy the dog.

CONTENTS

ACKNOWLEDGEMENTS

A ny book is a team effort: from the pitch process and initial research to editing, design, printing, marketing and distribution, there are always many behind the scenes whose vital work receives less attention than its importance deserves.

There are a few people whose contributions are particularly worthy of note regarding this publication and our sincere thanks go to: author Harry Harris and editor Alan Beck; Liverpool FC chief executive Peter Moore and UK licensing manager Christina Morley; Richard Freed, Ben Duffy, Stephen Mitchell, John Lewis and the rest of the team at publisher St James's House; and a host of Red legends who kindly gave their time for exclusive interviews.

Thank you to Jürgen Klopp, and Ian Rush and Jordan Henderson for supplying our foreword and afterwords, respectively, and to all the players, backroom staff and club employees who made the whole thing possible.

Credit must also be paid to numerous sources in print, online and broadcast that we have used to help complete the story of the 2018/19 season including, but not exclusively restricted to:

LFCTV, liverpoolfc.com, BBC Sport, BT Sport, Sky Sports, YouTube, The *Daily Telegraph*, *The Guardian*, *Daily Mail*, *Daily Mirror*, *Daily Express*, *The Independent*, *Evening Standard*, *Liverpool Echo*, Wikipedia, Twitter, uefa.com, lfchistory.net, lfcstats.co.uk, football-lineups.com, 11v11.com, transfermarkt.com, The Players' Tribune.

Finally, the deepest gratitude is due to you, the fans, for reading this account of the journey through an unforgettable football season and for your continued, dedicated support for Liverpool FC. You really are the point of it all.

CHIEF EXECUTIVE'S MESSAGE

It has been such a hectic time since we became European champions. We have been organising so much behind the scenes that it has been surreal at times, but well worth it all. And I am sure this book will be a worthy memento of such an epic and exciting season.

What has struck me in my second full season here at the club is that the chemistry and the talent within the squad, all brought together by a world-class manager, provides us with great optimism that they will bring even more silverware to this wonderful club.

Let's hope that like the old saying about London buses, when one comes along there are always two or three close behind. There's so much to look forward to from this brilliant team. You really cannot help but see us winning more trophies, although it is easier said than done. Having said that, we have the right infrastructure at Liverpool FC to give us a chance of making it happen.

I cannot be prouder of the Liverpool fans. They have been a credit to the club all season, never more so than when tens of thousands of them descended on Madrid and gave it a carnival atmosphere. There was not a hint of trouble and it was the perfect backdrop to a sixth European Cup win.

It has been an amazing journey this season, and I hope you enjoy reliving every step.

Peter Moore, CEO, Liverpool FC

FOREWORD

BY JÜRGEN KLOPP

The 2018/19 season is one everyone with Liverpool Football Club in their hearts will remember with joy. And not just because of how it ended in Madrid. Yes, of course this was a landmark moment for everyone involved; it's number 6 – it's history.

But this journey had so many moments we loved at the time and will be with us for generations. The destination is the most important part of any trip, but the route there can be something amazing also, if you allow it to be.

This season meant so much because we experienced these moments together. Players, supporters, management, staff – the whole LFC family. We came together as a community to create and share something special.

There are many parts that make a great club, but without doubt the most important two are the team and the supporters. At Liverpool we are blessed to have world class in both. And they share so many qualities. Both have passion and courage. Both are filled with belief and desire. Both understand the hard work you need to achieve something worthwhile. Both embrace the values of supporting your own team and helping your mates. Whatever they do, they do it together and for one another. That's how our story came to be this season.

My players this year did remarkable things. I called them mentality giants after we beat Barcelona, but that's not saying enough. Skill, intelligence, emotion, fitness – they have it all.

The most important thing for Liverpool fans when reliving the memories of this season is to remember it's the start – not a conclusion. Madrid wasn't the final chapter for us – I think we're still writing the introduction.

When we were travelling around Liverpool with the European Cup on that magical Sunday, the words that I heard sung the loudest were "We're never gonna stop!" That's what this team and club has to live by. We arrived at this point because we were hungry for moments like 1 June.

Take all the joy from this campaign and do so in the knowledge we want it again. Love the memories and use them to shape our future. Thank you again for the amazing support and happy reading!

You'll Never Walk Alone.

Jürgen Klopp

INTRODUCTION

INTRODUCTION

Does it matter when you embark on a story that you know how it ends? Many of us will have a favourite film that we've seen half a dozen times or more times, or a book that we return to after a few years, and while the experience is subtly different, it's no less enjoyable. The shock of the new is replaced by deeper understanding: awareness of details that weren't obvious the first time around, or anticipation of a delicious twist in the plot, all set against a backdrop of familiar characters who, over time, become old friends.

Similarly, we hope this review of Liverpool's 2018/19 season also brings a measure of joy in recounting one of the most extraordinary campaigns in the club's long history. The final tally adds a sixth European Cup to elevate the Reds even higher as the nation's leading representative in the competition. It also delivers sole tenure of third place in the Continental rankings ahead of Bayern and Barcelona and behind only Real Madrid and AC Milan. An epic title race was ultimately fruitless, yet it provided spellbinding entertainment from the first day to the last and we hope to have captured something of that excitement in the pages that follow.

We may not have got everything right. VAR may be coming to the Premier League next season but even with the advent of video evidence, football is still a game as much of opinions as it is of fact. A good proportion of what we love about the game is the post-match analysis on the sofa or the shop floor. So your own experience as a fan means you may not always agree with our version of events. And across an entire season there may be the odd blip in timings or personnel – a metaphorical misplaced pass or wrong number on the subs' board. For these, in the proud tradition of journalistic teamwork, your author and editor will seek to blame each other.

We have striven for accuracy and balance through numerous sources: print, online and broadcast media, including the invaluable documentation of the season by the club's official media outlets liverpoolfc.com and LFCTV. More detailed credits can be found at the back of the book.

And while we have also tried to build the story beyond events on the pitch, certain elements of the matchday experience may not realistically be included game-by-game. We're thinking here of important initiatives such as Fans Supporting Foodbanks (@SFoodBanks on Twitter), which has collected much-needed supplies for the local area throughout the season at home games, and to the ongoing efforts to deliver funds for the rehabilitation of injured fan Sean Cox.

Beyond these specific regulars we must also acknowledge the immense input of staff and players beyond those involved with the senior men's team – at Anfield, Melwood and in offices beyond: LFC Women, Academy, Foundation, coaches, physios, scouts, groundsmen, security, cleaners, bar staff, cooks, hospitality, stewards, administrators, press team, presenters, tour guides, technicians and many more. This book focuses almost exclusively on the achievements of the senior men this season but is dedicated to everyone who works for and on behalf of Liverpool FC.

Last but absolutely by no means least, we should recognise the contribution of the fans, from season-ticket holders and diehard travellers to every away game, to the locals who fill the pubs or pay their TV subs, and the millions of members of supporters' branches around the world who lend their voice to the amazing community of Reds. You have been the club's 12th man this season and none of it would have happened without your passion, pride and energy.

Let's get on with some football. And we begin, not quite at the beginning, but a little bit before – winding back to Kiev and defeat to Real Madrid in the 2018 Champions League final. It was a night when misfortune with injury, a couple of high-profile errors and, arguably, the finest goal ever seen in UEFA's showpiece final all conspired to deny Liverpool a sixth European Cup.

Those incidents – featuring Mohamed Salah, Loris Karius and Gareth Bale respectively – were the lightning rods for fans' regret; but it's easy to forget now just how much the Reds had outperformed pre-season expectations in even having the chance to return "Ol' Big Ears" to the Anfield trophy cabinet.

The mid-season loss of Philippe Coutinho to Barcelona was compensated for in spades by the astonishing form in front of goal of summer signing Mo Salah. The Egyptian's previous, comparatively quiet, spell in England with Chelsea had given few clues to his full potential beyond his searing pace on the flank. And even the rise in goal return with Roma that led to his signing on Merseyside was insufficient for any commentator to predict quite how effective Salah would be in his debut season.

Salah's 32 league goals represented a Premier League record for a 38-game season. Add 11 in 15 Champions League games and one in the club's only FA Cup tie and the tally reaches 44 goals from 52 appearances. These are numbers that elevate an attacker to a plateau of excellence in top-level European club football occupied in recent times only by serial Ballon d'Or winners Cristiano Ronaldo and Lionel Messi.

Reaching the final was a significant achievement in itself – a huge step forward for Jürgen Klopp's project. But on the home front, the league title was never a realistic proposition in 2017/18. Both Manchester clubs came flying out of the traps in the autumn: first United set the pace, then City took over and after 10 games Liverpool were 12 points behind the leaders in sixth. Tellingly, while City's goal difference at that point was +29, Liverpool's was +1. Scoring goals wasn't the issue; conceding them – 16 in 10 games – was. The stirring 4-0 win over Arsenal in August was followed by just one league win in six, including a 5-0 defeat at City (mitigated by the early sending off of Sadio Mané) and a 4-1 reverse to Tottenham at Wembley. Alongside draws against Burnley, Newcastle and Manchester United, inconsistency of performance allowed City to jump clear.

In the end, no one would come close to catching Pep's men. Records were sent tumbling as City reached 100 points, with 106 goals and only two league defeats all season. This last stat, though, contains the spark that ignited Liverpool's run to the Champions League final. On 14 January, with the Sky Blues serenely cantering towards the title, Jürgen Klopp's side showed they weren't invincible. They could be disrupted. And they could be beaten. In a crazy 10-minute spell at Anfield, Liverpool scored three goals to lead 4-1; and though a late rally brought the score back to 4-3, it proved that with sufficient pressure high up the pitch, City's defence – committed to a passing style come what may – was capable of errors.

Though it meant little on the context of the Premier League, as Liverpool refocused efforts on Europe, that result was banked by Klopp and his players and paid out over two fearless legs of the Champions League quarter-final in April. Precision on the break, plus a thunderbolt finish from Alex Oxlade-Chamberlain and a clean sheet, helped seize control with a 3-0 win at Anfield. And despite a fast start from City at the Etihad – Gabriel Jesus scoring inside two minutes – a determined defensive display was capped by away goals from the irrepressible Salah and Roberto Firmino. Over four games between England's most effective side and its most entertaining, the final score was 9-8 to Liverpool. The title was all but settled, but it was the Reds looking forward to a semi-final against Roma (another goalfest) and eventually that date with Real Madrid.

As much as the goals were flying in from Salah, Firmino and Mané, the second half of Liverpool's season was also notable for the way January signing Virgil van Dijk settled immediately into a leadership role at the heart of the defence. Strengthening at centre-half had been a priority for Klopp and the Dutch international from Southampton became a virtual ever-present from the end of January to May. His abilities both in the air and on the deck brought an increased solidity to the team – qualities that only increased in influence during his first full season on Merseyside.

The emergence, too, of young, pacy, direct full-backs in Andrew Robertson and Trent Alexander-Arnold gave much cause for optimism in the defensive ranks for 2018/19. Much more on this, of course, to follow.

But to pack away season 2017/18, we can reflect that while Kiev hurt, Liverpool were not outclassed. It was a testament to Klopp's efforts in his first two and a half years in charge that his side looked worthy of a place back at the very top table of the European game.

And far from dwelling on defeat, many of the squad soon had other footballing matters on their minds, joining up with their national squads ahead of the World Cup in Russia.

A patched-up Salah went out in the group stage with Egypt, as did Mané with Senegal, while Firmino scored for Brazil against Mexico but fell to Belgium in the quarter-finals. England duo Jordan Henderson and Trent Alexander-Arnold enjoyed the renaissance and ride to the semis under Gareth Southgate; but only Dejan Lovren was left as the last Liverpool player standing, reaching the final with Croatia.

Meanwhile, back at Liverpool FC's training ground Melwood, planning was in earnest for the new campaign. It had become self-evident over recent years that for so long as the summer transfer window overlapped the start of the league season, it was strongly in the interest of clubs to conclude their transfer business in good time. But with this summer's Premier League deadline day brought forward to 9 August, and a World Cup to play for many transfer targets during the window, that focus intensified further.

The only high-profile departure from the club in summer 2018 was that of German midfielder Emre Can, who left to join Juventus when his contract expired at the end of June. Four players were on their way in. Naby Keïta, a dynamic Guinean central midfielder whose signing was arranged in summer 2017 finally arrived from RB Leipzig on 1 July. He joined Brazilian Fabinho, also strengthening the midfield, who was signed from AS Monaco. A desire for depth in creativity prompted the signing of Swiss playmaker Xherdan Shaqiri from relegated Stoke City; while Roma's Alisson Becker was the target sought and acquired to fill the number 1 role between the Anfield sticks.

A truncated pre-season leaned heavily on match practice. Nine matches were compressed into the month between 7 July and 7 August, including the International Champions Cup in the US, where a 3-1 defeat to Borussia Dortmund was followed by wins over both Manchester City and United.

Leg-stretchers they may have been before the main event kicked off, but the goals, encouragingly, were flowing. Two against City and four in that defeat of United – including a stunning bicycle-kick by new boy Shaqiri – in front of a crowd of more than 100,000 in balmy Michigan.

As it happened, the Reds attackers were just getting warmed up.

CHAPTER 1

—

AUGUST

"WE ARE STILL ROCKY BALBOA,
THEY ARE IVAN DRAGO"

A short time spent in an empty press box at Anfield is a rare and peaceful experience. On match day the rows of swing-out seats are packed with journalists and the tabletops alive with sounds of furious typing and broadcast chatter, but now all is quiet. Or quiet-ish. Even in the summer months the stadium doesn't sleep.

Across the widely striped pitch, two groundsmen push their humming mowers in opposite directions. Distantly there is a piped-in roar and a fragment of "The Fields of Anfield Road" from some time when the stadium was filled with 50,000 souls in unison.

Over in the Kop, a group of teenagers on a stadium tour starts singing. It's hard to make out at first – a terrace anthem? – but slowly becomes familiar, if a little unexpected. They're belting out the French national anthem, "La Marseillaise". The kids give themselves a round of applause and wander out of the arena laughing.

Cotton-wool clouds drift overhead, their shadows flitting over the turf and up row after row of empty seats. Except they are not so much empty as presently unoccupied. There's a difference. Most of these numbered spots represent a personal home from home, season tickets for the journey, a small but highly prized tenancy with a terrific garden. Soon they will fill again in eager anticipation of the first whistle and the season ahead – the Reds faithful called back to the temple on the hill. But not yet; not quite.

The Liverpool squad returned from the States for the final two fixtures of pre-season with Britain still basking in temperatures in the high twenties. But en route back to Merseyside there was a stopover in Ireland for August's first fixture, the team taking on Napoli at the Aviva Stadium in Dublin in the penultimate pre-season clash of the summer.

And the team continued just as they had concluded in Ann Arbor with goals aplenty. Clad all in purple, the "Reds" made short work of one of Italy's Champions League contenders. Klopp's men were two-up in 10 minutes through James Milner and Gini Wijnaldum; and the match became a procession in the second half, with thunderous strikes from Mo Salah, Daniel Sturridge and – with the pick of the lot – Alberto Moreno.

The only downside was a nasty head injury sustained by James Milner in a collision with Portuguese defender Mario Rui that required 15 stitches. It was a serious wound, although not so much as to dampen the overall good humour. Jürgen Klopp joked that Milner was in a positive frame of mind as he had not yet been handed a mirror.

Now it was back to Anfield, for the final warm-up game against Torino – the first time the teams had ever met – and another stylish display in front of a buoyant homecoming crowd. Fabinho was given the chance to mark his first appearance in L4 with a goal but dragged an early penalty kick wide. However, Roberto Firmino soon put Liverpool ahead with a hooked shot into the top corner.

A lightning break sent Wijnaldum through to slide the ball under Torino keeper Salvatore Sirigu, and although the Italians hit back almost immediately with a bullet header from Andrea Belotti, a much-changed second half line-up for the Reds – including Jordan Henderson's first outing since the World Cup – signed off final preparations, with Sturridge nodding home Shaqiri's glorious dinked cross. A fine flourish.

The manager expressed his satisfaction at a job – and pre-season – much to his liking. "The players from last year are responsible for the excitement, and then we brought in a few new players as the icing on the cake," he said post-match. "I'm happy that we came through the pre-season so far, so good."

"Now we have to make the last step, we have to bring ourselves into the competition, in a championship mood, really being 100 per cent focused in all situations," he added. "Obviously in the offensive department we are able to do some nice things but that's only one part of the game. We have [only] a few days but I like that. I'm happy we can start at the weekend because pre-season is good but the season is even better."

How much better, time would tell.

In the lead-up to the season opener against West Ham, Klopp set the tone for the season with a typically inventive sound bite. Much had been made in the media of Liverpool's spending over the summer. More than in recent seasons and more, by estimated total, than any other club in the Premier League in this transfer window. Did this – added to the epic run to Kiev – make the Merseysiders favourites for the league title?

Klopp was having none of it: "We are still Rocky Balboa. They are Ivan Drago. We are the ones who have to do more. We have to fight more. That must be our attitude. We have to be like Rocky."

That summed up the epic struggle to topple champions Manchester City. Klopp's message at the outset was that Liverpool were determined to chase down the title favourites and the season lived up to the billing on the card. Punch followed punch as the league lead changed hands multiple times

– fortunes swaying as each sought to gain the upper hand, to establish a dominant momentum and, hopefully, deliver a knockout blow.

City manager Pep Guardiola was laconic in his response to Klopp's suggestion the holders were still clear front-runners for the league crown. "For nine years I've lived with [the favourites tag], no problem," said the Spaniard. "Every season except the first one when I arrived at Barcelona, when I had people who didn't know I was a manager. Since then we have always been the favourites. But thank you, Jürgen. You are so kind."

Defending the Premier League title, however, is no mean achievement. In the decade since Manchester United won three in succession from 2007 to 2009, no one had since managed the feat. Pundits, though, were virtually unanimous in their belief that City would be unstoppable n 2018/19.

Guardiola was guarding against complacency. "It's a challenge [to defend the title]," he argued. "If we play well, we have the chance to repeat it. If we are going to win, we have to prepare to be better. It's a big mistake to think about last season or that we are going to win. The best way is the training session, next game and then the next one. We'll see at the end of the season. I don't think too much about back-to-back, defending the title. The main thing is to improve. Then? We will see."

From a purely statistical perspective, Liverpool had acres of ground to make up. A fourth-placed league finish in May 2018 left Klopp's team 25 points behind City, yet that also should be put in the context of a staggering achievement by Pep's men. That title race featured City, fresh air and then everyone else.

It was the subplot of league and European wins over the Sky Blues that suggested Liverpool were much closer than the points gap suggested. "You all ask me about the gap to City and what we have to do, [but] it has nothing to do with City," Klopp said. "City took three points from us, we took three points from them, but we lost them in other games. Win all of them and it is good, but it is pretty difficult to do because not only the other Big Six – you see how Wolverhampton acts, how Fulham acts and how Everton acts – they are all ambitious."

"I don't think too much about what we have to do," he added. "I thought about it [in] pre-season but now we have to be in this championship mood. It is like [when] you jump in the water and dive and then you don't have enough air anymore and you have to go up again. That is the plan – that we really go for it."

It was a lung-busting mantra that would impose intense demands upon Klopp's players over a gruelling campaign but one that spoke to a demonstrable truth about title-winning sides. They are never outfought; never outrun.

So what about this side? Once the manager had taken the chance to run his rule over them in pre-season, what was his verdict on the squad and its additional strength through summer acquisitions?

"My own expectations are always pretty high," he said. "I think for us it was pretty normal there would be one point where we spend more money. The last few years I've had to sit here and defend our transfer behaviour [when] we sold more than we brought in. It all makes sense, we had to create a squad which is strong enough and wide enough to cope with the Premier League.

"People ask me is it the best squad I've ever had? I don't think about that. It's about what we make of it, how often we deliver, how often we bring ourselves in a mood to fight against all these Premier League teams who want to have our points."

Klopp's summer business in midfield in securing the services of Naby Keïta and Fabinho was intended to back-fill and then strengthen in the absence of Emre Can, after the German international rejected the offer of a new contract and left on a free for Juventus. On the departure of his countryman for Italy, the manager had a pragmatic view: "I have no problem with a player leaving," Klopp told the *Liverpool Echo*. "The only problem I had for the club was that I wanted to get some money: 'Sign a new contract and then we'll sell you!' But that wasn't really realistic.

"There was never a problem between Emre and me. [He] is 24 now. Playing in another country can be a life target: 'I've spent four years in England, now I want to go somewhere else.' Why not? He's a top player and he's gone to a top club."

A shake-up in the goalkeeping department was all but inevitable once the club's acquisition of Alisson from Roma was confirmed; hence Danny Ward departed for Leicester City the following day, while Loris Karius joined Turkish side Beşiktaş on a two-year loan deal. Simon Mignolet stayed and was joined by academy graduate Caoimhin Kelleher to complete the first-team keeping cohort.

In attack, the tying of Mo Salah to a new deal was the first and most crucial order of business, sorted in early July, but the performances of an injury-free Daniel Sturridge in pre-season were also a boost.

"I can't remember a bad game off him in pre-season," said Klopp. "When Daniel is fit, nobody doubts him. I do not. He's here, he's in a good shape, hopefully he can bring that into the season."

Sturridge would be deployed mostly as a substitute – eventually making only four league starts – given the settled nature of the team's first-choice front three. But alongside Divock Origi, he gave a depth to the forward-line so critical when chasing silverware on multiple fronts.

Ensuring sufficient squad depth is a familiar enough item on the managerial checklist but some of Klopp's preparations fly somewhat under the radar. Consider the appointment of specialist throw-in coach Thomas Grønnemark – the subject of some media scepticism but very much of a piece with the modern recognition of marginal gains as critical to top-level sporting success.

The Dane had previously worked with Midtjylland and Bündesliga sides Schalke and Hertha Berlin and also worked with Denmark's athletics and bobsled teams. He holds the world record for the longest throw-in, at 51.33 metres, but his brief was not to turn Liverpool's wide players into latter-day Rory Delaps. More it was to understand and master the range of attacking potential at restarts – and also to avoid situations where the team could be put under pressure from their own throw-ins and, likewise, take advantage of teams that are less well drilled.

Klopp estimated that Liverpool take or defend around 50 throw-ins per match, and felt his players squandered possession too often from these set plays. Grønnemark told the BBC: "If you are expecting professional footballers to be world-class throwers without coaching then you are pretty optimistic. Generally the standard is quite poor.

"A focus on throw-ins can save the life of small clubs, as a technique to survive. But at the top of the league, it can help with a more fluent style of play. No matter what position in the league, throw-ins are an advantage."

Such innovations appearing in Klopp's instruction manual for Liverpool should come as no surprise to those who know something of the German's rise to his current lofty position. He's on record as ascribing any success and longevity in his playing career as a triumph of brains over ball skills. When he was appointed as head coach by Borussia Dortmund in 2008, he was asked by a German newspaper why he never made it to the top flight as a player. "I had fourth-division talent and a first-division head," he quipped. "That resulted in the second division."

In 11 years with Mainz 05, Klopp made 325 league appearances, mostly up front, before reinventing himself as a central defender in his later years. After hanging up his boots in 2001, aged 33, he moved into the dugout, saved the team from relegation with one game to spare in his first season; and within three years had guided them into the Bündesliga for the first time in their history.

Although Mainz were subsequently relegated in 2008, bigger clubs had seen enough of Klopp's potential to add him to their managerial shortlists and he was immediately appointed by Dortmund.

There, his high-pressing style took immediate effect, lifting BVB from 13th in 2007/08 to sixth, then fifth and eventually, in 2010/11, to the league title itself. He then went one better with a league and cup double in 2011/12 and came within a whisker of the Champions League in 2013, losing 2-1 to arch rivals Bayern Munich and a last-minute Arjen Robben goal at Wembley.

These were the peaks, the most visible result of Klopp's managerial expertise. But alongside the trophies, what was emerging – and this is perhaps more significant to the wider game – was a distinctive style, a rapid-transitioning type of football that lay almost in direct opposition to the dominant "tiki-taka" style that had earned so much success for Barcelona and the Spanish national team in preceding years.

With Marco Reus and Mario Götze (for line-up purposes at least) either side of the prolific Robert Lewandowski, Klopp in fact deployed his numbers 9, 10 and 11 in 2012/13 as a fluid and interchangeable front three who could break at pace. They filled their boots with a shared 62 goals in all competitions. Sound familiar?

For that front-line, now read Mané, Firmino and Salah – a new trio with which Klopp could implement his vision of attacking, entertaining football, this time in England.

In August, the German was asked by *France Football* magazine how he would describe his style of play. His response suggested that, while on the surface his strategy may look like a template drawn from one club to another, Klopp prefers his framework to be seen to be seen as one designed to give the game more feel. He leans less on a dogmatic insistence on possession and more on an instruction to "go and play".

"What is my style? Well, you know what? I have been a coach for 18 years and I haven't even thought about this question," he said. "I don't really get what it means. I love the game, it's as simple as that. When I watch a match,

I always see things I like, if not, it would be a waste of time.

"Entertainment is the most important part of football," he added. "There are too many serious problems in the world to make football boring, too. I want to see happiness with my players, passion in their eyes and a desire to fight. I want to see them bursting [with energy], to surprise me, to look what's on their right, to try and make a pass to their left – that sort of thing."

On the matter of the upcoming season, Klopp was keen to manage expectations and also stress the privilege he felt at being at the helm of this iconic club.

"Liverpool's history is made up of battles," he said. "And when you battle, you never expect it to be easy. Why would it be now? Yes, we're aiming for the stars, but we respect the game. I feel the size of the club and above all the honour given to me to lead the team. Last year, I turned 50 and I invited quite a lot of people to celebrate. I hadn't seen some of them for 20 years. The words that I heard most were: 'Who would have thought it? That you would, one day, be manager of Liverpool?' It's true that when you're born in the Black Forest and you have played in Germany's seventh division, it seems improbable. I didn't even dream of being a professional or having a career in football... so for me, I'm at the club that suits me to achieve every goal."

The league campaign kicked off on Sunday lunchtime of the opening weekend – so after the bulk of the fixtures but ahead of Manchester City's trip to Arsenal – and changeable, blustery conditions greeted the Reds and visitors West Ham United.

There was a good deal of novelty for the home supporters to drink in during a freewheeling 4-0 win. Naby Keïta was the standout performer in midfield, snapping into tackles and showing a fine range of distribution. The *Liverpool Echo*'s Ian Doyle enjoyed the debutant's display, writing:

"Almost 12 months have passed since Naby Keïta agreed a move to Liverpool, a time during which hype and anticipation among supporters grew to almost unprecedented levels. So when the Guinea international finally stepped out at Anfield for his competitive debut, expectation weighed heavily on his shoulders. Has Keïta been worth the wait?

"On this initial evidence, the answer is most certainly in the affirmative. Having caused a stir with some early performances in pre-season, a neck injury had the welcome effect of shifting the spotlight away from the former RB Leipzig man. Here, though, he was centre stage. And how.

"Keïta keeps it simple when he has to, knows when to make a run and isn't averse to the flamboyant. This wasn't a perfect debut – some needless loose play and one wild shot saw to that – and early predictions are always fraught with danger. But rarely can a player have looked so at home after such a short period."

New keeper Alisson was barely troubled, James Milner – sporting a large bandage to protect the head wound sustained against Napoli – was a constant threat from his new station on the right wing, and Klopp was able to summon Henderson, Shaqiri and Sturridge from a notably strong bench. Sturridge, who had top scored in pre-season, rounded off the goalfest with his first touch, mere seconds after coming on.

The manager was thrilled with how his side were able to maintain their momentum in a first competitive test of the campaign. "You cannot wish for better," he said in his post-match press conference. "It was a fresh start from the first minute, everything looked like it should have been.

"It's a good day. It's only the start, and we know that, but for a start it was really good. We all know West Ham have a lot of individual quality. In all other situations we were really concentrated defensively. It's a good game, but for the moment, it's no more. It's a nice moment, and we can enjoy it for two, three hours, and then prepare for Crystal Palace.

On Sturridge's instant impact: "What was it, 10 seconds? 12 seconds? Ha! Sometimes you need luck in life. He didn't need luck in that situation; he only has the nose for it in those situations. It's brilliant. Sturridge had a fantastic pre-season, the best since I've been here, and it gives us unbelievable new options."

A trip to Selhurst Park to face Crystal Palace was quite a different undertaking, with the Eagles having won away at Fulham on the opening day – a positive start entirely at odds with the previous campaign's goalless losing streak that ended Frank de Boer's short reign at the club.

With former Reds and England boss Roy Hodgson in the dugout, Palace recovered from stone-last to finish 11th and boasted vibrant attacking options in the pacy Wilfried Zaha and Andros Townsend, the hulking physical presence of Christian Benteke and captain and dead-ball specialist Luka Milivojević.

Jürgen Klopp was particularly mindful of Zaha, given how he had tested Trent Alexander-Arnold in the previous season's fixture. "Zaha is exceptional, that's true," he said. "If you leave any full back alone, nobody is able to defend Zaha. But we will not do that. Trent is very smart, a very serious football player. He wants to play, perform, and show his best."

In a rare occurrence Klopp named an unchanged side, one that would undergo a far stiffer examination than that posed by West Ham. Andros Townsend smacked one long-range shot against the bar in the first half, while Alisson had to be at his most alert to scramble behind his wall and claw the ball away when a Milivojević free kick seemed destined for the top corner.

Liverpool's back-line was given a stern test, and afterwards Reds defensive stalwart Jamie Carragher was effusive in his praise for Virgil van Dijk, suggesting the Dutchman had the potential to be as influential to this side as Alan Hansen was in the 1980s.

"[Van Dijk] should be disappointed if he's not alongside Hansen when in 20 years' time we're thinking of great Liverpool central defenders," said Carragher on Sky Sports' *Monday Night Football*.

"I don't there is another centre back who can almost tick every box. You think of the presence, the pace, the strength, ability on the ball. Normally a player will have a couple of those and are lacking somewhere else and they'll have to cover up for that. You'll have different strengths, but he's got all of them at the moment and players like him in this team now need to be the ones, those leaders who take Liverpool to something bigger and to when they win something big."

Co-presenter Gary Neville concurred: "He's a far better defender than I thought he was. The impact is far greater than I thought it was. He's a monster. He reminds me a little bit of what Jaap Stam was doing at United in terms of his level of performances."

In the end, the result was swung by two fouls, both on Mo Salah: the first was by Mamadou Sakho as the Egyptian twisted in the box. James Milner tucked away the spot kick in first-half injury time; the second was by Aaron Wan-Bissaka as Salah sprinted clear with 15 minutes left. Deemed the last man, the defender was shown a straight red.

The points weren't safe, though, until the third minute of added time, when Sadio Mané finished a lightning break by rounding Hennessey and tucking the ball home.

Post-match, van Dijk sought to emphasise the team element: "It is all about adapting the style of play. It is about being comfortable at the back. We have an amazing team and amazing manager." But it was increasingly clear how vital an individual presence – in terms both of defensive ability and leadership – the Dutchman was becoming in this side.

"It [was] a very tough game," he added. "We knew before the game it would be. We know how direct Crystal Palace are looking for Benteke and then [Zaha]. I don't think the big teams ever win here comfortably. I think [it's] a well-deserved three points and clean sheet.

"We showed a lot of good things today – we need to be proud of ourselves today. We've got to try to win everything. It's been a while but we don't need to think too much ahead. We've only played two games, it'll be a very long road and a tough year."

Wise words. Just how long and tough was emphasised by the fact even two wins, six goals and none conceded wasn't enough to stay top of the table. Manchester City had hammered Huddersfield Town 6-1 on Sunday to sneak ahead by one goal. Even at this early stage, the shape of the title race to come was beginning to emerge.

Sadio Mané's three goals delivered the headline stat from the Reds' opening two fixtures and his manager suggested that he was beginning to realise his full potential.

"Now [Sadio] is much more secure that this is his level," said Klopp. "The players surprise themselves sometimes – 'Wow, really? That's how good I am?'! We all need to show our best and get used to it.

"We have to make sure we can show that every week. Who scores the goals is not too important, but it was very important for us and very nice for him that he could do it in the last game. Sadio's a very consistent player for us. His work rate is great."

Meanwhile, James Milner believed the difference between the West Ham and Palace games showed team were getting better at grinding out results.

"That's something we have to work on: winning all different types of games," he told the club's website. "We know with the players that we have going forward, if we keep those clean sheets then we've got every chance of nicking a goal at the other end. So, it comes from the keeper and all the way through the back four and all the way through the team and the way we play. Everyone defends together."

Next up were Brighton & Hove Albion and the need to approach every game with the requisite focus was highlighted sharply by the fact Chris Hughton's men had put a dent in Man United's early-season hopes with a surprise 3-2 win at the Amex. Sluggish defending cost José Mourinho's team three first-half goals and Klopp was keen to ensure no such complacency affected Brighton's visit to Anfield, not least since it was only three league games ago – on the final day of 2017/18 – that they last met on Merseyside, a 4-0 home win.

"I don't want to compare the last game of last season to this game," Klopp said. "Brighton saved [themselves from relegation] the week before and we had to fight for our lives [to stay in the top four]. It's a very good team, I respect a lot what Chris is doing. Not only the Manchester United game, [although] we used it for our analysis – it was impressive. Very organised, United were unlucky in one or two situations. I have a lot of respect, we have been warned, we have to be awake. So much positivity around here at the moment, and I like that, but we have to be awake and ready to work. It's good, but we play a very good Brighton side with an obvious good result last week."

The manager said he considered changes to the starting XI for the first time this season – with Alberto Moreno, Fabinho and Jordan Henderson all awaiting a first start – but decided again to name an unchanged side.

"I don't think it makes sense to stick to a team only because we won. We have quality in the squad and there can be different reasons to change the line-up, so that's possible of course."

Klopp said he wanted Fabinho to follow the examples of Alex Oxlade-Chamberlain and Andy Robertson, who overcame slow starts at the club before establishing themselves as first-team regulars.

"It is about players understanding the position and who else is available as well, otherwise Fabinho would have been involved in the squad as he was in the first week. It is different football to what he is used to, but he is improving already with big steps. I can see that in the sessions and that is cool. He is used to playing at a high level in France. It is not about who we play but about how we play. It is all fine. For sure, it is not nice for a new player [not to be playing]. It never was. But you see Andy Robertson running around here at Melwood now and he's a completely different person to the one who was here in the first three months. That's how it is. And everything will be fine with Fabinho."

An early evening start at Anfield allowed the fans to size up rivals' fortunes earlier in the day and they welcomed news from Molineux that Wolves had held Man City to a 1-1 draw in the lunchtime kick-off. And though Liverpool were never at their fluent best against the Seagulls, a scrappy 1-0 win was enough to restore them to the league summit.

A match of few chances was decided by a single passage of excellence, as Brighton's otherwise obdurate defence played themselves into trouble and a one-touch combination between Mané, Firmino and Salah resulted in a neatly taken winning goal from the Egyptian.

Brighton might have stolen a point at the death, but substitute Pascal Gross's header was palmed away superbly by Alisson, meaning a third clean sheet out of three, despite a few anxious moments – including one tribute to his Brazilian heritage in a cheeky chip over the onrushing Anthony Knockaert after Virgil van Dijk left a back pass short.

"If it works, then it's cool," Klopp said after the match. "I had a few centre-halves who were able to do things a centre-half should not do, like Mats Hummels [at Borussia Dortmund] constantly doing things which made no sense, but he was really good in there. Alisson is obviously a goalkeeper who can play football, which is good. He's confident enough to do it. He didn't do it for showing off, he did it to sort the situation. He has a nice level of confidence, so he uses that. I like the save from the header more than the chip, but the chip was the right thing to do in that situation."

Of more concern to the manager was the noticeable drop in intensity that afflicted Liverpool's performance after half-time. "In the second half we lost the plot," Klopp admitted. "The freshness, the intensity, the legs – all these things. We had outstanding counter-pressing situations in the first half. In the second half we had none. We were still around but we didn't win the balls.

"It's not because the boys didn't want it but because they felt the intensity. After winning 4-0 we didn't run around Melwood for the rest of the week with our arms in the air! We will not do it this week. We will prepare for Leicester. We have a lot of things to improve but it's clear that still winning on a not perfect day gives you different opportunities."

In other words, winners know how to "win ugly". "That is clear", agreed Klopp. "I've spoken about this a lot – [before] if we are good then we win, if we are average then very often, we lost. That is what we have to change. We want to be brilliant all the time but, if that doesn't happen, that doesn't mean we don't go for a result. We fought for this result and so I am really happy."

The final tally for the month read three wins, seven goals, none conceded, but beyond the bare stats was the knowledge that Liverpool had found three different ways to win in three very different games.

At the end of August, Liverpool managing director Billy Hogan gave an interview to the *Liverpool Echo* in which he claimed this "sleeping giant" of a club had been awoken. The club had undergone a dramatic transformation off the field in the six years since Hogan joined as chief commercial officer, with owners Fenway Sports Group overseeing the redevelopment of Anfield and the impending move to a new training ground, while Jürgen Klopp led a resurgence on the pitch.

"There's a huge desire to return the club to where we believe it belongs at the top of world football," Hogan said. "Sitting here today, the club is in a tremendously positive place. The football is terrific, the team is playing great and we're all excited about the future."

Hogan paid tribute to the impact Klopp had made to the club on and off the field. "Jürgen is a big personality and he's also tremendously supportive. The 'Klopp factor' is more than just about his interaction with football, it's across the whole club. He's a tremendous fit and we're so happy that he's here. We're starting to see the culmination of the strategy we've been following. Getting to this place, seeing the way this team is playing and the amount of talent in the squad – seeing what the guys have done at Melwood and the academy – is fantastic. If you go back to when FSG first started looking at Liverpool as an opportunity, people were referring to the club as a sleeping giant. I think that's something that's been proven to be true."

People at all levels of the club were enthused by the bright start to the new campaign that they had all hoped for. Club CEO Peter Moore was one among them. Born locally, brought up a Red, the 63-year-old Chief Executive considered this his dream job.

"I am Liverpool born and bred," said Moore proudly. "My dad managed a local pub; my mum was a nurse at Alder Hey Children's Hospital. I watched my first match at Anfield in 1959 when I was four. I can still remember the score – Liverpool 4 Leyton Orient 3 – Phil Taylor was the manager. The next month some Scotsman called Shankly took over! Back then the club was languishing down in Division Two but how things have changed.

"My love for the club has remained, it has never diminished and never will. I've followed the family tradition from my grandad to my dad and it's a part of me.

"I grew up knowing Liverpool's Scotland Road near the stadium like the back of my hand; but in the mid-60s, when I was eight years old, we moved to North Wales where my dad became a licensee. Fast-forward through a short career as a PE teacher and I moved to the US as a soccer coach. In those days it was hard to find out the results as the newspapers hardly bothered covering 'soccer'. Now, of course, the Premier League is big news over there, it is covered much more widely, and NBC Sport have been showing the games for some time now."

Peter was a huge success in his career Stateside. From football coaching he completed a master's degree at California State University, Long Beach and then began a career in sports merchandise with French football boot company Patrick. After 11 years he rose to president of the company before taking charge at Reebok as head of global sports.

It was with Reebok that he secured a standout deal with Liverpool in 1996 but after a long spell in Boston, he sought a change of scenery. This brought him to the west coast, where he began work with SEGA, then Microsoft and Electronic Arts where he became Chief Operating Officer in August 2011. He resigned from EA in February 2017 to become CEO of Liverpool Football Club.

Now he has arrived at his beloved Anfield, what does his role entail? "I run the business of the football club, making sure all the variety of operations run efficiently. I know some people think we put on a football match almost with our eyes closed, that it must be a simple process of opening the doors, and everyone strolls through! In reality, it is a massive logistics operation.

"My main role is driving commercial revenues, plus overseeing the club's civic and community responsibilities, something that we take extremely seriously; and are, in fact, very proud of what we do and what we have achieved with LFC Foundation and Red Neighbours, helping the local people in and around Anfield, in one of the most impoverished areas of the city and indeed the country.

"We take on some big projects with an emphasis on education and assisting young children. We have food banks in and around the area of the stadium. It is surprising how many people drop off food on their way to Anfield and we have a number of drop-off points around the stadium. It is saddening, in 2018, just how many people still have a problem putting food on the table for their families.

"Red Neighbours is an initiative to work on the three postcodes L4/L5/L6 and help the most deprived 1 per cent in and around our stadium who need food and assistance. It's an irony that we have such a magnificent stadium and millions of pounds worth of players, but we are also surrounded by some of the most socially and economically stressed parts of the country.

"Our objective is to break that cycle of poverty, otherwise the kids in these areas won't have the chance to break away from it. The use of our badge is a powerful motivational tool. You can see the kids' faces light up when they see our staff enter the room in the tracksuits with the liver bird club crest, and how they react and participate is very important to us. It's vital we give them some opportunities in life, and if we can make the children happy, then there is every chance their parents will also be happy."

Peter is also immensely proud of that fact the football club is one of the biggest employers in the area. He explained: "Liverpool FC is the number one tourist attraction in the city. We commissioned an economic impact report in the Metro region with Deloitte Sports Group, and it found that we generate over £700 million a year for the Metro Liverpool area, which includes the money people spend that we attract into the area, the amount of wages we pay, et cetera. We have more than 700 employees, while on match days we have an army of 2,500 workers, including stewards, retail stores, office staff, ticket office staff, people pulling pints, supplying the catering from burgers to upscale hospitality."

One of Peter's most popular initiatives has been a campaign to embrace all former Liverpool players under the umbrella "Forever Reds". "When I arrived at the club, there were many legends involved in numerous activities some employed for hospitality purposes and forums, but I felt it was worth bringing them all together. So we set about locating every single player, even if they had played only one game for the first team, with our search being worldwide, but with today's lines of communication it wasn't that difficult to track down virtually everyone.

"We have found more than 300 Liverpool first-team players, embracing the likes of Ian Callaghan to Jamie Carragher and everyone in-between. The objective is to keep them informed of club activities, opportunities to bring them together and invite them to our games.

"Roger Hunt and his wife came to a game and he was one of my heroes. I asked him why, when you look at the pictures of the time, he has spun away when Geoff Hurst's shot hit the bar in the World Cup Final. His answer was that he knew it had crossed the line and had no reason to stop to ask the question. What a gentleman.

"And all the players we invite to the games love to be remembered. For my part I believe the club has an obligation to cherish their memory. This club has a fine and rich history, it is in fact, a unique history, and we owe that to our former players. We have entertained Phil Neal, Chris Lawler, David Johnson, and many others, and they have all enjoyed the experience of returning to Anfield."

AUGUST MATCH REPORTS

SUNDAY 12 AUGUST 2018 | PREMIER LEAGUE | ANFIELD | ATTENDANCE: 53,235

LIVERPOOL 4
(Salah 19, Mané 45+2, 53, Sturridge 88)
WEST HAM UNITED 0

The Hammers would not pick Anfield as their favourite destination and definitely not one at which to set out their stall for a new Premier League season. One win in 46 previous visits is an extraordinary statistic and borne out by another unfulfilling trip for the travelling fans from east London. For their pains they endured a 4-0 thumping.

Mohamed Salah registered his 29th goal in as many league games after 19 minutes, tapping home Andy Robertson's cross at the far post to give Liverpool a deserved lead. West Ham threatened only sporadically, with Alisson comfortably saving a Fabian Balbuena header, one of only two efforts on target all afternoon.

Lone striker Marco Arnautović was well marshalled by the central defensive pairing of Virgil van Dijk and Joe Gomez, the latter proving his fitness to ease a mini-crisis at centre-half, as none of Joel Matip, Dejan Lovren or Ragnar Klavan was available. The young England player showed the qualities of composure and game-reading that characterised his rapid rise to the national side and it was encouraging to see him back in action after ankle surgery ruled him unfortunately out of a place at the World Cup in Russia.

The Reds created numerous chances to extend the lead but it wasn't until first-half injury time that a second was forthcoming, Sadio Mané turning in James Milner's cut-back when unmarked, six yards from goal.

Needing more attacking impetus, Hammers manager Manuel Pellegrini brought on creative Scot Robert Snodgrass after the break for the more defensively minded Declan Rice, but only seven minutes into the second period, the visitors found themselves three behind.

Mané appeared offside as he collected Firmino's pass in the box, but the flag stayed down and he drilled his effort beyond new West Ham goalkeeper Lukasz Fabiański.

Pellegrini turned to Javier Hernandez and Ukrainian summer signing Andriy Yarmolenko to try to turn the game in the visitors' favour but still Alisson remained largely untroubled and Liverpool notched their fourth late on through Daniel Sturridge, scoring with his first touch only 24 seconds after coming on.

A Milner corner found its way via a deflection all the way to the back post, where Sturridge was lurking to bundle home.

So Liverpool finished the first round of fixtures top of the pile, one goal ahead of Chelsea, who had won 3-0 at Newcastle and two ahead of Manchester City, winners at the Emirates against Arsenal.

TEAMS

LIVERPOOL

Alisson; Alexander-Arnold, Gomez, van Dijk, Robertson; Milner, Wijnaldum, Keïta; Salah (Sturridge 87), Firmino (Henderson 69), Mané (Shaqiri 82)

WEST HAM UNITED

Fabiański; Fredericks, Balbuena, Ogbonna, Masuaku; Noble, Rice (Snodgrass 45); Anderson (Hernandez 62), Wilshere, Antonio; Arnautović (Yarmolenko 67)

MATCH FACTS

- Sadio Mané became the first Liverpool player to score in three consecutive opening top-flight fixtures since John Barnes between 1989/90 and 1991/92.
- Mo Salah had now scored 20 goals in his 20 Premier League games at Anfield.
- The win over West Ham was Liverpool's 500th of the Premier League era.

THEY SAID

James Pearce, *Liverpool Echo*: "This is what you call packing a punch. Liverpool got their Premier League campaign off to a flyer with a genuine heavyweight performance at Anfield. Belief in what the crop of 2018/19 are capable of delivering will only rocket after such an emphatic start. This was the Reds' biggest opening-day win at Anfield since Wolves were thrashed 5-1 way back in 1932. If it had been a boxing match the towel would have been thrown in long before the end."

MONDAY 20 AUGUST 2018 | PREMIER LEAGUE | SELHURST PARK
ATTENDANCE: 25,750

CRYSTAL PALACE 0
LIVERPOOL 2
(Milner pen. 45, Mané 90+3)

Jürgen Klopp was full of praise for his players after they killed off a tough, draining game in front of a bouncy south London crowd, completing the weekend's schedule on a Monday evening.

Leading by a single goal in second-half stoppage time, the Reds were defending a corner as Crystal Palace threw men forward in search of an equaliser. The ball broke to Mo Salah, who released Sadio Mané on a 50-yard run, muscling past Patrick van Aanholt and rounding Wayne Hennessey to seal the points.

Klopp said it showed guts and desire to get forward and score a second despite being physically tired. "In these moments the fuel is really low and maybe the players need a bit of help from an angry manager – 'run or I will kill you!' – and they did that with a fantastic counter attack."

It spoke much for Palace's efforts that centre-half Virgil van Dijk was made man of the match, as he and the whole back four were given a stringent test of their mettle by the Eagles' attackers in Wilfried Zaha, Andros Townsend and Christian Benteke.

Liverpool began brightly, though, on a balmy evening in the capital and had the ball in the back of the net on 20 minutes when Wayne Hennessey spilled a Trent Alexander-Arnold cross. The ball dribbled gently over the line; but the effort was ruled out for a foul by Sadio Mané on the Palace keeper.

Next, Naby Keïta span away from his marker Townsend and delivered a gorgeous, 60-yard pass into the path of Mo Salah, who controlled deftly, but his attempted lob was heavy and flew into the fans behind the goal.

Shortly after, though, Townsend brought the Palace fans to their feet as he cut in from the right and unleashed a dipping, left-footed drive that beat Alisson and cannoned off the crossbar.

The first half was ticking down when Salah found a small pocket of space in box, turned neatly and was clipped by Mamadou Sakho. Referee Michael Oliver pointed to the spot and James Milner slotted the ball coolly into the bottom-right corner as Hennessey dived the other way.

Palace boss Roy Hodgson contended that it was a soft award by Oliver – "Sakho is a defender and he has to try and defend, which I think he did well" – but Sakho used his arm to obstruct Salah and the referee was in no doubt.

Early in the second period Keïta nearly registered a first Liverpool goal, clipping narrowly wide from Salah's square ball, but Palace came even closer. On 53 minutes, Luka Milivojević's deft free kick was curling into the top-right corner of the visitors' goal, but Alisson made excellent ground to scramble across behind his wall and push the shot clear.

The chances kept coming. A crisp Salah volley was on target but deflected wide by the head of Jeffery Schlupp. Trent Alexander-Arnold missed a defensive header in his own box and the ball fell to Zaha, but the winger could only fire straight at Alisson as the defensive cover closed in.

On 75 minutes – a key decision. Salah was through on goal and Aaron Wan-Bissaka clipped his heel just outside the box. Arguably, a heavy touch by Salah meant the ball had gone, but it was still a foul tackle and the referee brandished the red card.

That lack of numbers was exposed at the end as Mané applied the finishing touch.

TEAMS

CRYSTAL PALACE

Hennessey; Wan-Bissaka, Sakho, Tomkins, van Aanholt; Schlupp (Meyer 83), Milivojević, McArthur, Townsend (Ward 79); Zaha, Benteke (Sørloth 70)

LIVERPOOL

Alisson; Alexander-Arnold, Gomez, van Dijk, Robertson; Milner (Henderson 67), Wijnaldum, Keïta (Lallana 87); Salah, Firmino (Sturridge 90+4), Mané

MATCH FACTS

- James Milner became the first player to score eight consecutive Premier League goals from penalties.
- Sadio Mané became the first Liverpool player to score in three successive meetings with Palace. His six goals in eight games against the Eagles was the most he'd scored against any opponent.
- Palace had now won only two of their last 20 Premier League games against Big Six sides at home, losing 16.

THEY SAID

Chris Sutton on BBC Radio 5 Live: "That is a big three points for Liverpool. Palace will feel aggrieved and they gave it a real go, but is this a different Liverpool we're going to see this year."

SATURDAY 25 AUGUST 2018 | PREMIER LEAGUE | ANFIELD | ATTENDANCE: 53,294

LIVERPOOL 1
(Salah 23)
BRIGHTON & HOVE ALBION 0

Anfield was bathed in early evening sunshine for this tea-time kick-off but despite the glorious stage, the match as a whole failed to sparkle. Despite a lively start by the Reds, this turned into a gritty battle more befitting the dark days of an English winter.

Liverpool engineered two early chances. One was created by Mo Salah, who went on a mazy run down the right flank before teeing up Sadio Mané. The shot from the edge of the box, however, slid narrowly wide. For the second, a wicked cross from the left by Andy Robertson landed plumb on the head of Roberto Firmino, but Brighton keeper Matt Ryan reacted brilliantly to keep the Brazilian's effort out at the near post.

With 14 minutes gone, Trent Alexander-Arnold then went close as his free kick – earned when Naby Keïta was barged over by Dale Stephens – dipped over the Seagulls' defensive wall and thudded against the crossbar with Ryan beaten.

The goal came from loose defensive play by Brighton. Leon Balogun's pass from centre-half was poorly controlled by Yves Bissouma and Liverpool seized the opportunity in a flash. Mané touched the ball to Firmino, who laid in Salah on the right edge of the box. The Egyptian's shot was eased just beyond Ryan's right hand and in off the far post.

Liverpool continued to press, while Chris Hughton's side were mostly happy to contain until the break. Ryan blocked a fierce shot from Gini Wijnaldum at the near post, while Mané's stopping header lacked the power to trouble the keeper.

The visitors emerged with more purpose in the second half and came close to restoring parity after persistent work by Glenn Murray in the box fashioned a chance for Anthony Knockaert. Although the Frenchman got his shot away on the turn, he couldn't direct his effort on target.

What followed was scrappy fare as the Reds misplaced passes in the final third and Brighton threw themselves into their defensive work with relish but had little to offer in an attacking sense. That single goal lead was fragile, though, and the stadium became increasingly nervous as the minutes ticked down.

Those fears so nearly proved justified. Pascal Gross's header from a Martin Montoya cross in the final minute of the 90 was firm and well directed but just within the reach of Alisson, who stretched to push it aside.

It was a mighty relieved Anfield that acclaimed a third straight win of the season on referee Chris Kavanagh's final whistle.

TEAMS

LIVERPOOL

Alisson; Alexander-Arnold (Matip 89), Gomez, van Dijk, Robertson; Milner, Wiljnaldum; Keïta (Henderson 67); Salah, Firmino, Mané (Sturridge 80)

BRIGHTON & HOVE ALBION

Ryan; Montoya, Duffy, Balogun, Bong; Knockaert (Jahanbakhsh 76), Stephens, Bissouma (Gross 80), Propper, March (Locadia 75); Murray

MATCH FACTS

- Liverpool named the same starting XI in three consecutive Premier League games for the first time since May 2017.
- Liverpool had kept 11 clean sheets in the Premier League in 18 games since Virgil van Dijk's debut in January 2018, more than any other side in that period.

- Gini Wijnaldum completed 75 of his 76 attempted passes (98.7 per cent).

THEY SAID

Brighton manager Chris Hughton: "It's a performance to be proud of but we're disappointed as well. With the form Liverpool are in, you don't get too many opportunities to get something out of the game. You know they are going to have chances, but we had chances as well. We finished strong and we won't have many better opportunities."

PREMIER LEAGUE TABLE AT END OF AUGUST 2018

Pos	Team	Pld	W	D	L	GF	GA	GD	Pts
1	Liverpool	3	3	0	0	7	0	7	9
2	Tottenham Hotspur	3	3	0	0	8	2	6	9
3	Chelsea	3	3	0	0	8	3	5	9
4	Watford	3	3	0	0	7	2	5	9
5	Manchester City	3	2	1	0	9	2	7	7
6	AFC Bournemouth	3	2	1	0	6	3	3	7
7	Leicester City	3	2	0	1	5	3	2	6
8	Everton	3	1	2	0	6	5	1	5
9	Arsenal	3	1	0	2	5	6	-1	3
10	Crystal Palace	3	1	0	2	3	4	-1	3
11	Fulham	3	1	0	2	5	7	-2	3
12	Brighton and Hove Albion	3	1	0	2	3	5	-2	3
13	Manchester United	3	1	0	2	4	7	-3	3
14	Wolverhampton Wanderers	3	0	2	1	3	5	-2	2
15	Cardiff City	3	0	2	1	0	2	-2	2
16	Newcastle United	3	0	1	2	2	4	-2	1
17	Southampton	3	0	1	2	2	4	-2	1
18	Burnley	3	0	1	2	3	7	-4	1
19	Huddersfield Town	3	0	1	2	1	9	-8	1
20	West Ham United	3	0	0	3	2	9	-7	0

CHAPTER 2

—

SEPTEMBER

"THIS IS GOING TO BE SOME KIND OF SHOW"

F or all of August's encouragement, the football season never feels properly under way until it's officially autumn. Now you get a full programme – Premier League, League Cup, Champions League and, yes, the first international break – with all the attendant stresses and strains that accompany the task of managing a leading European football power.

With three wins from three already under the belt, Jürgen Klopp was eyeing a fourth straight league success – a sequence not recorded by Liverpool since 1990-91 – and it was a bright and warm Leicester that welcomed Liverpool's travelling fans for the lunchtime fixture on the first of the month.

All set fair then? Not really. The Foxes had beaten Liverpool at the King Power in each of the past three seasons – twice in the Premier League and once in the League Cup – and were on a three-match winning run of their own, having overcome Wolves and Southampton in recent weeks and then eased past Fleetwood Town in the League Cup five days previously. Something had to give.

Leicester, though, had cause to rue the suspension of striker Jamie Vardy, who had scored an extraordinary seven goals in his last five games against the Reds, including his 40-yard wonder-volley in the title-winning season of 2015/16. Vardy would be serving the last of a three-match suspension after being sent off in the win over Wolves.

And Liverpool could also fall back on the memory of last season's trip – a five-goal thriller that the visitors edged 3-2, with a goal from captain Jordan Henderson proving the difference. Henderson was the sole change to Klopp's starting XI, replacing Naby Keïta in a bid to freshen the midfield after those three matches with an unchanged line-up.

"Bringing back Jordan Henderson makes sense for the game today," Klopp argued. "We have to be rock solid in all departments as Leicester are a good footballing team. So we need to defend very well, be really compact.

"So it helps that the boys are used to it; this midfield [Henderson, Milner, Wijnaldum] played the last third of the last season unchanged. It's about being fresh and being desperate to be on the pitch. We have to improve in each department; and be ready today, to show we are here for the three points. We want to defend and fight. Thank God I have a selective brain so I forget the losses against Leicester! But we have won here as well. It's clear they have quality; it's a difficult place."

In the end, Liverpool's perfect start was preserved with a 2-1 win, but this was as gritty and scruffy a performance as the previous effort against

Brighton, with a similar dynamic of a fast start followed by a drop in intensity.

Goals from Sadio Mané and Roberto Firmino opened up a cushion at the break, albeit the second was against the run of play. But Leicester were far better in the second half and Claude Puel's team would have imagined themselves unlucky not to pick up at least a point for their efforts overall.

Klopp's team invited pressure and it was an individual error by goalkeeper Alisson that summed up the collective loss of focus. With just over an hour gone, Virgil van Dijk's back-pass was misplaced, but Alisson's decision to Cruyff-turn past substitute Kelechi Iheanacho proved extremely ill-advised. The Nigerian robbed the keeper and played in Rachid Ghezzal, who promptly halved the home side's deficit. The visiting fans – who may have gasped back at Anfield when Alisson chipped the ball over Brighton's Anthony Knockaert – were this time aghast.

His manager at least found the positive spin that it was a lesson learned without costing any points. "It was clearly going to happen one day," Klopp said, noting the similarity in how the incident developed. "I didn't think it was going to happen in the next match [after Brighton]. He knows he could have cleared the situation.

"I said last week we need to get used to it. Don't constantly give the goalkeeper the ball – there are other solutions. He's a fantastic goalkeeper who makes fantastic saves and of course in this situation he did not do what he should have done, but he knows it was his mistake. Of course, he is man enough to get that. I told him this is the best game to do it in because we won it. Now we tick that box – don't play all the balls to Alisson. But how cool he was after that, when the crowd tried to make him a bit nervous? It was good that we could still use him."

Klopp added that the match as a whole was a good learning experience for his players. "If you are flying constantly, you are not prepared for the difficult moments," he said. "I told the boys immediately after the game in the dressing room that if winning away games in the Premier League [was] easy, then everybody would do it constantly. It's difficult and to do it in the way we did it – we caused ourselves problems, we could've done better – but in the moments when did what we actually wanted to do, we were really strong."

With Manchester City beating Newcastle and Chelsea winning at home to Bournemouth, Liverpool led the Londoners on goal difference heading into the international break. For the next week, at least, all Reds would have their fingers crossed for the safe return of our raft of international stars.

Joe Gomez and Jordan Henderson both started in England's 2-1 Nations League defeat to Spain, while Xherdan Shaqiri faced England back at the King Power as Marcus Rashford's goal earned England a 1-0 win. Henderson came on for the last 20 minutes.

There was a chastening first experience of international captaincy for Andy Robertson, though. Playing left wing-back he was unable to help a callow Scottish back-three that was torn apart by Belgium. The 4-0 defeat was Scotland's worst home reverse since 1973. Thankfully, morale was restored by a 2-0 win over Albania in the Scots' Nations League opener.

Meanwhile, Roberto Firmino was on the scoresheet for Brazil against USA in New Jersey, while Fabinho also started.

Klopp believed Fabinho might be ready for his debut after the international break. "The team is good, he needs time to adapt," the German said. "It is different football to what he is used to, but he is improving already with big steps. I can see that in the sessions and that is cool. Fabinho is used to playing at a high level in France. It is not about who we play but about how we play. For sure it is not nice for a new player. It never was, but it is all fine."

And so to Wembley – where Jürgen Klopp had not yet won a competitive match – and a match-up with Tottenham Hotspur, an occasion with a certain rawness around the edges for Liverpool after a 4-1 defeat in the corresponding fixture in 2017/18.

Pre-match, Klopp reflected on that performance: "Last year we made it too easy for them. We lost the ball and they only had to play one pass behind our lines. It is Tottenham. It is a top team in Europe, not only in England. We should be much better organised this time. You get nothing for an average day at Tottenham. We needed to be on our top level. It was a wake-up call."

As ever with the German, though, he was able to summon some positivity about how his side bounced back: "After that we had pretty good results and I don't think we conceded a lot of goals. We learned – the experience was that one game can be completely different from another. But on the other side we still knew we had a good team. It was the moment where we could show that we are convinced about what we are doing, we just had to do it more often and in a better way."

The Reds squad had emerged from the international break more or less unscathed, but that was not the case for Tottenham, as key midfielder Dele Alli picked up a muscle strain in England's match against Spain and was ruled out. Captain and keeper Hugo Lloris was also absent with a thigh strain.

45

Whereas Spurs had stunned Liverpool with their fast start the previous season, on a sun-baked London lunchtime it was the visitors who came out firing. The ball was in the Tottenham net within a minute, but Firmino's glanced finish was ruled out due to Mané lurking offside at the back post.

Mo Salah then spurned an effort when through on goal after a mistake by Eric Dier, while for Spurs a Christian Eriksen free kick was easily fielded by Alisson.

The breakthrough came from an unexpected quarter. Tottenham keeper Michel Vorm's attempt to clear a corner was untidy, and Gini Wijnaldum looped a clever header towards the top corner. Although Vorm clawed the ball out, referee Michael Oliver confirmed it had crossed the line.

In the second half, the home side's Lucas Moura smacked a shot against the foot of Alisson's post, but it was Liverpool who extended the lead when Sadio Mané's cross was deflected on to the post by Jan Vertonghen and the ball rolled gently along the goal-line, where Firmino was able to convert from inches out.

Although Erik Lamela's clever finish in stoppage time gave the hosts faint hope and there were a few hearts in mouths when substitute Son Heung-Min subsequently went down in the box, the points were secured to make it perfect nap hand – five out of five.

"It's fantastic that we've won all five games," said Jürgen Klopp afterwards. "We've improved, and this was by far our best performance of the season, so I liked that development. Now we have to do it again and again.

"Over 85 minutes we were really dominant. With and without the ball we caused them massive problems. The things they usually do usually work, but they didn't today. The boys stuck to our plan – everybody worked so hard.

"The performance was much better than the result. That was a tough game, man! Two good teams, two big teams, football as it should be. We won the game and [winning] at Tottenham is a big result. The players did the job and they worked unbelievably hard, and I'm really proud of them."

The only concern for the manager was the well-being of Firmino, who came off after 74 minutes after being gouged in the eye by a Jan Vertonghen finger. Liverpool said a hospital examination confirmed it as an abrasion, but that there would be no lasting damage.

Welcome news, with just the first match of a severely testing period safely negotiated. Next up, the second of seven games in 23 days: PSG in the Champions League.

The draw had handed Liverpool a tough course to navigate, with Group C arguably the hardest section of all, including Paris Saint-Germain, Napoli and Red Star Belgrade.

PSG were up first, coming to Anfield; and with two of the pre-eminent forward lines in European football on display, the one thing you could guarantee? It wasn't going to be dull.

Visiting captain Thiago Silva was anticipating something special. "We've got to be prepared because I know the fans are going to be in for a great spectacle," said the Brazilian. "It's going to be a real show of football. You are looking at probably the two strongest club forward lines in world football – three attackers on each side that can entertain and provide a threat all the way through the match. We'll be talking between now and [the game] and the best way of approaching the game tactically, but as I say, this is going to be some kind of show."

So it proved. There was a crackling, old-school atmosphere at Anfield for the visit of the French champions – a first chance for Jürgen Klopp's men to move on past the experience of Kiev and lay the foundations for another tilt at European football's greatest prize.

Both sides were managed by Germans, with the impressive Thomas Tuchel in charge of PSG, and the links went further than mere nationality as both men had showcased the talents that secured their current employment while at Borussia Dortmund. Tuchel had taken the reins at Dortmund when Klopp left for Merseyside and had moved to Paris earlier in 2018, replacing Arsenal's new boss Unai Emery.

PSG's talisman Neymar had been rested for the Friday's Ligue 1 match against Saint-Etienne, while Kylian Mbappé – the star of France's World Cup win – also sat out a 4-0 win with a suspension. So both threatened freshness in attack.

The French, like Liverpool, had won all their league games so far, in their case scoring 17 times in the course of five wins. "Paris are one of the favourites for the competition, for sure," Klopp said. "This team is built for winning the Champions League. They have unbelievable quality. I like these challenges, but I only like it because I have a really good football team. If I was not a manager, I would watch this game. We play at Anfield and it can be an advantage. We hope we can use that."

One by one, Klopp reeled off the names and highlighted each superstar's quality, as he became increasingly animated. "I watched them last year and this year. It is impressive. They are good. Really good and not only for Paris. Kylian Mbappé? Come on! What a World Cup he played. Neymar? We know about his quality. Angel Di Maria… maybe he didn't have the best time at Manchester United, but all the rest of his career was outstanding. Edinson Cavani? An outstanding goalscorer… In the preparation, I have to make sure that we know about it. We have to respect them."

Respect, yes. Fear, no. And Klopp was quick to point out that while he admired PSG's strengths, they in turn were unaccustomed in their domestic league to facing anyone with the talents at his own disposal. "I can't prepare a team to face Paris Saint-Germain without showing them [their] strengths," he said. "But it's quite difficult for them to prepare as they have never played against us. Us playing them will look different to what they have faced so far this season. That's the truth."

The absence of Roberto Firmino from the starting XI looked like a big loss. He already had two goals and two assists this season and scored 10 in 13 Champions League games in 2017/18; but Klopp was wary of his eye injury and left the Brazilian on the bench. In came Daniel Sturridge to lead the line – it had been six years since the Englishman's last Champions League start.

As evening drew in and a full house gathered, the flags waved around Anfield, songs reverberated around the stands, anticipation tangible among the Reds' faithful. And it was a match quite befitting the occasion: quality aplenty, five goals and a last-gasp winner to send the home fans away breathless.

Sturridge gleefully marked his return to Champions League action with a headed opener from Andy Robertson's pinpoint delivery. James Milner tucked away a penalty in his customary, nerveless fashion.

PSG hit back with an opportunistic volley from full-back Thomas Meunier and it seemed all of Liverpool's hard work might be undone when Mbappé struck with just about his only clear opportunity of the night.

But there was a final twist to round off a thrilling night's entertainment. Notwithstanding the discomfort in his left eye, Roberto Firmino rose from the bench – replacing Sturridge at 72 minutes – and provided the *coup de grâce* with as clear-sighted a piece of finishing as you could imagine. A hand placed over the damaged eye in celebration was icing on the cake for delighted Reds fans. The campaign was up and running and the tone was set for a topsy-turvy Group C to come.

Klopp was overjoyed by the performance of his returning and substitute strikers. "Daniel played a super game," he said post-match. "I have never seen him as fit as he is in the moment and I said to him before the game, 'You are in the best shape since I've known you – now you have to use that.' He was everywhere. He helped left and right and he was in the box when he was needed. Then you can bring Bobby Firmino on and that helps a lot. I can't say enough good things about Bobby. I loved his goal celebration.

"[The performance] was really good in all departments. It's so difficult to defend [against] them, but we did. Organisation and big heart are always a good combination for defending. All 11 players were involved in that. It was a good performance against an outstandingly strong team, it was necessary that we played well. The atmosphere was fantastic. It's so special to do these things in that stadium."

The club's 100 per cent record was still intact; if Liverpool could beat Southampton at Anfield it would be the best start to a season in the club's illustrious, 126-year history. The current run of six consecutive victories hadn't been achieved since 1961/62 under Bill Shankly in the old Second Division. That run ended in the seventh game with a 0-0 draw against Brighton. In 1990/91, the Reds won their opening eight top-flight matches and two League Cup clashes in a triumphant 10-game run. However, that winning run only came after the season had started with a 1-1 draw against Manchester United in the Charity Shield.

The condensed schedule towards the end of the month meant Jürgen Klopp was already thinking of changes to his line-up – and one player in particular – to freshen his selection. Summer signing Xherdan Shaqiri had made an instant impact in pre-season and impressed the manager in training, but his game-time thus far was limited to a mere 27 minutes of Premier League action in four matches, plus a five-minute cameo in the Champions League. He was a likely starter for the upcoming Carabao Cup clash with Chelsea, but Klopp was ready to spring a surprise by including him against the Saints.

"He is very lively, very positive," said Klopp in his pre-match press conference. "It's not only from the performances but also as a guy in the dressing room. Everyone loves Shaq. That is more my mistake than his [that he hasn't played more]. We are going to have to use the boys now. They are in good shape. They all want to play.

"We have to create something where the boys not only push from the bench, but they push with their performance on the field as well. We have to give opportunity – then it is my job to decide who will start."

Meanwhile the media were making play of Mo Salah's perceived lack of goals – he'd not scored since netting the opener against Brighton four matches ago. Klopp, understandably, disagreed with the idea that his striker was off-form.

"Everybody expects things because of last season but no one remembers [how he started in 2017/18]," said Klopp, recalling that at the comparative stage he had just one more goal than at present.

"It is a completely normal situation for an offensive player that they have times when they don't score. But he is still a threat, has fantastic situations and he is in good shape."

"On the defensive side he was outstanding in the last two games," he added. "That says everything about him, that he's always ready to work for the team. At the end of the season we will see how it is, not at the start."

Klopp reported frustrations that inclement weather had curtailed training at Melwood on Friday, as he was experimenting with a 4-2-3 system that would allow Shaqiri a free role in behind Salah, who would operate as a number 9, with Firmino and Mané either side.

He needn't have worried. Shaqiri took his opportunity to start brilliantly – always on the move, impossible for the Saints' defensive midfielder Oriol Romeu to pin down and linking effortlessly with the Reds' rejigged attacking trident.

For the opener, he popped up on the left wing, after being slid in superbly by Sadio Mané. And though there was a huge slice of luck in the double deflection that took the ball past Alex McCarthy, the way the defence was opened up suggested new options at the manager's disposal.

Now teams were learning you couldn't just sit deep against Liverpool and prevent rapid counter-attacks. Klopp had the tactical sensitivity to adapt to the differing demands of a see-saw tie against European heavyweights and the massed ranks of a tightly drilled defensive outfit in the league.

It was a good day, too, for another player who had shown patience while Joe Gomez and Virgil van Dijk established their partnership at centre-half. Towering Cameroonian Joel Matip was – like Shaqiri – making his first start of the season and crowned an assured defensive display with a fine headed goal from a corner.

By half-time it was effectively "game over". Shaqiri swerved a wicked free-kick against the Southampton bar and Salah was there to poke the rebound in. Whatever whisperings there had been pre-match about a loss of form, here was the riposte – this was Salah's 30th goal in 31 games at Anfield across all competitions since joining from Roma.

A delighted team sprinted to acclaim Shaqiri, who was then substituted at half-time with one eye on him starting in midweek.

"I said to [him] at half-time that I had never brought a player off after such an influential time without an injury," said Klopp. "It was not easy, to be honest. It's my job to sometimes deliver news nobody wants to hear. That's how it was at half-time; but he is a fantastic boy."

The second half was something of a stroll against Mark Hughes's men, who struggled for cohesion in attack and never looked likely to score with lone striker Shane Long and then substitute Charlie Austin isolated against Matip, van Dijk and latterly Gomez, who came on for the Dutchman early in the second half.

Seven wins in a row, then. In typical style, the manager wasn't getting carried away – he'd seen sufficient ups and downs in football to know the trajectory isn't always upward.

"I once lost seven games in a row and that felt much different," said Klopp. "Yes, it is a surprise but the performances we showed so far were good enough to win all the games. Different styles and different opponents but the boys were always there."

Now Liverpool would face the same opponent twice in the space of a few days. Back-to-back games against Chelsea would offer a much stiffer test.

A tough draw in the League Cup always presents the manager with a dilemma. The opportunity is there to give players game-time if they haven't been starting regularly – and as record eight-time winners there is an innate respect due to the competition. But multiple changes are a gamble against capable opponents, who may switch up their selection to a greater or lesser degree, leading to uncertainty from a tactical perspective.

Those in the frame for Liverpool included Dejan Lovren, Fabinho, Nathaniel Clyne and Alberto Moreno – although neither Adam Lallana nor Divock Origi was sufficiently fit to be considered. Ahead of the game, Klopp was keeping his team-list to himself, with one exception.

"The only position I will confirm today is Simon [Mignolet in goal]. Simon will start. All the rest, you have to wait until tomorrow. But it will be a good team, believe me!" said Klopp.

"It will not be the maximum and it will not be the minimum. One I have already confirmed, so it cannot be nil, and it will for sure not be 11."

Meanwhile, Chelsea's assistant manager Gianfranco Zola admitted that while Chelsea would have one eye on the league game to come the following Saturday, they would take the Cup match "seriously".

"It's an opportunity to see players who didn't have many games so far," said the Italian. "The game on Saturday is going to be huge – the type of game [that] means a lot. We are greedy, [so] we want to win both of them if we can."

Liverpool's recent record against the west Londoners offered thin pickings. Just two wins in the past 14 meetings (away wins in the league at the Bridge in 2015 and 2016), and the last time they'd met in the League Cup in January 2015, Chelsea won a semi-final in extra-time. Branislav Ivanović scored the winner in extra time.

In 2017/18, the Reds had been knocked out at the first time of asking by Leicester City, so the onus on the players to perform against Chelsea was threefold. First, to show the manager each was worthy of a regular starting place; second, to improve on last season; and third, to maintain the momentum of a 100 per cent start to the season ahead of a big-league game against a title rival.

Jordan Henderson's column in the match day programme picked up the theme of selectorial issues. "There's been a lot said and written about the strength of our playing squad for this season, but I don't think anything highlights it better than the result and performance [against Southampton]," he said. "Joel Matip and Xherdan Shaqiri both made their first starts of the season and made massive contributions. Likewise, Daniel Sturridge midweek against PSG, by the way. I don't envy for one second the gaffer and the coaching staff having to the pick the team, because seeing the level of the lads in training means that there's a case for about 23 players to get a start every time."

In the event, a first defeat of the season was a story of missed opportunities and one standout moment of exquisite skill from the visitors' best player, Eden Hazard. Eight changes by each side leant a certain disjointedness to the play but Liverpool had numerous chances to establish a lead over the course of the first hour, none clearer than when Daniel Sturridge was unable to steer the ball into an empty net, having rounded Willy Caballero shortly after the break.

Otherwise, the Reds found Chelsea's back-up keeper in inspired form, keeping out a host of good opportunities, notably from Naby Keïta and Sadio

Mané. Sturridge did break the deadlock with a flying volley on 58 minutes, but the Blues hit back through Emerson – the goal upheld after review on VAR. Álvaro Morata and César Azpilicueta were standing offside at the point Hazard's free kick was struck, but the key figures in the goal – Ross Barkley and Emerson – were not and referee Kevin Friend's initial verdict stood.

Then, in a blur of acceleration from the right wing, Hazard beat Keïta and Moreno – the latter twice – before slamming the ball home for the winner. The 100 per cent run was ended and Liverpool were out of the competition at this stage in consecutive years for the first time since the 1990/91 season.

The disappointment was tangible in the stadium; but the defeat needed to be seen in the context of the wider campaign. The *Liverpool Echo*'s James Pearce wrote: "A sense of perspective is important. This was always fourth on Liverpool's list of priorities. As serious contenders for the Premier League title and the Champions League crown they have bigger fish to fry. And now they need to turn a negative into a positive by taking advantage of the fact they only have two competitions to focus on until January. Certainly, no harm should be done to morale as Klopp plots an instant revenge mission down at Stamford Bridge on Saturday night. That contest certainly means more than this one."

Just three days, then, were afforded to Jürgen Klopp and Maurizio Sarri to refocus, reassess and develop a tactical plan for their top-of-the-table clash. It turned out to be an enthralling contest, with Daniel Sturridge again on the scoresheet, this time as a late substitute delivering a world-class goal in the final minutes of normal time to stun Stamford Bridge and send the away fans into delirium.

The past few years had been testing for Sturridge. Back in 2014 he had been England's first-choice centre-forward in the World Cup in Brazil. Fast-forward four years and in the run-up to Russia 2018 he was on loan at soon-to-be-relegated West Brom and barely featured at The Hawthorns after pulling his hamstring.

Back now on Merseyside, he had impressed in pre-season, scoring four goals, but the emergence of Klopp's first-choice front three meant Sturridge would have to be patient and take his chances when they came.

The 90 minutes he played against Chelsea in the League Cup was his first full game since September 2017. The next step was to play at such intensity for an entire league game. "That is the target," his manager stressed. "He played for 60 to 70 minutes against Paris Saint-Germain with high intensity. He could have played longer, but we had Bobby [Firmino to come on]. It must always be the target, to play high intensity over 95 minutes.

"Daniel does not want us to change our style for him," Klopp added. "He plays exactly how we want him. He makes moves in the right places and judges situations and scores goals. Daniel is tactically a very, very smart player. He did not have to improve a lot. Since we [have] worked together, he has had spells when he was fit, but they were not long enough. When he was fit, he was always an important part of the team and so he is now."

The striker himself was keen to stress his part in a whole team effort. "All I'm doing is focusing on the team being successful," he said. "I take every day as it comes and train hard. Everyone is pushing themselves to the limit."

His goal, earning the Reds a deserved point, was a reminder of the quality the Englishman possesses when given a stage on which to express himself. Accepting a pass from Xherdan Shaqiri on the left, 10 yards outside the area, Sturridge was confronted by five blue shirts and the Chelsea goalkeeper standing no more than a yard off his line. He took one touch to set, had a little look up, and then sent a sweet, curling shot into top-right corner – the only spot Kepa couldn't reach. It was the very definition of a "postage stamp" goal.

The contrast could not have been starker with his last encounter at his old club Chelsea. It was only three minutes into West Brom's visit to the Bridge in February that his troublesome hamstring had let him down, leaving him to trudge disconsolately back down the tunnel.

Klopp was naturally thrilled with the turnaround in his striker's fortunes. "[Daniel is] in the best shape since I've known him. I'm really happy for him. When he came in the dressing room it was pretty loud. The boys were really happy for him because he's in a good moment. What a spectacular football game. If we play like that, we will win plenty of games."

Sarri believed Chelsea were "closer than [he] thought" to Liverpool after both teams maintained their unbeaten starts in the league. He now believed the Blues could narrow that gap in his inaugural season, having faced Liverpool twice in four days without losing. Chelsea ended the round of fixtures for the week in third place, two points behind Klopp's side and defending champions Man City. City went top on goal difference with a 2-0 win over Fulham at the Etihad that manager Pep Guardiola described as "outstanding".

The scenes on the touchline between Klopp and Sarri at the final whistle were more reminiscent of old friends catching up than rivals in the heat of battle, and Sarri later revealed the contents of the two coaches' touchline conversation. "There are moments when the grand spectacle of it all convinces you to put aside any regrets," he told Italian newspaper *Corriere dello Sport*. "Even if you concede in the last minute or five minutes into stoppage time. That was an extraordinary show. Just 10 minutes earlier, I saw Klopp looking at me with the game going on. I asked: 'Why are you smiling?' He replied, 'Aren't you having fun?' I said, 'So much!' and he added: 'Me too!'. He was losing at the time. Even after the equaliser, remembering that moment, we hugged like two old friends. I'm sure he would've done the same even if Liverpool hadn't equalised. The Premier League has this joy of football."

SEPTEMBER MATCH REPORTS

SATURDAY 1 SEPTEMBER 2018 | PREMIER LEAGUE | KING POWER STADIUM
ATTENDANCE: 32,149

LEICESTER CITY 1
(Ghezzal 63)
LIVERPOOL 2
(Mané 10, Firmino 45)

An early start on the first of the month as Liverpool and Leicester kicked off the weekend programme and the visitors moved quickly into high gear. With just three minutes gone, a crisp pass around the corner from Mo Salah was brilliantly taken into his stride by Roberto Firmino and though the Brazilian's attempt to slip the ball past Kasper Schmeichel was thwarted by a big Danish paw, the ball fell right into Salah's path. Surprisingly, he dragged the chance wide. It wouldn't be the Egyptian's day to shine.

A lead came soon enough, though. On 10 minutes, left-back Andy Robertson showed bull-like strength to shrug off Ricardo Pereira – dumped on his backside, quite fairly – before cutting the ball across to Mané. The striker's touch was a little heavy off the knee; but he stretched to poke the ball left-footed firmly past the advancing Schmeichel. With that, Robertson's contribution in his last nine league games for Liverpool was one goal and five assists.

That was not the cue, however, for the Reds to press home their advantage.

Leicester pressed in midfield and the eye-catching Demarai Gray forced a good save from Alisson down to his right after his pacy diagonal was found by Rachid Ghezzal's reverse pass to give the youngster a sight of goal.

It was against the run of play, therefore, that Liverpool doubled the lead as half-time approached. James Milner whipped over a corner from the right flank, while Firmino drifted easily away from his marker James Maddison to plant a free header in at the near post. Spirits sagged in the home stands, but the visiting fans were jubilant at the break.

Leicester, to their credit, came out for the second half with real purpose and gave Liverpool's defence a genuine test. The goal was only kept intact by some fine work from Virgil van Dijk and Joe Gomez, the latter flinging himself into a brilliant block for Maddison when the Leicester playmaker looked certain to score.

Then Wes Morgan should have done better when a fine cross from Marc Albrighton fell to him at the front post, but the centre-half couldn't sort his feet out sufficiently to fashion a shot.

Eventually, the Reds cracked but the wound was entirely self-inflicted. A slightly wayward back pass from van Dijk took Alisson wide but the keeper opted against a simple clearance up the line, scuffed his attempted Cruyff turn and was dispossessed by Kelechi Iheanacho. The substitute striker skipped away to pull the ball back past the covering defenders. Maddison missed it, but Ghezzal made no mistake and spanked a finish past the desperately scrambling stopper, who punched the post in frustration at his error.

Leicester continued to press, with Ghezzal and Maddison bright throughout, while Salah was replaced by Xherdan Shaqiri and Jordan Henderson made way for Naby Keïta. But despite a nervy last 10 minutes, Klopp's side survived without any serious alarm or test for the much-relieved Alisson.

TEAMS

LEICESTER CITY
Schmeichel; Pereira, Morgan, Maguire, Chilwell; Mendy, Ndidi; Ghezzal, Maddison (Amartey 83), Albrighton (Iheanacho 61); Gray (Okazaki 76)

LIVERPOOL
Alisson; Alexander-Arnold (Matip 89), Gomez, van Dijk, Robertson; Wijnaldum, Henderson (Keïta 71), Milner; Salah (Shaqiri 71), Firmino, Mané

MATCH FACTS

- This was a match between the two youngest teams in the league. At kick-off, the average age of Liverpool's starting XI in 2018/19 was 25 years, 228 days, while Leicester's was even younger at 25 years and 174 days.
- James Milner became the fourth player to play 100 Premier League games for three different clubs. He also registered his 80th Premier League assist, equalling David Beckham.
- Man of the match Joe Gomez made five clearances and three interceptions among his 76 touches of the ball and won 100 per cent of his aerial and ground duels.

THEY SAID

Martin Keown, *Match of the Day:* "Gomez is a real talent. Today he was better than van Dijk and that's some compliment. His mobility, the way he floats across the pitch, he can pass the ball, has the technique and the vision. He has everything in his game. [England boss] Gareth Southgate must be licking his lips to work with him."

SATURDAY 15 SEPTEMBER 2018 | PREMIER LEAGUE | WEMBLEY STADIUM
ATTENDANCE: 80,188

TOTTENHAM HOTSPUR 1
(Lamela 90+3)
LIVERPOOL 2
(Wijnaldum 39, Firmino 54)

With more than 80,000 fans packed into Wembley and the sun beating down, this felt more like a Cup Final than a league clash in mid-September, but the Liverpool fans who'd made the trip down to the capital weren't complaining. They revelled in the occasion.

In fact, they'd barely taken their seats when the hosts' net bulged. Roberto Firmino applied the faintest of touches to a Milner cross and the ball eluded keeper Michel Vorm but Mané had tried to prod it in, too, from an offside position. Despite no appearance of a touch from Mané, the officials ruled the attempt out because of his proximity to the play.

Shortly after, Toby Alderweireld had to be alert to block a Firmino shot from a tight angle, but had a chance himself from a curling Christian Eriksen free kick. His header, though, was wayward.

Firmino was in effervescent mood, dropping deep to direct attacking play, while Spurs went unusually long in search of Harry Kane, seeking to bypass the midfield.

Mo Salah shot straight at Vorm after a typically penetrating run but as Tottenham grew into the game, Eriksen's next free kick offered a mouth-watering chance, just right of the "D". The Dane's effort was crisp; but Alisson was well placed to collect.

Liverpool's opener came from a set piece when Milner curled in a corner and Vorm tried to punch clear under pressure from van Dijk but failed to make proper contact. Eric Dier headed away – but the clearance lacked power, allowing Wijnaldum to attempt a looping header of his own, which sailed over Kieran Trippier on the line and was clawed away by Vorm. The goal was awarded courtesy of goal-line technology, which showed the ball to be a couple of balls' widths over.

At the start of the second half, Vorm was scrambling again, this time as Andy Robertson's cross glanced off the face of the crossbar; but he was at his best to beat away a smart turn and shot from Sadio Mané a few minutes later.

However, he was powerless to prevent a second on 54 minutes. Tottenham had just come close to equalising, when Lucas Moura hit the outside of Alisson's post after a penetrating run. But then Liverpool's Robertson sent Mané free down the left and his pace took him to the byline. Vertonghen stretched to intercept his cross but could only deflect it on to the inside of the post. The ball rebounded across goal and slid between the arms of Vorm as he lay on the floor. Firmino reacted quickest to thump the ball into the net – and wheel away to celebrate in front of the Reds fans, packed over to the right-hand side of the goal.

Naby Keïta – selected for this match ahead of Jordan Henderson – should have confirmed the win just after the hour. With Mané striding down the centre, Liverpool had three-on-two with Keïta to the left and Salah to the right. Mané teed up Keïta but Vorm was able to parry over. The Dutchman was also equal to a curling Salah shot, with Mané unable to reach the rebound.

Erik Lamela engineered a fine finish in injury time from a narrow angle after a corner reached him at the back post, but Spurs were unable to create another clear chance to equalise. Son Heung-Min tumbled in the box after Mané's challenge, but play was waved on and then, moments later, brought to an end by referee Michael Oliver.

TEAMS

TOTTENHAM HOTSPUR

Vorm; Trippier, Alderweireld, Vertonghen, Rose; Dembélé (Lamela 60), Dier (Wanyama 83), Winks (Son 73); Eriksen, Kane, Moura

LIVERPOOL

Alisson; Alexander-Arnold (Matip 90), Gomez, van Dijk, Robertson; Milner, Wijnaldum, Keïta (Sturridge 83); Salah, Firmino (Henderson 74), Mané

MATCH FACTS

- Gini Wijnaldum's 19th Premier League goal was his first in an away game at the 58th attempt.
- Roberto Firmino had scored or assisted 61 Premier League goals for Liverpool under Jürgen Klopp (38 goals, 23 assists); 16 more than any other player.
- Since Klopp's appointment in 2015, Liverpool now boasted the most points per game against the other "big six" clubs (Man City, Man United, Chelsea, Spurs, Arsenal). Liverpool had 1.59 points per game, with United second on 1.46 and City third on 1.45.

THEY SAID

Robbie Fowler, *Sunday Mirror*: "It's far too early to get carried away, but that was almost the perfect performance from Liverpool at Wembley. They dominated Spurs [and] made a fantastic team look very ordinary. They suffocated them, which is a pretty impressive achievement given the quality in [Spurs'] midfield with Eriksen and Dembélé. It is perhaps the biggest compliment you could pay to Jürgen Klopp's tactics and his side's execution of them, that you barely noticed Eriksen – one of the best midfielders in the world."

TUESDAY 18 SEPTEMBER 2018 | UEFA CHAMPIONS LEAGUE – GROUP C | ANFIELD
ATTENDANCE: 52,478

LIVERPOOL 3
(Sturridge 30, Milner 36 pen, Firmino 90+1)
PARIS SAINT-GERMAIN 2
(Meunier 40, Mbappé 83)

A buoyant Anfield greeted French visitors bristling with attacking talent in Edinson Cavani, Neymar and World Cup winner Kylian Mbappé, but Jürgen Klopp had a shrewd plan from set pieces to exploit a comparative lack of interest in defensive duties, at least from the Brazilian.

After five minutes, a short corner routine on the right between James Milner and Mo Salah – with Neymar motionless as the play developed – released Milner into a yawning space in the box. His cut-back travelled all the way to Virgil van Dijk at the far post and the Dutchman's scuffed shot was destined for the top corner. Only a smart reaction from PSG keeper Alphonse Areola kept the scores level.

A similar interchange would bring Liverpool the lead with half an hour played. Gini Wijnaldum teed up an untracked Trent Alexander-Arnold, whose whipped cross flew across goal. It fell, however, to fellow full-back Andy Robertson, who also had time and space to measure a perfect centre. Where in recent weeks he had been arrowing the ball onto the forehead of Roberto Firmino, it was Firmino's replacement Daniel Sturridge who found space for a free header, expertly steered past Areola.

Previously set to a simmer, the match now sprang into life. Five minutes on, a mazy run from Mo Salah ended with Wijnaldum picking up possession on the edge of the box. PSG defender Juan Bernat stuck out a lazy leg and it was an easy decision for referee Cüneyt Çakir to award a spot kick. Milner – who had started the move with a typically committed challenge on the right flank – strode up purposefully to side-foot into the right corner.

The two-goal cushion didn't last long, however. A cross from Ángel Di María evaded Cavani's attempt at an overhead kick, but the Uruguayan did enough to distract Robertson; and when the ball bounced up off the Scot's knee, right-back Thomas Meunier swivelled to drive a volley into the corner. Game on – and more thrills to follow in the second half.

Just before the hour, Mo Salah put the ball into an empty net after Daniel

Sturridge seized on Wijnaldum's deflected shot, but replays showed a correct decision to disallow the goal as Sturridge's follow-through challenge on Areola delivered an eye-watering blow between the keeper's legs.

Sturridge had another free header, this time from an Alexander-Arnold cross, but this one was mistimed and bounced up for a comfortable save. With 10 minutes remaining, Mané fashioned an unlikely chance for himself with great persistence in the area; but the angle was too tight as he sought the far corner.

And those misses looked to be costly just two minutes later, when a loose pass from Salah was seized upon by substitute Julian Draxler, just on for Cavani. Draxler released Neymar to run at the heart of the defence and when van Dijk's attempted tackle fell to Mbappé, the youngster buried the chance.

The tie was not over, though. Despite the eye problem that prevented him starting, Firmino replaced Sturridge at 72 minutes and was determined to leave a lasting mark on the match. There looked to be little on when he picked the ball up on the right corner of the box, but two twists to set the PSG defence off balance and he had fashioned a sight of goal. A firm swing of the right boot sent the ball sailing into the far corner and Anfield into raptures.

TEAMS

LIVERPOOL
Alisson; Alexander-Arnold, Gomez, van Dijk, Robertson; Milner, Henderson, Wijnaldum; Salah (Shaqiri 85), Sturridge (Firmino 72), Mané (Fabinho 90+3)

PARIS SAINT-GERMAIN
Areola; Meunier, Thiago Silva, Kimpembe, Bernat; Rabiot, Marquinhos, Di María (Choupo-Moting 80); Mbappé, Cavani (Draxler 80), Neymar

MATCH FACTS

- Daniel Sturridge started a Champions League match for the first time in 2,379 days. His last was for Chelsea against Napoli in March 2012.
- On his 150th appearance for the club, Roberto Firmino moved equal third in Liverpool's European Cup scorers list with 12 goals. Only Ian Rush (14) and Steven Gerrard (30) were ahead of him.
- Three goals meant Liverpool had scored 34 times in the last 10 European

games at Anfield. Only FC Porto had prevented the Reds scoring in that run.

THEY SAID

Man of the match James Milner: "It's the perfect start for us and hopefully we can build on it. We would have been very disappointed [with a draw] and I can't say enough good things about Bobby [Firmino] to come off the bench and score a goal like that. There's a lot more to come from this team – you can see already how we're improving, staying in games and sticking it out."

SATURDAY 22 SEPTEMBER 2018 | PREMIER LEAGUE | ANFIELD
ATTENDANCE: 50,965

LIVERPOOL 3
(Hoedt 10 og, Matip 21, Salah 45+3)
SOUTHAMPTON 0

A seventh straight win from the start of the season – a first such sequence for Liverpool in 28 years – was delivered with a minimum of fuss against a Southampton side unable to match the dynamic pace and penetration of their hosts.

Playmaker Xherdan Shaqiri made his first competitive start under Jürgen Klopp and seized his opportunity with glee, making two goals and combining superbly with his attacking team-mates, including Roberto Firmino, fully recovered from his eye injury.

The opener was a bizarre, pinball moment of an own goal, as Shaqiri ran in behind to collect an incisive pass from Sadio Mané, checked back inside and his shot cannoned off Shane Long, then off Wesley Hoedt and the ball rolled into the corner past helpless keeper Alex McCarthy.

Playing a central role, Mo Salah was a constant threat and nearly doubled the lead after a pitch-length break. Facing away from goal he tried a cute back-heel that rolled inches wide. And he seemed certain to score after a one-two with Firmino on 20 minutes, but was denied by a committed recovery tackle by Cedric Soares. The visitors' relief was short-lived, however – from the resultant corner, swung in by Trent Alexander-Arnold, Joel Matip rose above Jannik Vestergaard to thump a header into the top corner.

Any chance that Southampton boss Mark Hughes might be able to rally his troops at the break was snuffed out in first-half injury time. Shaqiri smacked a brilliant dipping free kick against the underside of McCarthy's bar and Mo Salah reacted quickest to bundle the ball home.

It was Shaqiri's last involvement as the Swiss was replaced by James Milner and the second half was a curious affair, with the visitors showing little ambition to get back into the match. In fairness, Saints were short of attacking options: loanee Danny Ings was ineligible to play against his parent club, while Manolo Gabbiadini was out injured. Shane Long was left to spend much of the game as a lone – and lonely – presence up front.

Back in a familiar 4-3-3 formation, Liverpool gave little away and Southampton's only shot on target came in injury time, as substitute Charlie Austin's effort was easily collected by Alisson.

Salah thought he had a brace for the day, but his finish was disallowed as the Egyptian had returned from an offside position. The only note of disquiet for the hosts was Virgil van Dijk's withdrawal with a rib problem but it proved precautionary.

Though this match may have lacked the visceral thrills of midweek against PSG, Liverpool enjoyed a highly successful trial of a new attacking formation, and a worry-free second 45 minutes was much appreciated by players and staff amid a welter of challenging fixtures.

TEAMS

LIVERPOOL
Alisson; Alexander-Arnold, Matip, van Dijk (Gomez 55), Robertson; Wijnaldum (Keïta 70), Henderson; Mané, Shaqiri (Milner 45), Firmino; Salah

SOUTHAMPTON
McCarthy; Soares, Vestergaard, Hoedt, Bertrand; Romeu (Bednarek 55), Redmond, Højbjerg, Lemina, Targett (Armstrong 55); Long (Austin 79)

MATCH FACTS

- Liverpool hadn't conceded at home in the league in 751 minutes and had scored 23 unanswered goals in that time.

- Salah had been directly involved in 41 goals in 31 games at Anfield (30 goals, 11 assists).
- This was Liverpool's eighth consecutive clean sheet at home against Southampton.

THEY SAID

Mark Hughes, Southampton manager: "I'd like to think that, on our day, we can give the best teams a good go. Hopefully we will prove that along the way but you have to acknowledge that Liverpool have a settled way of playing, personnel who have been here a long time and a manager who has been here a long time as well. They are clearly building something here."

WEDNESDAY 26 SEPTEMBER 2018 | EFL CUP – THIRD ROUND | ANFIELD
ATTENDANCE: 45,503

LIVERPOOL 1
(Sturridge 58)
CHELSEA 2
(Emerson 79, Hazard 85)

Reflecting on a first Liverpool defeat of the season, you could assess the team sheet, see eight changes from the win over Southampton and conclude that Jürgen Klopp had taken one League Cup liberty too many against a high-class opponent.

The truth, however, is that the Reds had ample opportunity to win this tie and in the end it was a combination of wayward finishing, plus a moment of individual brilliance from Chelsea's Eden Hazard that made the difference.

To detail the raft of changes made by Jürgen Klopp, in came Simon Mignolet, Nathaniel Clyne, Alberto Moreno and Dejan Lovren – in his first run-out since the World Cup final – all making their first starts of the season in an unfamiliar back five alongside Joel Matip. Fabinho also earned a first start of 2018/19, joining the returning James Milner and Naby Keïta in midfield. Sadio Mané and Xherdan Shaqiri retained their places, while Daniel Sturridge was back as centre-forward.

Chelsea made eight changes of their own, with the headline news that key players Hazard and N'Golo Kanté were dropped to the bench. There was a rare start for Ross Barkley, while Álvaro Morata would play up front, flanked by Willian and Victor Moses.

The first clear sight of goal came to Morata, whose central run was deftly found by Cesc Fàbregas. Morata's lob was parried by Mignolet and the striker found the angle too narrow to squeeze in the rebound. Mignolet was also equal to another close-range effort from Morata shortly after, the ball deflecting behind for a corner.

On half-an-hour, Liverpool had appeals for a penalty waved away when Naby Keïta went down under a challenge from Gary Cahill. Replays showed minimal contact. Then Keïta drew a fantastic save from Blues keeper Willy Caballero, who palmed away a rising drive. Next, Caballero kept out a Mané header from Shaqiri's lofted pass, as the Reds' pressure mounted.

As half-time approached, Sturridge might have done better when a loose pass from César Azpilicueta was instantly turned into his path by Shaqiri, but his first touch went awry. And straight after the break, he absolutely should have scored when a no-look back-pass from Andreas Christensen let the striker in one-on-one with Caballero. Sturridge took the ball round the keeper but couldn't wrap his foot around it with the goal gaping.

Sadio Mané had an unexpected chance when Barkley's mistimed back-header fell to him on the penalty spot. Mané stretched to reach it under pressure from Christensen, but the finish flicked off Caballero's knee and slid past the post.

A corner-kick bounced off Dejan Lovren's back onto the roof of the net and, eventually, the lead that had seemed certain to be taken from one of these chances arrived through Sturridge. Mané played Keïta into a promising position in the area and the latter's shot stung the palms of Caballero. The ball looped up and Sturridge executed an acrobatic volley to make it 1-0.

Although Mané continued to threaten with his dribbling skills on the left flank, Liverpool couldn't press home their advantage and on 78 minutes, the Blues were level. When second-half substitute Hazard's free kick from the near the right touchline was nodded down powerfully by Barkley, Mignolet stuck out a hand to save but Emerson was closest in attendance to poke the ball over the line. A first Chelsea goal for the defender.

Sturridge nearly restored the lead with a long-range strike against Caballero's bar, but then Hazard took centre stage. Again from the right-hand side, one touch took him inside Keïta and Moreno, then he changed direction, nutmegged Moreno and fired a shot past Mignolet into the far corner that was past the keeper in a blink. It was a moment of extreme high quality worthy of winning any cup tie.

Liverpool's regret was that the home side could and should have been out of sight before the Belgian was even introduced.

TEAMS

LIVERPOOL

Mignolet; Clyne, Matip, Lovren, Moreno; Milner (Henderson 60), Fabinho (Salah 87), Keïta; Shaqiri, Sturridge, Mané (Firmino 71)

CHELSEA

Caballero; Azpilicueta, Cahill, Christensen (Luiz 73), Emerson; Barkley, Fàbregas, Kovačić (Kanté 64); Moses, Morata, Willian (Hazard 56)

MATCH FACTS

- Familiar foes: this was the 57th time Liverpool and Chelsea had met since 2000, making it the most-played fixture in English football since the millennium.
- Daniel Sturridge had scored 11 goals in his last 11 League Cup appearances.
- This was Liverpool's first home defeat since 27 January, when West Brom knocked the Reds out of the FA Cup in the fourth round.

THEY SAID

Gianfranco Zola, Chelsea assistant manager: "Eden [Hazard] is one of the best players in Europe and one of the best in the world. His goal is proof of that and he's getting better and better. But I don't think this game will have much impact on [the league meeting on] Saturday. It was a close game and Liverpool had their chances to win it."

SATURDAY 29 SEPTEMBER 2018 | PREMIER LEAGUE | STAMFORD BRIDGE | ATTENDANCE: 40,625

CHELSEA 1

(Hazard 25)

LIVERPOOL 1

(Sturridge 89)

Just as Chelsea had turned the result in their favour three days before with a late, exceptional piece of individual skill, here was Liverpool's response in kind. True, it was only to level the scores but most observers considered 1-1 a fair result after Daniel Sturridge's wonder-goal earned the Reds an away point at the Bridge.

Managers Klopp and Sarri embraced warmly at the end and both would have enjoyed the spectacle – with the two clubs' main cast restored to their respective starting XIs, this was a match with much quality to savour. The only niggle for Liverpool fans was that, as in the League Cup tie, enough chances were created to have come away with a win.

On a sunny early evening in the capital, Mo Salah and Sadio Mané both had efforts early on but each was skewed wildly off target. Roberto Firmino then had a promising opening snuffed out by the covering David Luiz.

Chelsea carved out a clear chance on 23 minutes as Luiz's 60-yard pass picked out the run of Willian in behind Andy Robertson. The winger had only Alisson to beat but the keeper – clad all in shocking pink – was alert and advanced quickly enough to block a dinked attempt to finish.

Respite was brief, though. Two minutes later, Eden Hazard was sent clear by Mateo Kovačić. The Belgian's pace meant Joe Gomez was unable to block the route to goal and a sure-footed diagonal across Alisson nestled inside the far post.

Salah came close after holding off Marcos Alonso when played in by Firmino. He rounded Kepa, but the angle was narrow and although he managed to squeeze a shot on target, Antonio Rüdiger had sprinted round to cover and was able to block on the line.

With half-time approaching, Mané tried a lavish overhead kick when a pass to the overlapping James Milner might have been the better option. He did much better early in the second half, wriggling elusively in the box and contriving a near-post finish that drew a superb, plunging save from Kepa.

Hazard nearly doubled the home side's lead when a quick free kick opened up an acre of space on the left. He drove towards goal, with Liverpool's back-four frantically scrambling to cover, but his shot clattered into Alisson's legs and flew over the bar.

Xherdan Shaqiri replaced Salah and should have levelled within four minutes of his introduction. Robertson took advantage of a slip by César Azpilicueta and his centre picked out the Swiss in a central position, 12 yards out. Shaqiri let the ball run across him and fluffed the chance wide.

Luiz needed to be in the right place when Milner shaped to shoot, but then delivered a deft cross to Firmino, whose downward header was goalbound. With Kepa beaten, the Chelsea defender stuck out a foot to clear.

With just four minutes of normal time remaining, Klopp withdrew Milner for Sturridge and the striker repaid his manager's faith with a dipping 25-yard drive that left the away fans and Liverpool bench in delighted disbelief.

TEAMS

CHELSEA

Arrizabalaga; Azpilicueta, Rüdiger, Luiz, Alonso; Kanté, Jorginho, Kovačić (Barkley 81); Willian (Moses 73), Giroud (Morata 65), Hazard

LIVERPOOL

Alisson; Alexander-Arnold, Gomez, van Dijk, Robertson; Wijnaldum, Henderson (Keïta 78), Milner (Sturridge 86); Salah (Shaqiri 66), Firmino, Mané

MATCH FACTS

- Sturridge had scored 17 Premier League goals as a substitute, level with Ole Gunnar Solskjær and behind only Olivier Giroud (19) and Jermain Defoe (24).
- Georginio Wijnaldum made his 100th appearance for Liverpool in all competitions.
- Eden Hazard was topping the Premier League scoring charts with six goals.

THEY SAID

Chelsea manager Maurizio Sarri: "It's very strange [that Liverpool haven't won the league for 28 years]. But the important thing is now they are ready. [Klopp] is one of the best coaches in the world at the moment. They have worked very well in the last season with these players. I think they are ready to win maybe the Premier League, maybe the Champions League, but ready to win something important."

PREMIER LEAGUE TABLE AT END OF SEPTEMBER 2018

Pos	Team	Pld	W	D	L	GF	GA	GD	Pts
1	Manchester City	7	6	1	0	21	3	18	19
2	Liverpool	7	6	1	0	15	3	12	19
3	Chelsea	7	5	2	0	15	5	10	17
4	Tottenham Hotspur	7	5	0	2	14	7	7	15
5	Arsenal	7	5	0	2	14	9	5	15
6	Watford	7	4	1	2	11	8	3	13
7	Leicester City	7	4	0	3	13	10	3	12
8	Wolverhampton Wanderers	7	3	3	1	8	6	2	12
9	AFC Bournemouth	6	3	1	2	10	11	-1	10
10	Manchester United	7	3	1	3	10	12	-2	10
11	Everton	7	2	3	2	11	11	0	9
12	Burnley	7	2	1	4	9	11	-2	7
13	Crystal Palace	6	2	1	3	4	6	-2	7
14	West Ham United	7	2	1	4	8	12	-4	7
15	Brighton & Hove Albion	7	1	2	4	8	13	-5	5
16	Southampton	7	1	2	4	6	11	-5	5
17	Fulham	7	1	2	4	8	16	-8	5
18	Newcastle United	7	0	2	5	4	10	-6	2
19	Cardiff City	7	0	2	5	4	16	-12	2
20	Huddersfield Town	7	0	2	5	3	16	-13	2

UEFA CHAMPIONS LEAGUE GROUP C AT END OF SEPTEMBER 2018

Pos	Team	Pld	W	D	L	GD	Pts
1	Liverpool	1	1	0	0	1	3
2	Red Star Belgrade	1	0	1	0	0	1
3	Napoli	1	0	1	0	0	1
4	Paris Saint-Germain	1	0	0	1	-1	0

CHAPTER THREE

—

OCTOBER

"IF WE DO NOT ENTERTAIN THE PEOPLE,
WHY DO WE PLAY FOOTBALL?"

Two teams with sky blue kits stood between Liverpool and the next international break, both boasting oodles of international talent and both posing highly credible threats to Liverpool's ambitions on two fronts. The Reds had faced both Napoli and Manchester City during their Stateside sojourn in pre-season – winning 5-0 and 2-1 respectively – but at full competitive strength these opponents would provide a far sturdier examination.

The Italians, managed by Carlo Ancelotti, had lost 3-1 away at the weekend to Serie A champions Juventus, so this tie was a test of their ability to bounce back against another high-end opponent.

The manager spoke in glowing terms about Liverpool at his pre-match preview and explained just what his side would need to do to achieve a positive result.

"Regardless of who plays, what remains the same is our strategy and the mentality of trying to impose our game. We need to keep a balance throughout," said Ancelotti.

"I think we have a strong team that's achieving levels of excellence in terms of its play and mentality. At times we're not able to maintain our consistency, but I'm confident because with time we can only improve.

"Liverpool will play with very high intensity so we'll need to be ready for that. It's important that we show bravery and personality, implement what we've worked on and be ready to withstand their counter-attacks. If we play the way we know how, we can cause Liverpool problems."

The key change in Ancelotti's line-up involved Polish striker Arkadiusz Milik starting up front alongside local favourite Lorenzo Insigne, with Belgian international Dries Mertens dropping to the bench. Skilful captain Marek Hamšík and tricky winger José Callejón were retained and would be central to the home side's attacking intentions.

Jürgen Klopp made just one change to the side that had started against Chelsea in the league, with Naby Keïta coming in for Jordan Henderson in midfield.

"Fresh legs and the opportunity to do it," Klopp told BT Sport when asked for his rationale behind the change. "Hendo has played a lot of games now and didn't have a perfect pre-season. I want to have Naby's specific skills in-between the lines."

That theory, however, didn't last long on the pitch. Less than 20 minutes into the first half, Keïta went down with no one around him in centre-field and was stretchered off after a lengthy delay. It later transpired that he had been whisked to hospital for scans amid worry about a potential spinal injury.

"[Keïta] got a flight to Liverpool at 2pm," said the hospital's cardiologist Ciro Mauro on Neapolitan radio, confirming that the player had travelled back separately from the rest of the squad. "He [had] a strong back trauma. He had an MRI and CAT scan to rule out any problems to his spine."

It's not the way Keïta would have chosen to end his Champions League debut; but for all connected with the club there was much relief at the news.

Back in the Stadio San Paolo, a balmy southern Italian day had given way to cloud and drizzle, but despite plenty of empty seats in the lower tiers of the ground, both sets of fans were giving full-throated encouragement to their teams.

Napoli had come close before Keïta's departure, with Insigne's shot from the left of the box flying inches wide. Then Liverpool keeper Alisson had to be alert to Milik's turn and shot that spun up off van Dijk's foot, but chances were scarce in the opening 45 minutes.

The home side, though, came on strong after the break. Milik forced a good save from Alisson down to his left, with Joe Gomez arriving just in time to tidy up. And Gomez again was in good position to clear off the line from Callejon. Dries Mertens crashed a finish into the underside of the bar and the goal was still – just – intact. But in the 90th minute, Insigne slid in to covert Callejon's cross and secure three points.

With PSG thumping Red Star 6-1 in Paris, Liverpool dropped to third in the group on goal difference and Napoli rose to top spot on four points.

The manager was typically honest in his appraisal of the performance. "We have to blame ourselves, that's how it is," said Klopp.

"The start of the game was okay, then the timing for our defensive movements were not good enough. We didn't close the spaces in the right moment, we didn't react in the right situation, so they could play through our formation. Things like this happen but not as often as they did tonight, and it costs energy. The second half was not good enough and it's always a bad sign when your goalkeeper is your best player."

Former Reds players on the BT Sport couch – Jim Beglin, Michael Owen and Steve McManaman – were less worried about the performance, Owen suggesting he wasn't bothered by the defeat because a cautious approach meant "[Liverpool] didn't lose playing their way". And McManaman was sure his old side would still progress from the group: "I thought it was a poor performance and they have to get better [but] Liverpool should qualify and quite comfortably. They should beat Napoli at Anfield, [so] it won't matter in the grand scheme of things.'

However, *The Telegraph*'s Chris Bascombe reflected much of the reaction from the travelling press pack, who believed Klopp's men had been well below par in Naples.

"Liverpool's front three brought tornadoes to the continent a year ago," he wrote. "In Naples they were sedated.

"Carlo Ancelotti, described by Jürgen Klopp as 'a smart fox' prior to the Italians' victory, lived up to his portrayal by proving the great pacifier of Mohamed Salah, Roberto Firmino and Sadio Mané. Liverpool's feared trio spent more time chasing than combining. For the esteemed coach – once interviewed for the Anfield job when Klopp was preferred – this was a tactical triumph.

"Perhaps more extraordinary than Napoli inflicting the first group game defeat of Klopp's Anfield reign was Liverpool's failure to have a shot on goal. It is certainly rare to see Liverpool so anaesthetised."

Two defeats and a draw over the course of a week were hardly ideal preparation for welcoming Manchester City to Anfield, but if the team returned somewhat deflated by their trip to Italy, there was no better incentive to redouble their efforts than a visit from the Premier League champions.

Since dropping points against Wolves in the last game in August, Pep Guardiola's men had been in peerless form in the league – four games, four wins, 12 scored, one conceded. The only blot on their September copybook had been an unexpected reverse at the Etihad against Lyon on Matchday 1 of the Champions League. But they quickly righted the ship with an away win at Hoffenheim before setting their sights on Merseyside.

As it happened, the respective form of both teams perhaps had less impact on the outcome of this match than the memories of last season's wildly fluctuating matches in the league and Champions League, when Liverpool proved one of the only puzzles that Guardiola's class of 2017-18 had been unable to fathom.

Klopp identified a weakness in City's defence. With the Blues' full-backs playing so high and wide, if Liverpool won possession back far enough up the pitch, the front three could attack the centre-halves before the full-backs were able to retreat and cover. Two belting finishes from Alex Oxlade-Chamberlain helped, obviously.

But Pep didn't get where he is without the nous to learn from his mistakes. "It's a team, Liverpool, the strong point is the quality of the players, the manager," he said. "When you make a mistake, they use it. This side, when you have some doubts and situations like that, they are so clinical. That's why they are one of the best teams in the world."

He would also have been aware that City had played 17 games at Anfield since they last won one. The last time the Blues had left here with the points was in May 2003, when their front two comprised Nicolas Anelka and a certain Robbie Fowler. Before that, the last win was on Boxing Day 1981. All teams have a bogey ground; City's is Anfield. Guardiola's guiding principle on this occasion was that Liverpool would not again be allowed to run riot on their home turf.

Klopp perhaps sensed this, too, with a note of caution present in his pre-match remarks.

"If we do not entertain the people, why do we play [football]?" he asked. "It's not always possible and it's always hard work but that's really an important thing. That's why we have to try and create as often as possible and Pep's teams are best at that.

"We are not bad [at] a few other things and that's why we were not the most comfortable opponents for City but that means nothing for Sunday. We need to be at 100 per cent, if not 110 per cent, to deal with the quality of City."

First place in the table was visiting second, so this was the most eagerly anticipated league fixture of the season to date – words that rarely deliver anything but a commentator's curse on the occasion.

Two of the best attacking sides in Europe managed to contrive an attritional, fractious 0-0, full of niggly fouls on a somewhat less-than-super Sunday.

But Pep's plan so nearly worked. A late penalty, earned when Leroy Sane was felled by Virgil van Dijk, would surely have pinched the points, had the chance not been spurned by Riyad Mahrez. With regular taker Sergio Agüero substituted, Mahrez overruled designated no.2 Gabriel Jesus on spot-kick duties, but his effort was blazed high into bank of City fans behind the goal.

Guardiola took responsibility on his own shoulders. "During training sessions every day I see Mahrez taking penalties and it [gives] me a lot of confidence," he said after the game. "It will be good experience for him – next time it will go in. Jesus wanted to [take it]. I apologise. It was my decision."

It was a cruel end to the game for Mahrez, who for much of the afternoon had been the exception to the scattergun action on display. Always willing to get on the ball and drive forward, he provided the few moments of alarm for goalkeeper Alisson and could have been forgiven for thinking his endeavours deserved some reward.

With the second international break now due, media reaction focused on taking stock. Just how good were Liverpool, compared to the team Klopp's men were trying to dethrone?

"Guardiola did not want his side undone by the attacking blurs that have come to define and decide these fixtures and admitted he intended to oversee a match of attrition rather than attacking splendour," wrote Melissa Reddy of joe.co.uk. "The comments from City and the honesty over their approach underscores Liverpool's elevation under Klopp, who celebrates his third anniversary on Merseyside this Monday. They are now genuinely title contenders – albeit with a lot of improvement still to ensure – and are treated as such."

The *Liverpool Echo*'s James Pearce reiterated this theme of respect: "A point apiece was the right result. Neither team did enough to merit anything more," he wrote. "Fatigue undoubtedly played a part after a gruelling run of fixtures, with both sides failing to come close to their fluent best.

"Respect was another factor with Pep Guardiola, who has now won just one of his last eight meetings with Klopp, clearly desperate to avoid a repeat of City's previous visit in the Champions League back in April when they were 3-0 down inside half an hour. The Spaniard, who has previously admitted to being "scared" of Liverpool's firepower, wasn't prepared to risk another mauling by leaving his backline exposed."

During the international break, Jordan Henderson and Dejan Lovren faced each other in a rerun of the World Cup semi-final in which Croatia had prevailed in the summer. The match was an eerie event played behind closed doors – the punishment after fans sprayed a swastika on the pitch before a Euro 2016 qualifier against Italy in Split – and more reminiscent of a training game as the players' voices echoed around the stands. A few hardy England fans found vantage points on high ground around the stadium, but otherwise it was players and staff alone.

A scoreless outcome summed up the rather featureless spectacle. One interesting side-note, at least, was that Jadon Sancho, the English youngster lighting up the Bundesliga for Borussia Dortmund, became the first player born after 2000 to play for England's senior men's team. All readers of a certain vintage are entitled to feel their age at this point.

Joe Gomez came in for the suspended John Stones as England then took on Spain in Seville and gave the Spanish quite a shock. Luis Enrique's team had battered Croatia 6-0 in their Nations League opener, so when England opened up a 3-0 lead on 38 minutes, home fans were shaking their heads in disbelief. Spain rallied in the second half but the 3-2 win for Gareth Southgate's men was a result of some historic note. The Spanish were previously unbeaten in 38 competitive matches at home (since losing to Greece in 2003), and had never before conceded three in the first half in their history.

Meanwhile, Gini Wijnaldum and Virgil van Dijk enjoyed a 3-0 win over Germany as the Netherlands' renaissance continued apace. The Germans went on to lose to France as well, and after their group stage exit in Russia, Jürgen Klopp's home nation were having a rare crisis of confidence.

Elsewhere, Andy Robertson's Scotland let a lead slip in Israel to go down 2-1 in their Nations League group, while Alisson, Fabinho and Roberto Firmino all saw action in friendlies held in Saudi Arabia: a 2-0 win over the hosts was followed by a 1-0 win over arch-rivals Argentina, the latter made all the sweeter by the winner coming in the 94th minute.

Returning to domestic matters, Klopp urged Liverpool not underestimate their next opponents – struggling Huddersfield – and his great friend and compatriot David Wagner.

While the Reds lay third as one of three teams as yet unbeaten in 2018/19, the Terries reflected a mirror image: third from bottom as one of three teams, alongside Newcastle and Cardiff, yet to win a game. It was hard to shake the conviction this was a game Liverpool could and should win with something to spare, yet the manager knew the pitfalls of this line of thinking from a team perspective.

"This game is a trap, a 100 per cent trap," Klopp argued. "We are third with 20 points, they are pretty much bottom of the table. That's why analysis is so important; if you only used the table to analyse a team, you would say 'They don't score a lot, they conceded a few and they are third from the bottom so obviously not a good football team'. Then we'd have a big problem. But, thank God, we have a lot of people working on analysis, not only against PSG. That's good, so we have all the information we need."

Wagner and Klopp played together in the 1990s at Mainz and also coached together at Borussia Dortmund, with the former taking charge of the second XI while the latter had the top job. The pair developed a friendship – along with a fondness for designer glasses and baseball caps – and became so close that Klopp was, in fact, the best man at Wagner's wedding.

"I've known Jürgen longer than I've known my wife," Wagner told *The Guardian*, shortly after taking the reins at Huddersfield. "We met up at Mainz and I took his place in the team, so he changed his role from a striker to a defender because it was much easier for him! He always thinks about football or his team, always. I think you do this if you are a good head coach. You can never stop your brain from thinking about what could happen tomorrow or next week or the next hour. It is not possible to close your brain to this in football."

When Wagner arrived in English football, it was a brave move from Dortmund – one of German football's heavyweights – to a club lying 19th in the English Championship. But all first-time head coaches have to make the step up somewhere and the familiar Dortmund style of high press and intensity was a conspicuous success at the John Smith's Stadium.

In his first full season in charge, Huddersfield were promoted through the play-offs to the Premier League, and though 2017/18 was always a battle near the foot of the table, Wagner's team ensured survival with draws against Manchester City and Chelsea during a fearsome sequence of fixtures in the run-in. Along the way they had also beaten Manchester United, so Klopp was right: whatever their current position, this was not a team to take lightly.

And the underdogs came so close to getting something from this game: a point – an end to the home goal drought that extended back to April; something for the home fans to cheer.

Captain Jonathan Hogg struck a post, referee Michael Oliver waved away arguable claims for a penalty for handball against James Milner and Steve Mounie missed a glorious opportunity near the end to equalise but fired over.

Huddersfield were, indeed, terrier-like in their efforts to disrupt Liverpool's passing and their proactive approach was highly impressive. Although Mo Salah's pinpoint strike on 24 minutes proved enough to earn the win for the visitors, most observers believed Wagner's team did enough to deserve a draw.

After the match, the two managers embraced warmly and then took the unusual step of being interviewed together.

"It is strange [to face Wagner] in the preparation, but only on a private level, as it's the only week of the year when we don't speak," said Klopp. "We could have scored in five, six, seven situations with one easy pass. The last pass was so often not good. We'll have to watch it again. We were not fresh. But mostly Huddersfield did really well and we had to fight; we did that really well and I am proud. I expect us to do better, and we will do."

Wagner responded: "I have seen this [type of] game before, against Tottenham and Burnley. We have played well, with passion and aggression, we pressed high and caused panic. The players have done well but without results. I would lie if I said it isn't a problem, but at the end it is a challenge, and the experience of turning performances into results will be exciting." Klopp said it was the first time in his career that one of his teams had been winning "average matches" – in reference to hard-fought wins against Brighton, Leicester and here – and expanded on the theme of a lack of freshness after the international break.

"I prefer the spectacular way, but I would take that [result] today completely," he said.

"When you come back from the international break there are many things no one asks about, like the time difference. That is why I was a bit more animated on the touchline today because if you are tired, you at least need to be afraid of your manager."

On his return to the side, Adam Lallana was pleased to come through more than an hour of first-team action with no ill-effects. After a difficult time with injuries in 2018 that contributed to his omission from the final England World Cup squad, he was looking forward to being a regular part of the Reds push for silverware

"It was nice to contribute, it's been so long," he said. "On that form, Huddersfield have a good chance to stay in the league and do well. But it's a huge three points for us. [The time off with injury has] been tough, just constant setbacks, but I feel I'm in a really good place now, I just want to play games. Everyone's going to have to contribute if we're going to achieve something special."

It's a widely accepted maxim of the Champions League group stage that if you win your home games, you'll probably qualify. There's no guarantee, of course – in 2013/14 Napoli failed to progress from Arsenal's group despite winning four games and amassing 12 points, losing out to the Gunners on head-to-head goal difference by one goal – but that was very much the exception to the rule. Nine points or above will generally ensure progress to the round of 16.

So as disappointing as defeat to Napoli on Matchday 2 had been, it needed to be viewed in the context of the group as a whole, and the visit of Crvena Zvezda – or Red Star Belgrade as they are better known here – was an ideal opportunity to get the Reds' European campaign back on track.

Winners of the European Cup in 1991 when still part of the former Yugoslavia, the Serbian side were back in the competition after a 26-year absence and it wasn't easy to assess what sort of team would present itself at Anfield. A valuable point had been eked out in a goalless draw their opener against Napoli, but the defence proved extremely porous against the quality of Neymar, Mbappé and Cavani in Parc des Princes. Paris Saint Germain ran out 6-1 winners.

After a tricky few weeks for Liverpool domestically and in Europe, was this a chance to loosen up a little and play with some more of the Reds' customary freedom? Klopp insisted the task at hand was to obtain three valuable points and that quality of performance was, in the end, commensurate with results.

"The first job we have to do is win football games and we have played really good stuff already this season," he said. "We all compare it with the best games from last year because nobody remembers the average games. For us, the most important thing is always to win and all the games we won so far we deserved. The two draws in the Premier League, we deserved a point. The game we lost against Napoli we deserved to lose."

On Red Star themselves: "I know they are able to defend and they are able to create as well. Their strengths are the different possibilities to line up, different strikers, tall, quick, good footballers, good headers, full-backs really on their bikes, very offensive-orientated, a clear structure.

"Offensively and defensively, Serbian teams are always well-organised, they know how to defend and are not bothered to be a bit more aggressive. So, we need to be ready for a really hard fight, we need to fight for each little square metre of space with all we have. For that, we need our crowd, that's very important. We learned last year especially that atmosphere can make the difference."

A noisy Anfield heeded this last call to arms (albeit the home fans had little atmosphere to battle against as Red Star were denied an allocation tickets due to a pitch invasion earlier in the season in Salzburg) and the team responded with a display of vibrancy, pace and power with which the visitors simply could not live.

A tactical rejig returned Liverpool to 4-2-3-1 – the formation in which they'd last overwhelmed an opponent, Southampton, in September. In this case Fabinho – a day after his 25th birthday – was handed a first European start for the club alongside Gini Wijnaldum. An attacking midfield three of Sadio Mané, Roberto Firmino and Xherdan Shaqiri lined up behind Mo Salah with a licence to go and play. Trent Alexander-Arnold was restored to right-back and Joe Gomez resumed his partnership with Virgil van Dijk at centre-half.

Ahead of the game, Alexander-Arnold said there was still much more to come from Liverpool this season. "There's always room for improvement," he said at the pre-match press conference. "It's something we're all really excited about and something we need to strive towards in putting in better performances and reaching our full potential as a team."

Reflecting on a couple of games out of the side he acknowledged that squad rotation was something players – especially young ones – had to accept.

"It's wrong to think you'll be going into a game and starting week-in, week-out," he said. "It's only right that there's rotation to keep everyone on their toes and get the best out of people."

With Alexander-Arnold offering width and a constant out-ball, Shaqiri had a virtually free role, able to tuck in centrally, get on the ball and create havoc in the Red Star ranks. The Swiss player created the openings for the first two goals, both with delightfully weighted passes, and was a menace throughout.

Firmino converted the first from Andy Robertson's cut back after Shaqiri's pass left Ben Nabouhane stranded; Salah the second after a killer touch from Shaqiri dropped a fizzing forward ball from Wijnaldum into the Egyptian's path.

Salah then celebrated his record-breakingly rapid 50th goal from the club after an emphatic finish from the penalty spot, to put the Reds 3-0 up at the break.

The home side had to settle for just one more in the second half but it could have been five or six, with Mané missing a penalty and a glorious late chance. In between, though he slid in a finish at close range from Sturridge's lay-off.

Over in Paris, PSG and Napoli drew 2-2, with the home side grateful to Angel Di Maria for a stunning injury-time finish that rescued a point. That was good news for Liverpool, too, as points dropped by both of their main rivals for qualification meant they ascended to the top of Group C at the halfway stage.

Klopp was asked about Fabinho's performance and suggested it was the change in system that helped get the best out of the Brazilian: "[He was] very, very good. The present for his birthday was not that he was in the starting line-up, it was that we played his favourite system with a double six [two holding midfielders]. He played really well. It was good to see. Very aggressive – everything was there. For the first game in a while, his second game from the beginning, it was good. It was quite impressive what people saw tonight. It always helps a player to play a good game, and that helped us tonight and helped him. That was the start, let's carry on."

Next up on the Premier League calendar were Cardiff City, promoted back to the top-flight under Neil Warnock and, at the time of this fixture, wrestling with a horribly difficult run. Over the course of seven games since 2 September, they'd faced Arsenal, Chelsea, Manchester City, Tottenham and now Liverpool, but they were at least coming to Anfield after a first win of the season – over fellow strugglers Fulham.

Before the Bluebirds' trip to Merseyside, it seemed maverick boss Warnock was adopting a novel psychological tactic – an attempt to kill the opposition with flattery.

"[Jürgen] is the sort of manager I would love to be at that level," he said. "He has so much enthusiasm, it's infectious. You don't lose that passion, just the way I don't think I will ever lose it – it is something you have from [when you are a kid] and it never leaves you. Some managers are quiet and introverted, thoughtful and so on, but I like to see the passion from a manager on the touchline.

"So much is talked about [Liverpool's] spending for this season alone, but I think they have spent wisely. From the goalkeeper to several other purchases, they have bought some super players and when you look at the money they generated from the Champions League alone, then you can see why they can spend it. With such a good manager and so many excellent players they are going to run Manchester City close for sure."

Klopp returned the compliment in his own pre-match remarks: "I'm really looking forward to meeting [Neil]. I've heard a lot about him and he's obviously very talented vocal-wise!

"[I know] he's one of the most experienced managers in the world of football and it's unbelievable some of the things he has achieved. My respect for the Championship [has grown] so much since I've been here – such a difficult league – and it seems like he could do pretty much whatever he wanted and got promoted.

"So we are aware of the way Cardiff and Neil Warnock play. It's a challenge, as it always is after a [European] game, to adapt to the new situation and last week [winning against Fulham] would have given them a big boost. But even before they were not that bad. All the games they lost were close. They deserve all our respect and they will get it."

Leaders City were not in action until Monday night, so this was a chance for Liverpool to go back to the top of the Premier League pile – temporarily at least – and apply some pressure to Pep's men, who faced a tricky trip to play Tottenham at Wembley.

Klopp was still without Jordan Henderson and Naby Keïta but returned to 4-3-3, with Fabinho and Gini Wijnaldum joined by Adam Lallana in midfield as Xherdan Shaqiri dropped to the bench. In defence Dejan Lovren was preferred to Joe Gomez at centre-half and Alberto Moreno came in for a first start of the season at left-back.

The bald statistics of scoreline, possession and shots – all weighted heavily in favour of the home side – were somewhat unreflective of the general play as for 55 minutes Liverpool were unable to add to their early lead, delivered by Mo Salah after the ball rattled around in the box from Trent Alexander-Arnold centre, then squirted to the striker at the back post.

Cardiff threatened frequently on the break and came close to restoring parity early in the second period when a set-piece routine was bundled in but rightly called offside.

The second goal came via Sadio Mané after Roberto Firmino made an intelligent run into the left channel and laid the ball off to the supporting Moreno, who found Mané on the edge of the area. The Senegalese twisted past two challenges before unleashing an unstoppable drive past keeper Neil Etheridge.

Cardiff weren't done, though. Warnock made two changes, bringing on the fresh legs of Loïc Damour and Kadeem Harris for Aron Gunnarsson and Josh Murphy and within three minutes the visitors were back in it. After a neat link-up with Bobby Reid, Junior Hoilett sent in a cross that was converted by striker Callum Paterson and Liverpool had conceded a home league goal for the first time since February.

Unfortunately for the travelling fans, Liverpool's two-goal lead was reinstated six minutes later by substitute Xherdan Shaqiri, rolling in his first for the Reds after good work by Fabinho and the ever-dangerous Salah. And Mané chipped in a fourth from another Salah pass as Cardiff tired late on.

Warnock took the defeat on the chin, rueing individual errors rather than any lack of collective effort. "I think [the scoreline's] a bit harsh but you get punished for making mistakes," he said in a BBC interview. "I thought we had some great opportunities in the first half, breaking away; and we made the wrong decision so many times.

"I said to them at half-time if we could just improve that in the second half and get the next goal, we could give them a good game. Unfortunately we didn't, but all credit to the lads – they fought back. Anfield's an intimidating place and our fans have been fantastic. They know we were up against it. It was so quiet in the ground apart from our fans when [Paterson's goal] went in. I think it's the first goal I've ever scored here as a manager!

"It's difficult for [a promoted team] against the top-five teams unless you've spent an awful lot of money [but] they've given me everything today."

Klopp noted that it had been a tough match against a side that didn't "give away space" and suggested conceding a goal had actually helped, both to sharpen the team's concentration and to create that extra space as Cardiff pushed forward for a second.

He was particularly pleased that Shaqiri had netted his first goal in Red after coming on as a substitute. "Having a good footballer [like Shaqiri on the bench] helps," Klopp said. "Four games in a row he has played with us and his country, so [it was] clear he would not start today. Bringing him on is a good thing to do. We have a good squad – if they stay fit we have a lot of players who can play. [Shaqiri] had a good impact."

The Reds could take much satisfaction from a return to attacking ways, but the importance of form and results were rather put in context later that evening. The football world was shocked by the news that Leicester City chairman, Vichai Srivaddhanaprabha, had been killed in a helicopter crash outside the King Power Stadium after the Foxes' match with West Ham, along with three other passengers and the pilot. Fond tributes were paid to a man who had been hugely well respected in the club and, just as notable, for his generosity in the community at large. This was an overseas owner with a truly local touch, and one whose underdog club had, in 2015/16, pulled off a feat for the footballing ages.

Manchester City's narrow win at Tottenham in the Monday night game took Pep Guardiola's team back to the top of the table, but across the first 10 games of the league season it had been clearly established that Liverpool were credible title contenders.

Late in October, John Barnes – twice a league-winner with Liverpool and part of the last side to achieve the feat in 1989/90 – reflected on the club's progress under Jürgen Klopp and potential for the current campaign and a for the future.

"This is the first time since the late 1990s that I've thought we have a chance of winning the title. Brendan Rodgers' team finished second [in 2013/14] and had an incredible run, but I never felt there was quite enough there to sustain it; they didn't have that balance despite having such superb players like Luis Suarez.

"Now there is a lovely balance to the team. Not only can they compete with – and beat – the top teams, they also look far more comfortable against the lesser lights – teams that caused them so many problems even last season.

"Jürgen Klopp addressed many of the [defensive] issues with the purchase of Alisson and van Dijk and made them a much bigger threat as a result. It is just unfortunate that they have to overcome such a formidable force as Manchester City, a club with the financial resources, a wonderful manager and massive squad of hugely talented players with the money to buy more if they need them.

"Klopp is the main reason for this feeling of optimism. He is currently a reflection of the club's passion and commitment, and that's why the Liverpool fans love him, and why the fans respond to him.

"If the players don't perform, then that is not a problem for the manager, he seeks out the solutions. He brings in the players he believes will be right to bring that balance to the team, so they may not be the world's biggest names, costliest players, the names the fans might be wanting and expecting, but the ones he feels is right for his team.

"For example, James Milner might not have been right for Guardiola. But he's right for Klopp. That doesn't mean Milner is better under Klopp and worse under Guardiola. It means they have different ideas about players and how they form the right balance to their teams. Kevin de Bruyne and David Silva are important to Guardiola, but I don't think they are Klopp-type players; whereas Guardiola might not go for Naby Keïta or Gini Wijnaldum because they are Klopp-type players.

"If Liverpool can win the title, they will continue to challenge to win it again and again. [But even] if they don't win it this season, they will be high among the likely winners next time and time after time. There was a time when it was Manchester United and Arsenal first or second, or Manchester United and Chelsea, and Liverpool's best hope was finishing in the top six or top four at best. Now Liverpool are going to be first or second for the foreseeable future because they have all the ingredients – the finances, the manager and a great team."

OCTOBER MATCH REPORTS

WEDNESDAY 3 OCTOBER 2018 | UEFA CHAMPIONS LEAGUE – GROUP C
STADIO SAN PAOLO | ATTENDANCE: 37,057

NAPOLI 1
(Insigne 90)
LIVERPOOL 0

Hometown hero Lorenzo Insigne struck late to snatch the points on Matchday 2, just when it seemed Liverpool had ridden out a second-half storm in Naples.

Insigne stretched to reach Jose Callejon's cross and slide the ball past Alisson with 30 seconds of normal time remaining in the Stadio San Paolo.

In fairness, it was no less than the home side deserved. They created all the best chances and had been unlucky not to go ahead a few minutes earlier, when substitute Dries Mertens saw his shinned effort crash back off the underside of Alisson's bar after full-back Mario Rui's delicious centre from the left.

The visitor's careful preparations were disrupted in the first half as Naby Keïta – selected in place of Jordan Henderson – was stretchered off with a back problem. It looked serious but after a trip to hospital Keïta was later given the all clear.

Henderson resumed his role in central midfield, but there was little of the early-season fluency about the Reds' play. Passes were misplaced, forward runs were either not being read or were well covered by the Napoli defence. It was a highly unusual occurrence that Jürgen Klopp's side did not muster a shot on target all evening and only had four attempts in all.

Napoli were tidy on the ball and crisp in their movement and passing. Mohawk-sporting captain Marek Hamšík kept control in the centre of the park while Callejon and Rui offered plenty of width.

Fabian Ruiz and Arkadiusz Milik both drew good saves from Alisson; and Joe Gomez was on hand twice in rapid succession to clear danger in the box, once from a rebound off the keeper, once blocking on the line.

Mo Salah pulled a snap shot wide of goal and there was little else to encourage the travelling fans, despite their buoyant support.

Klopp introduced Fabinho for James Milner as Liverpool sought to preserve a point but it was the hosts who had the final word, Insigne sending a feisty home crowd home happy and Napoli to the top of Group C.

TEAMS

NAPOLI

Ospina; Maksim, Albiol, Koulibaly, Mario Rui; Callejon, Marques Loureiro, Hamsik, (Zielinskiat 81), Ruiz (Verdiat 68); Insigne, Milik (Mertens 68)

LIVERPOOL

Alisson; Alexander-Arnold, Gomez, van Dijk, Robertson; Milner (Fabinho 76), Wijnaldum, Keïta (Henderson 19); Salah, Firmino, Mané (Sturridge 89)

MATCH FACTS

- Liverpool recorded no shots on target in a Champions League match for the first time since February 2006 against Benfica.
- Joe Gomez played his 50th game for Liverpool in Naples.
- Roberto Firmino had featured in every European game for Liverpool under Jürgen Klopp, 30 in total.

THEY SAID

Michael Owen, BT Sport: "Liverpool are at their best when they commit so many bodies forward and have so many choices, more players in attacking positions, everything opens up it is like a chain reaction. Away from home you need good touches but it's difficult if you don't play the way you usually do."

SUNDAY 8 OCTOBER 2018 | PREMIER LEAGUE | ANFIELD | ATTENDANCE: 52,117

LIVERPOOL 0
MANCHESTER CITY 0

After a near-perfect display in central defence, Virgil van Dijk had cause to be relieved when Riyad Mahrez missed a late penalty and parity was preserved in this Sunday afternoon clash between the league's top two.

Van Dijk had mistimed his tackle on City's elusive wide-man Leroy Sané and Anfield feared the worst as Mahrez – the visitors' best attacking player on the day – put the ball on the spot. But the Algerian got right under his attempt and the ball sailed over the bar into the bank of visiting fans behind the goal.

Naturally the game was preceded by a much-hyped build-up but both sides were conspicuously more compact and less gung-ho than in last season's editions of the fixture.

Klopp made two changes from the starting line-up, with Trent Alexander-Arnold – on his 20th birthday – dropping to the bench and Dejan Lovren coming in. That meant a switch to right-back for Joe Gomez and hinted at a broadly more defensive set-up. Jordan Henderson started, with Naby Keïta sufficiently recovered from the back problem he sustained in Naples to make the bench.

City meanwhile had a wideranging reshuffle, with Raheem Sterling switched to the left and Mahrez in for Sane, Bernardo Silva came in for Ilkay Gundogan in the midfield three – Kevin de Bruyne was still unavailable, though back in training. John Stones replaced Vincent Kompany at centre-half, while Aymeric Laporte switched over from left-back to replace Nicolás Otamendi and Bernard Mendy took the left-back berth.

Liverpool began brightly and Mo Salah came close with four minutes gone, dragging a shot wide of the near post. Then Sane found some space to measure a cross for Salah, lurking at the far post, but Mendy was well stationed to clear.

It took the best part of 20 minutes for City to impose themselves on the match and they nearly profited from a moment of lost control by Gomez, when the young defender volleyed the ball back towards his own goal and City predator Sergio Agüero. Lovren snuffed out the danger, but risked giving the referee a decision to make as the Argentinian tumbled under his challenge. Sterling, nearby, appealed loudly for the decision but none was forthcoming.

With half an hour gone, James Milner was withdrawn with a muscle problem and replaced by Naby Keïta, and there followed a scruffy passage of play up to the break, featuring plenty of needly fouls but no shots on target for either side.

It took an hour for City to significantly threaten Liverpool's goal and Mahrez had two chances only a minute apart. His first was pulled narrowly wide, the second – after a loose touch from Andy Robertson – saved by Alisson.

Salah tried to lift the ball over Ederson after a collecting a long pass from Robertson but the lob was too heavy and flew out for a goal kick.

Sane and Jesus were introduced for Agüero and Sterling and the German's intervention was typically incisive, drawing a foul in the box from the hitherto flawless van Dijk. The execution from 12 yards was, however, wild.

TEAMS

LIVERPOOL

Alisson; Gomez, Lovren, van Dijk, Robertson; Wijnaldum, Henderson, Milner (Keïta 29); Salah, Firmino (Sturridge 72), Mané

MANCHESTER CITY

Ederson; Walker, Stones, Laporte, Mendy; B. Silva, Fernandinho, D. Silva; Mahrez, Agüero (Jesus 66), Sterling (Sane 76)

MATCH FACTS

- Riya Mahrez had now missed four of his last six penalties, for Leicester and now Manchester City.
- The Reds had scored in each of the last 24 league encounters with Manchester City at Anfield. The last time they had failed to find the net was in a goalless draw in August 1986.
- Sergio Agüero had failed to score in all 10 matches he'd played at Anfield (Man City 8, Atletico Madrid 2).

THEY SAID

Pep Guardiola, Manchester City manager: "If it is an open game at Anfield, you don't even have one per cent of a chance. We controlled it through Riyad Mahrez, Bernardo Silva, the guys to give the extra pass. Up and down [Liverpool] are the best team in the world in these transitions, offensive, defensive – it is built for that. In that situation they are much better."

OCTOBER

SATURDAY 20 OCTOBER 2018 | PREMIER LEAGUE | ANFIELD
ATTENDANCE: 24,263

HUDDERSFIELD TOWN 0
LIVERPOOL 1
(Salah 24)

David Wagner's Terriers may have been languishing in the Premier League's bottom three and without a goal at home all season, but this display against the high-flying Reds belied their position in the table and pushed the visitors to their full extent in their pursuit of Manchester City. The champions had eased past Burnley 5-0 earlier in the day to retake top spot from Chelsea.

The team news for this early-evening kick-off was that Liverpool made three changes from the starting XI against Manchester City. Naby Keïta and Sadio Mané were both out injured, while Roberto Firmino and Gini Wijnaldum dropped to the bench.

In came Xherdan Shaqiri and Daniel Sturridge, but the most eyecatching inclusion was that of Adam Lallana, the England international making his first appearance in a Reds shirt since August – and a first league start in 10 months – after recovering from a groin injury. James Milner had shaken off a hamstring problem in just 10 days to take his place in midfield.

Mo Salah's 50th goal in English football (including two for Chelsea) secured the points in the end – the Egyptian scoring his first in five matches with an angled drive after a neat piece of interplay between Joe Gomez and Shaqiri – but this win was far from straightforward.

Shortly after Salah's strike, a clearing header by Andy Robertson was controlled by Huddersfield captain Jonathan Hogg and struck brilliantly on the half-volley from 25 yards. The ball was still rising as it cannoned into the post, with Alisson well beaten. The search for a first home goal of the season went on.

Philip Billing sent a free-kick narrowly wide of the post, then the home side were vociferous in their claims for a penalty against James Milner for handball but referee Michael Oliver was unmoved. Alex Pritchard thought he had finally ended the drought just before the break but he was ruled offside after a lobbed finish bounced gently over the line.

Klopp brought Gini Wijnaldum on for Henderson at half-time, a precautionary measure as the Englishman had felt a tight hamstring, but Huddersfield still maintained a measure of control in midfield, preventing clear communication between Liverpool's forwards and their supply line. And the home side continued to threaten: Laurent Depoitre's header just before the hour required Alisson to move smartly across his goal to save.

Lallana was struggling with cramp and was replaced by Fabinho – on for his league debut – and Huddersfield made attacking changes, bringing on striker Steve Mounie, to play two-up-front with Depoitre, and winger Isaac Mbenza. It nearly worked for Wagner.

On 82 minutes, Virgil van Dijk and Dejan Lovren got in a tangle dealing with Mbenza's cross and the ball dropped to Mounie, eight yards from goal. The Benin international should have scored but shinned his effort over the bar.

TEAMS

HUDDERSFIELD TOWN

Lössl; Jorgensen, Schindler, Löwe; Hadergjonaj (Mbenza 69), Mooy, Hogg (Diakhaby 90+2), Billing (Mounie 70), Durm; Pritchard; Depoitre

LIVERPOOL

Alisson; Gomez, Lovren, van Dijk, Robertson; Shaqiri, Henderson (Wijnaldum 45), Milner (Firmino 77); Salah, Sturridge, Lallana (Fabinho 69)

MATCH FACTS

- Alisson had kept six clean sheets in his first nine Premier League starts (second only to Petr Cech's seven in nine for Chelsea).
- The 23 points reached by this win equalled Liverpool's best start after nine games in the Premier League (also 2008-09).
- The last time Huddersfield beat Liverpool was in November 1959, when they were managed by an aspiring young coach called Bill Shankly. It was his last game before joining the Reds three days later.

THEY SAID

Ian Doyle, *Liverpool Echo*: "[Salah's] display at a boisterous John Smith's Stadium was intriguing given it was for the most part without his usual attacking pals, the benched Roberto Firmino and absent Sadio Mané. He was Liverpool's liveliest attacker, constantly running at the Huddersfield defence, drifting in off the right and often providing a much-needed outlet for a Reds side surprisingly under the cosh during the second half."

WEDNESDAY 24 OCTOBER 2018 | UEFA CHAMPIONS LEAGUE – GROUP C | ANFIELD
ATTENDANCE: 53,024

LIVERPOOL 4
(Firmino 20, Salah 45, 51 pen, Mané 80)
RED STAR BELGRADE 0

The Reds were back to their fluent best against Serbian side Red Star Belgrade, with a comprehensive win taking Jürgen Klopp's side back to the top of Group C.

Mo Salah scored his 49th and 50th goals for the club and by doing so in his 65th game became the quickest to reach that total in Liverpool's history. Give the illustrious names that have graced the Anfield frontline over the years, it was quite some achievement.

The Egyptian came close to opening his account on 10 minutes. Through on goal after superbly pulling in a lofted pass from Xherdan Shaqiri, Salah hit the legs of keeper Borjan, who had raced out to smother the chance.

Shaqiri was in terrific, impish form and instrumental in Liverpool's opener. Tracking back to win possession near halfway with 19 minutes played, he drove forward and measured a perfectly weighted pass inside Ben Nabouhane for Andy Robertson. The Reds left-back cut the ball back towards the penalty spot and Roberto Firmino checked once to unbalance to covering defence before slamming the ball home via a slight deflection.

On half an hour, Sadio Mané executed an outrageous back-heeled through-ball to Salah, who was again through with only Borjan to beat. The keeper saved once more and in any case the offside flag was raised; but the Mané's skill was emblematic of the more fluid, carefree attacking play that was Liverpool's hallmark under Klopp, but less evident in recent weeks.

With half-time approaching, Shaqiri again showed his subtlety of touch, cushioning a pacy pass from Gini Wijnaldum into the path of Salah, who this time gave Red Star's keeper no chance, thumping home at the near post.

Not long into the second half, Liverpool were awarded a penalty when Mané went down under a challenge from Filip Stojković – intriguingly, as the referee seemed to change his mind – but that was of little concern to Salah, who seized the chance eagerly to bring up his half-century for the club from the spot with relish.

A lovely link-up between Fabinho and Trent Alexander-Arnold – two of five changes from the weekend – nearly led to a goal for the Englishman. Had his volleyed lob been a foot higher, it might have been one of the great Anfield goals. As it was, Borjan was able to stretch up and collect in relative comfort.

With a quarter of an hour left to play, Red Star conceded another penalty through Ben Nabouhane's handball. Salah had been replaced by Daniel Sturridge, so Mané assumed responsibility for the spot kick but Borjan produced an extraordinary save, tipping the ball onto the underside of the bar and out. The rebound was scrambled away to safety.

Soon after, though, Mané made amends and it was 4-0. Red shirts flooded into the box as Wijnaldum broke forward, Sturridge fed Mané and the latter poked the ball in from seven yards out.

One final chance was presented to Mané, as Firmino sent him clear deep into stoppage-time, but his shot hit the side netting, sparing Red Star any further punishment.

TEAMS

LIVERPOOL
Alisson; Alexander-Arnold, Gomez, van Dijk, Robertson
(Moreno 82); Wijnaldum, Fabinho, Shaqiri (Lallana 68); Firmino,
Mané, Salah (Sturridge 73)

RED STAR
Borjan; Stojković , Degenek, Babić , Gobeljić; Krstičić, JovetiBen Nabouhane (Simić
81), Ebecilio (Jovančić 65), Srnić , Boakye

MATCH FACTS

- Liverpool had scored 48 goals in the Champions League since the start of 2017-18, 10 ahead of the next best record (Real Madrid, 38).
- During that time Roberto Firmino was directly involved in 19 Champions League goals (12 goals, seven assists), more than any other player in the competition.
- Salah's record of quickest to 50 goals eclipsed the record of post-war

Anfield legend Albert Stubbins, who achieved the mark after 77 games, 12 more than Salah.

THEY SAID

Tom Kershaw, *Independent*: "Shaqiri [created the] space to unlock the Serbians' defence for Liverpool's first and his dainty flick set ball unto platter for Salah and Liverpool's second. Those were the statistical highlights, but the Swiss man was wondrous throughout, orchestrating the relentless attacks in front of him like a malevolent conductor."

SATURDAY 27 OCTOBER 2018 | PREMIER LEAGUE | ANFIELD
ATTENDANCE: 53,373

LIVERPOOL 4
(Salah 10, Mané 66, 87, Shaqiri 84)
CARDIFF CITY 1
(Paterson 77)

While the scoreline suggests something of a procession for the Reds, a positive outcome was not at all secure here until the final few minutes. Sadly for Cardiff's travelling fans this was very much the story of their season so far – much endeavour for little reward against high-quality opposition. They had now lost to all of the league's top five in their first 10 games.

Centre-halves Sol Bamba and captain Sean Morrison directed a doughty rearguard effort but the match stats were indicative of Liverpool's dominance. The hosts enjoyed a rarely seen 80 per cent of possession and fired in 19 shots to Cardiff's two.

Mo Salah started and finished the opening goal, as his cheeky backheel put Trent Alexander-Arnold in space on the right flank. The youngster's dipping cross was blocked by Bamba but the rebound fell to Sadio Mané, leading to an almighty scramble as first the Senegalese's snap shot was blocked, Gini Wijnaldum also tried to force home and the ball eventually broke into Salah's path as he sprinted to the back post. Neither covering defenders nor keeper Neil Etheridge could prevent the striker's left-foot shot from rippling the net.

Shortly after, Virgil van Dijk nodded a header from Salah's lofted pass against the right-hand post and then Etheridge came smartly off his line and out of the box to prevent another chance for the Egyptian.

Morrison was well placed to clear Adam Lallana's header off the line in the final seconds of the first period so the lead remained slender at the break.

In between times, Roberto Firmino raised a smile with a remarkable feat of escapology by his own corner flag. Under pressure from Victor Camarasa, the Brazilian was sitting down with seemingly no option but to put the ball out of play. He then executed a circus skill of a backheel, nutmegging the Spaniard and setting Alberto Moreno free to clear his lines. Anfield roared with approval at the Brazilian's improvisation.

Six minutes into the second half, Cardiff thought they had equalised through a well-worked set-piece and a combination of Morrison and Camarasa, but the offside flag was raised.

Mané established a two-goal cushion on 65 minutes with a thunderous drive after he twice looked like losing possession in the box but somehow nipped the ball away from defensive challenges.

But then a truly rare occurrence in 2018: an opposition Premier League goal at Anfield. Junior Hoilett's cross from the right took a nick off van Dijk's toe, presenting Callum Paterson with the chance to slip the ball between Alisson's legs and in. The Scot's strike ended a 918-minute-long shut-out in the league at Anfield and left the home fans momentarily stunned.

Buoyed by the sniff of a result, Cardiff pressed forward in search of an equaliser but were soon undone at the back. Salah played in substitute Xherdan Shaqiri and with a shimmy of the hips and a wave of the left foot, the Swiss rolled in his first Liverpool goal.

The irrepressible Salah then capped arguably his best performance of the season to date with another assist. On a swift counter, he found Mané's diagonal run and a deft chip over Etheridge wrapped up proceedings in style.

TEAMS

LIVERPOOL

Alisson; Alexander-Arnold, Lovren, van Dijk, Moreno; Wijnaldum, Fabinho, Lallana (Shaqiri 61); Salah, Firmino (Milner 71), Mané

CARDIFF CITY

Etheridge; Ecuele Manga, Morrison, Bamba, Bennett; Hoilett, Camarasa, Gunnarsson (Damour 73), Murphy (Harris 74); Reid (Zohore 83); Paterson

MATCH FACTS

- Liverpool conceded a league goal at Anfield for the first time in eight months.
- Mo Salah's opener was his 22nd goal in his past 19 appearances at Anfield.
- The Reds' attacking trio of Mané, Firmino and Salah had scored 18 goals between them in the first 14 games of the season.

THEY SAID

Phil Neville, *Match of the Day*: "When you've got a big squad, you've got to trust them in games like today's. I thought [Alberto] Moreno was outstanding on his first start for nearly a year and Adam Lallana was always trying to make things happen when he got on the ball. Fabinho was also quietly effective after being outstanding in midweek [against Red Star].

Liverpool can be serious title contenders because they play fast, open, attacking football and they've got the squad to deal with the amount of games they [have to] play."

PREMIER LEAGUE TABLE AT END OF OCTOBER 2018

Pos	Team	Pld	W	D	L	GF	GA	GD	Pts
1	Manchester City	10	8	2	0	27	3	24	26
2	Liverpool	10	8	2	0	20	4	16	26
3	Chelsea	10	7	3	0	24	7	17	24
4	Arsenal	10	7	1	2	24	13	11	22
5	Tottenham Hotspur	10	7	0	3	16	8	8	21
6	AFC Bournemouth	10	6	2	2	19	12	7	20
7	Watford	10	6	1	3	16	12	4	19
8	Manchester United	10	5	2	3	17	17	0	17
9	Everton	10	4	3	3	16	14	2	15
10	Wolverhampton Wanderers	10	4	3	3	9	9	0	15
11	Brighton and Hove Albion	10	4	2	4	11	13	-2	14
12	Leicester City	10	4	1	5	16	16	0	13
13	West Ham United	10	2	2	6	9	15	-6	8
14	Crystal Palace	10	2	2	6	7	13	-6	8
15	Burnley	10	2	2	6	10	21	-11	8
16	Southampton	10	1	4	5	6	14	-8	7
17	Cardiff City	10	1	2	7	9	23	-14	5
18	Fulham	10	1	2	7	11	28	-17	5
19	Newcastle United	10	0	3	7	6	14	-8	3
20	Huddersfield Town	10	0	3	7	4	21	-17	3

UEFA CHAMPIONS LEAGUE GROUP C AT END OF OCTOBER 2018

Pos	Team	Pld	W	D	L	GF	GA	GD	Pts
1	Liverpool	3	2	0	1	7	3	4	6
2	Napoli	3	1	2	0	3	2	1	5
3	Paris Saint-Germain	3	1	1	1	10	6	4	4
4	Red Star Belgrade	3	0	1	2	1	10	-9	1

CHAPTER FOUR

—

NOVEMBER

"THE MANAGER HAD SOMETHING DIFFERENT ABOUT HIM.
HE LOOKED AT THE BIGGER PICTURE"

A couple of big wins at Anfield at the end of October had brought some home comfort to Reds fans, but November would prove an extended test of Liverpool's roadworthiness. The five-match schedule featured four away games: two in London, one in Paris and one in Belgrade.

The first was a trip to Arsenal, where the home team had quickly found their feet under new manager Unai Emery. The Spaniard had taken the best of his inheritance from Arsène Wenger in an attacking sense and allied it to more steel in midfield. Defeats in their opening two league fixtures of the campaign against Manchester City and Chelsea had been followed by seven straight wins (11 in all competitions), with that run only being brought to a halt the week before as Crystal Palace earned a 2-2 draw at Selhurst Park.

It was a respectful Gunners boss who spoke ahead of the game – a first meeting with Jürgen Klopp since the Europa League final of 2016, when Emery's Sevilla side prevailed 3-1 in Basel to record a third successive win in the competition.

"This [Liverpool] team is developing a lot," he said. "With Klopp and with signing new players in the last year. Three seasons ago, they were playing in the final in the Europa League. Their development was to last season play the final in the Champions League. Now, for us, it's a good example for how you can improve. We have a lot of respect for them also.

"We want to not allow them to do their jobs," he added. "They have quality with individual players and also their collective and tactical capacity. They can progress on the pitch with a lot of quality, starting with Alisson, the centre-backs and the midfield, and also, when they are playing in the transition and attacking moments with very quick players like Mané, Firmino and Salah. We need [to match them] in individual duels and also tactically. It's very difficult and not possible for 90 minutes to impose our style in every moment but in moments in the game, we need to impose our style and ideas."

That night in Basel was seen by many as a major staging post in Klopp's development of the current Liverpool side. Before the Champions League final against Real Madrid, Jordan Henderson had spoken to *Guardian* correspondent Andy Hunter and recalled how the German had fought against the personal disappointment of a fifth cup final defeat in a row (including his time at Dortmund) and his determination to look forward.

"It was the worst feeling ever," said Henderson. "I remember after the game [Henderson was an unused substitute, recovering from injury], the manager was obviously down but when we got back to the hotel he had something different about him.

"He was proud of the players that got to the final and how much we had improved since he came in. He had, I felt, a vision that in the future we would get to another final. He was obviously disappointed with the result but he looked at the bigger picture and the future and he felt it could be a big moment in our careers if we learned from the experience."

An extensive overhaul of the squad was undertaken that summer and the Reds – having finished eighth in league in 2015/16 as Leicester City claimed an unlikely title – secured Champions League football with a top-four finish the following May, leading eventually to the final in Kiev.

The attacking thrust so characteristic of that European run seemed to be back and, as Liverpool and Arsenal had shared 27 goals in their last five meetings, it was a fair bet there would be plenty of goal-mouth action at the Emirates.

"Arsenal are very good offensively and score a lot of goals, so it will be up to us [to stop them]," said Klopp. "They win balls back high up the pitch, they have the speed to use each little mistake you [make]. But it's nice to prepare for these types of games because you need the full package. You need to be ready to cause them problems with the ball and when they have the ball."

He also paid tribute to Emery, of whose qualities he was well aware, even if the Spaniard wasn't the highest-profile of managerial names to an English audience before his arrival in north London.

"[Everyone] in football knew how good he is," Klopp said. "He might have been under the radar for some fans because he wasn't at one of the biggest teams in Spain, and he was in France [with PSG], but he won eight trophies in the last two-and-a-half years, so that's pretty big."

As this match loomed, the Arsenal boss was having to contend with numerous injury worries, notably in defence, where Laurent Koscielny and Konstantinos Mavropanos were definitely unavailable, and there were doubts surrounding Hector Bellerin, Nacho Monreal and Sead Kolašinac. Bellerin and Kolašinac were deemed fit enough to start, either side of centre-halves Shkodran Mustafi and Rob Holding. In attack, a trio of Henrikh Mhkitaryan, Mesut Özil and Pierre-Emerick Aubameyang would look to feed central striker Alexandre Lacazette.

Liverpool made three changes, with Joe Gomez back in place of Dejan Lovren, Andy Robertson displacing Alberto Moreno, and James Milner back in midfield, with Jordan Henderson and Naby Keïta still sidelined.

Before kick-off, a minute's silence was well observed in memory of the late Leicester City chairman Vichai Srivaddhanaprabha, tragically killed in a helicopter crash the week before. The mood was sombre and reflective but soon dispelled by a frantic feast of attacking football. Vichai would have loved it.

A pulsating match swung from end to end, full of narrowly missed chances, goals ruled out for marginal offsides and last-ditch defending against two forward lines bursting with creativity.

The key decision in the first half surrounded Sadio Mané's disallowed goal on 17 minutes. Replays showed the Senegalese was in an offside position, retreating, as Trent Alexander-Arnold ball was played through to Roberto Firmino.

"It should have been a goal," said Klopp said. "He runs to the ball because he doesn't think he is offside and then the referee whistles."

Virgil van Dijk put in a colossal performance and not only at centre-half. He popped up as a centre-forward to control Mo Salah's long-range pass on his chest and side-foot for goal, only to be denied by Bernd Leno's brave block. The Dutchman then beat the keeper to a free kick and hit the post. And Leno again thwarted van Dijk in the second half, tipping over a powerful header from a corner.

It was a mixed performance from Arsenal's new stopper, who was arguably at fault for Liverpool's opener. He palmed away Sadio Mané's cross but only to the edge of the area, where Milner was able to advance and drill the ball home.

The Gunners had chances throughout the match, though, and eventually Liverpool's defence cracked. Substitute Alex Iwobi found Lacazette's angled run into the box and though Alisson seemed to have closed off the striker's options, the Frenchman swivelled to find a shooting angle and bent a terrific finish just inside the far post. Honours even, then, and a result accepted with grace by both managers as a fair outcome.

"The performance [was] good, we pushed and we worked... with our supporters pushing us with energy," Emery told BT Sport. "For the supporters it is a great match and a good spectacle but I am only 50 per cent happy because we wanted to win."

"The first half I was not happy with defensively," said Klopp. "Offensively we were okay because when we had the ball we were a real threat and caused them real problems. And we had a lot of good set pieces as well. We changed the system a bit in the second half to be more compact but one time we didn't close [Alex] Iwobi and he's able to make the pass to Lacazette [for the goal]. I think we deserved a point, we could have had more, but it's okay."

One interested observer of events at the Emirates was former Reds midfielder Nigel Spackman. A league title winner with Liverpool in 1987-88, Spackman still keeps a close eye on the club in his roles as a pundit for BT Sport and LFCTV and was particularly impressed by the contribution of Fabinho.

"As a new signing, coming from the French league where the pace was much slower, and the league less competitive, it's taken some time for Fabinho to adapt, and he's had to bide his time to make his mark in the role that Jürgen Klopp wants for him, and [also] for the manager to have the belief in him for such an important role," said Spackman.

"I think there is still a lot more to come from him. He's great in that defensive midfield role, with his intelligent interceptions, getting his toe in when it matters, breaking up the play. But I watched him a lot when he was at Monaco, and there is much more to his game. He has a wide range of passing and once he believes in himself even more I am sure that aspect of his game will also flourish."

Jimmy Carter – one of only 11 men to have played for both Liverpool and Arsenal – agreed with Spackman's assessment.

"I thought Fabinho did really well against a very competitive midfield duo of Granit Xhaka and Lucas Torreira, who were both excellent. It's taken [the Brazilian] a while to settle but he's looking like a player now," said Carter, who was signed by Kenny Dalglish towards the end of his reign and went on to join the Arsenal squad that would lift the FA Cup, League Cup and Cup Winners' Cup under George Graham.

"The performance wasn't Liverpool's most fluent of the season and they weren't at their flamboyant best. Mo Salah, although electric at times in the first half up against Kolašinac, lacked a little of the decisiveness we see so often from him.

"But you have to give credit to Arsenal – defensively Liverpool looked competent marshalled by the impressive van Dijk, and they will be disappointed to have conceded late in in the manner they did. Liverpool caused enough problems on the night and could easily have walked away with the three points."

Next up was a trip to Serbia and no game all season would be as representative of the different challenges faced home and away than Matchday 4 against

Crvena Zvezda (Red Star Belgrade). Red Star were looking forward to testing opponents who they'd met last – and for the only time – 45 years previously.

Liverpool's travelling fans, meanwhile, found Belgrade basking in unseasonably warm temperatures for November and a red-hot atmosphere for the visitors inside the Stadion Rajko Mitić, also known as the "Marakana".

The club invited members of that 1973 team, who had won 2-1 home and away for a 4-2 aggregate success in the old European Cup second round, to a parade on the pitch and heroes' acclaim from the boisterous crowd.

Liverpool left-back Andy Robertson reflected that the hosts would be a very different proposition on their own turf. "At Anfield we scored at the right times and we were at 100 per cent. I think they're a different beast when they're at home. They proved that against Napoli, getting [a] draw. They'll be hoping to use that to their advantage and hopefully we'll quieten the crowd."

No such luck. Red Star's low, wide bowl of a ground is not the kind of steep-sided venue you'd usually associate with intimidation of visiting teams, but the support from the home fans was committed, constant and very, very loud.

An early chance for Liverpool to settle was spurned by Daniel Sturridge, brought in to play centrally in place of Roberto Firmino. The Englishman was unable to convert at the back post after good interplay between Adam Lallana and Sadio Mané.

Then the home side struck twice in quick succession. Milan Pavkov – an old-school, physical centre-forward – rose unchallenged to power in Marko Marin's corner on 22 minutes. Then Pavkov showed the other side to his game, holding off Georginio Wiljnaldum in midfield after Marin had pinched possession in near halfway and unleashing a bullet drive from 25 yards. The team that had seemed meek at Anfield were – as Robertson predicted – utterly transformed when playing at home.

Marin had an instrumental role in this change. The German had spent four years at Chelsea after signing from Werder Bremen in 2012, but was sent out on loan by a succession of managers to four different clubs (Sevilla, Fiorentina, Anderlecht and Trabzonspor) with varying degrees of success. Here he showed the quality on the ball and ability to control midfield that had tempted Chelsea to secure his signature seven years previously.

After those two blows, Klopp's team had to regroup and seek a way back. There was still near enough three quarters of the match to play and plenty of time to score at least two goals. But though Liverpool bossed possession and fashioned numerous opportunities, Red Star's goal remained stubbornly unbreached.

Roberto Firmino replaced Sturridge at the break and posed a new threat by running into the left channel to combine with Andy Robertson, but when he carved out a chance for Sadio Mané on the edge of the six-yard box, the hosts threw bodies in the way to block.

With 20 minutes remaining, Mo Salah hit a shot that deflected wickedly but keeper Milan Borjan was able to readjust and save. And from the corner that followed, the Egyptian hit the outside of the post. But that was as close as Liverpool came to scoring.

After the final whistle, the home side enjoyed a lap of honour on the running track around the pitch amid delirious scenes around the stadium.

For the Reds it was another shut-out on the road in Europe and a thoughtful Jürgen Klopp who faced the media.

"I saw a few games like this already and it is really difficult to find your mojo," Klopp told the BBC. "We made life a bit too easy. I don't say it is already serious if you lose twice but we have to make sure it will not happen again.

"We had a lot of moments when we could get in control of the game and we didn't do it, we just made the wrong decision. The boys are very disappointed, I'm very disappointed and we have to do better because we can."

Full-back Robertson reiterated his manager's sentiments in his own post-match remarks.

"There's no hiding [the disappointment]," he said. "I think it's one of those periods we need to get through.

"Last season everyone was used to us scoring four or five goals. That can't be possible every single game. At times we've dug out results, in the Premier League more so this season. Maybe it's not been as good to look at but we've been effective at it.

"Away from home last season, we were very good in the Champions League. This season we've found that a bit difficult. But arguably we're still to play the best team away and we need to go there and put in a much better performance than we have done."

The test of PSG away would be doubtless be very much in the manager's thoughts but – with European and domestic stories unfolding side by side – there was little time to dwell on defeat in Serbia before recalibrating the tactical sights for the visit of Fulham to Anfield at the weekend.

The match was scheduled for a noon kick-off on a Sunday that promised considerable significance in the title race. Of the league's top five, only Tottenham played on the Saturday – winning away at Crystal Palace – with Arsenal, Chelsea and Liverpool all in action at home on the Sunday, as well as Pep Guardiola's champions welcoming United across town for the first Manchester derby of the season.

On paper, Liverpool appeared to have the most straightforward assignment of the four fixtures. Fulham had thus far struggled to turn the flowing, easy-on-the-eye football that earned their promotion from Championship into a formula that could secure results in the top flight. After 12 games, they were bottom of the pile, with only one win and five points to show for their efforts. In recent weeks, the Cottagers' defence had been alarming leaky. Three goals had been conceded to Everton, five to Arsenal, four to fellow strugglers Cardiff and three to Bournemouth. Even encouragement at only conceding once in defeat at Huddersfield was tempered by the fact the Terriers hadn't scored more than once against anyone in the league all season. It wasn't a run of form to bring Fulham's travelling fans to Merseyside with a great sense of optimism.

Meanwhile, Arsenal faced Wolves – who were making a better fist of their first season back in the Premier League. With their mix of Portuguese imports and battle-hardened homegrown talents, they had reached as high as eighth in the table after eight games – drawing with both Manchester clubs – and despite a mini-blip were, and would continue to be, dangerous opponents in 2018-19. Chelsea would face Everton, who were on a bright run of four wins in five, the only blot being a narrow defeat to Manchester United.

Kicking off first, Liverpool had a great chance to apply pressure to their title rivals, but Jürgen Klopp was on combative form in the press room when asked if – due to Fulham's hitherto porous defence – this match was a chance to improve Liverpool's goal difference.

"Whoa! I would really be an idiot to talk about goal difference before this game," he said. "I don't know if you have watched many whole Fulham games but they have been playing really good football in a lot of moments. They are a really skilled team offensively. Yes, they have conceded some goals but you're never going to win a game against them by going in with the attitude of scoring, scoring, scoring. This game is a big challenge for all of us."

Xherdan Shaqiri was back in the side, and hoping to reprise the starring role he had last played against Red Star at home, when part of an attacking midfield three behind Mo Salah. The Swiss also spoke before the match and said he believed the club was going in the right direction but also stressed the need for consistency of performance

"The process [Liverpool has] had for a few years is going very well. That's the most important thing," said Shaqiri. "Everybody sees that and of course in the near future it's important to try to challenge for titles, but at the moment we just have to look to ourselves and to try to stay on the highest level. We will see what happens, but if we keep going like this it's going to be an interesting year for everybody I think."

A drizzly morning on Remembrance Sunday gave way to a low, wintry sun peeking between the stands before kick-off. The teams were led out by military staff holding a giant red poppy before a minute's silence was observed impeccably by the 50,000-plus present.

Fulham were a match for their hosts in the first half and wholly unfortunate to go in at the break a goal down. Ryan Sessegnon should have tested Alisson when through on goal courtesy of Aleksandar Mitrović's flick-on, while Andre Schürrle's low shot was spilled by the goalkeeper but fell safely to Virgil van Dijk. Meantime, Cottagers keeper Sergio Rico was being kept busy by Mo Salah, who twice brought saves from the Spaniard.

The game's main incident – and one that caused much consternation in Fulham ranks – came with 40 minutes played. A well-worked short corner routine led to Tom Cairney clipping a delightful inswinging cross to the far post, where Mitrović couldn't miss. The offside flag went up, but Mitrović was shown to be just onside. Taking advantage of the distraction caused by goal celebrations being cut short, Alisson fired a quick pass out to Trent Alexander-Arnold, who in turn played a first-time ball to Mo Salah, the striker lurking on halfway, alert to the possibility of a counter. Suddenly the Egyptian was running free, one-on-one with Rico and rolled a composed finish into the far corner.

The points were effectively sealed not long into the second period, when Alexander-Arnold showed great vision – and underscored some slack marking from Fulham – when picking out Shaqiri at the back post. He made a cushioned-volley finish from close range look exceedingly simple.

Afterwards, Klopp was again full of praise for Fulham and under-pressure boss Slaviša Jokanović.

"I have absolute sympathy for [Slaviša] in his situation. I think today they changed their approach for the first time; in the end it was not the result they wanted but you see this team has a lot of quality and they work really good together," said Klopp. "I watched them last year a lot in the Championship and it was brilliant."

The Fulham manager declared himself frustrated with the result and with decisions that he felt went against his side.

"I've looked [at the replay] and Robertson didn't squeeze up enough so we scored a legal goal," said Jokanović. "Liverpool deserved the three points because they were the better team, but the decisions made a really complicated situation for us. We have to encourage ourselves and believe we made half a step forward to improving our situation."

That half a step was evidently insufficient, however, to persuade the Fulham board that Jokanović remained the man to help the team towards survival. The following Wednesday, he was sacked and replaced by former Chelsea and Leicester boss Claudio Ranieri.

So Liverpool went back to the top of the table and Reds fans were cheered by the news that Arsenal and Chelsea had both been held to draws. Manchester City, though, made no slip up against United, winning 3-1 to return to the Premier League summit ahead of November's international break.

This was a busy one for the Reds – with as many as 21 of the first-team squad heading off to represent their countries – and it provided two headlines from an English and Liverpool perspective. First, Trent Alexander-Arnold had the pleasure of scoring a first international goal in England's 3-0 win over the USA at Wembley, making him the youngest Reds scorer for the Three Lions since Michael Owen in 1999.

Sky Sports pundit Jamie Redknapp was glowing in his assessment of the full-back.

"He is such a good footballer," said the ex-Reds midfielder. "The way he passes the ball; a good player passes it with pace and purpose, because they know the quicker you get it to someone, the more time they've got. That's what he does so well. It's effortless for him. He's got it all, this young man. He's going to go right to the top."

Second, although Alexander-Arnold dropped to the bench for the crucial Nations League decider against in Croatia, Joe Gomez was brought in at centre-stage, confirming his status as a first-choice pick in manager Gareth Southgate's strongest side.

During a composed and widely admired performance at the back, it was as an attacking weapon that Gomez changed the course of the match. His long throw on 76 minutes sparked panic in the Croatia box, leading to Jesse Lingard's equaliser after Andrej Kramarić had scored first for the visitors. Harry Kane then scored late to ensure England topped the group.

Having missed the World Cup through injury, Gomez was delighted to be back in the team and part of a young, exciting national side.

"It was a great feeling to come back from one down," he said. "Credit to the boys, we kept fighting and I think it's that spirit that they showed in the summer."

Crucially for Liverpool, everyone came back fit and available as minds returned to the Premier League and another trip to North London, this time to face Watford – the first fixture in a run of 11 games in 40 midwinter days that would go a long way to defining the shape of the season.

"We know how important it is and how tough it's going to be with the amount of games [there are] in a short period of time, but we're ready," said Gomez. "All teams in the Premier League face this same task and we've just got to be ready for it and try to get as many points as we can."

At Sopwell House Hotel, a quaint Georgian retreat in the Hertfordshire countryside, Liverpool CEO Peter Moore was relaxing in the bar his red club tracksuit, while upstairs Jürgen Klopp and his team were preparing for the game ahead.

"For away games such as this one," he said, "the team and the entire entourage flew directly from Liverpool to Luton airport last night, where a number of buses were waiting to ferry us all to the hotel, chosen because it is quintessentially English in style, nothing too ostentatious. There is plenty of outside space for the players to take a stroll and loosen the limbs.

"In this hotel, the players occupy the ballroom upstairs where they dine. We have a nutritionist, dietician, and much of what the players eat and when they eat it, is dictated by the kick-off times.

"For a game with this schedule [a 3pm kick-off], the players arrive for something to eat at 9am. Gone are the days of steak and chips, as Kenny Dalglish would tell us, in fact some of his tales are hilarious, as they didn't think about what they would eat in those days. It is far more regimented now, indicative of the speed of the game today.

"Of course, the modern player also has the benefit of perfect Premier League pitches, compared to the old days of mud heaps."

After nearly five months in the job, Moore was getting to know Klopp well. He was impressed by his personality as well as his managerial acumen. "You will know when Jürgen is coming, you will hear his loud laugh before he is 100 yards from us!" Moore said

"It's a laugh that is infectious. He has an enormous smile, and a laugh that you respond to whether you a player or local kids he wants to reach out to in the community.

"At Liverpool Cathedral on a Monday night he was there for a club fundraising event with young, local children. He spent 45 minutes answering questions from invited guests. Every time he told them a story, and there were lots of stories, he would laugh. Sometimes he knows what's coming, of course, and starts to laugh before he even gets the chance to tell the story and can hardly get the story out.

"He is a charismatic, larger-than-life character, but it's backed up with his incredible motivational skills and his technical know-how. He is perfect for Liverpool, and Liverpool is perfect for him."

Before heading off to change out of his informal tracksuit into the official club suit, Moore reflected on Watford as opponents now and in the past: "This is a great test for us today," he said. "Even in the days of Graham Taylor, when they had the likes of Luther Blissett and Barnesy in the late 70s, it was never easy, and even for the great Liverpool teams of the Shankly era, to win here.

"I watched Jürgen's press conference yesterday and it was clear he knew what to expect and he was ready for this one. He was also acutely aware that this game kicks off a very cramped run of games before we take on Manchester City away on January 3rd. How we do in this period, though to mid-January, could determine the outcome of our season. It's a tough assignment with Paris on Tuesday, the Merseyside derby, followed by Burnley before we face Manchester United at Anfield – they all have the possibility of becoming defining games.

"The reality is Manchester City are setting the pace. You feel as though we have got to be perfect this season to be in the frame at the end of it."

Watford had made their best start yet to a Premier League season. After 12 games they were sitting in seventh place, above Manchester United on goal difference. Spanish manager Javi Gracia had his side playing with real freedom, drawing on creative flair from players such as Argentinian international Roberto Pereyra and mercurial Spaniard Gerard Deulofeu, and with goals being shared throughout the team.

The Hornets were led by rugged, talismanic centre-forward Troy Deeney and the skipper's programme notes summed up his team's approach – respect but no fear. "You don't need me to tell you what a team [Liverpool] are," he wrote. "The league table and the stats say it all, and we know each and every one of us will need to be at the top of our game to get some points off them. But we don't fear any team in the division. Spurs and Chelsea have both gone away from here with nothing this year and we believe we can add to that list today."

Jürgen Klopp sent his team out in the same 4-2-3-1 formation as against Fulham, with Xherdan Shaqiri retaining his place and Jordan Henderson replacing Fabinho on his return to the captaincy. Joe Gomez had sustained a minor ankle knock in training so gave way to Dejan Lovren in defence.

Watford were quick off the mark and thought they had scored inside two minutes, but Deulofeu's effort was ruled out for offside. And the Spaniard later combined well with Pereyra to give the Argentinian a sight of goal, but Alisson was equal to the shot, palming clear.

Liverpool were made to work hard by their energetic hosts and although the stats for possession and shots on target were overwhelmingly in favour of the visitors, this was by no means a case of one-way traffic.

The home side and crowd howled for a penalty when – on 55 minutes and the game still goalless – Will Hughes went over Andy Robertson's challenge but referee Jon Moss waved play on. Soon after, though, the Reds went ahead through Mo Salah, converting Sadio Mané's low cross, before Trent Alexander-Arnold's stunning free kick opened a clear advantage.

Roberto Firmino's late header finished off a lightning counter and gave a sheen to the scoreline that was somewhat unrepresentative of the play at large.

Klopp praised his players for a "mature" performance. "I am not sure if we had [so much of] the ball in the past when we've played here," he said. "They were much more open games – especially the 3-3 we played here. We've never controlled games like this in the manner we do it now. I like that."

And he cited a lack of preparation time as one reason why Watford had been able to cause significant problems in the first half.

"I know you always expect perfection but we had exactly one session to prepare this game because [some players only] came back on Thursday – the Brazilians and [Andy Robertson], for example," he said. "One session, with the specific demands of Watford's set-pieces; you saw what they did with routines and how they play around, where they chip the balls and where they block the guys. It's difficult. You need to work on your own set-pieces and you need to focus on the specific quality of the opponent."

In the end, the manager was able to reflect on a job well done and a record broken for Liverpool's best-ever start in the Premier League.

"With the outstanding [Liverpool] teams of the past, that this group of players can get this record is nice," he said. "We all know the season is not finished… but if somebody wants to have this record in the future they must beat this team. It's just a nice moment but of course we will carry on."

Among the title rivals, Manchester City continued their good run of form with a 4-0 thumping of West Ham at the London Stadium, but Chelsea had a first wobble under Maurizio Sarri. A 3-1 defeat by Tottenham at Wembley ended their unbeaten run and dropped them a place to fourth as Spurs leapfrogged into third.

The first Merseyside derby of the season lay ahead in the Reds' league programme, but first there was the matter of a trip to Paris and another date with the all-star line-up of Paris Saint-Germain.

Losing two away matches in the group stage was a concern to this point, a perplexing counterpoint to Liverpool's domestic form and a source of some anxiousness ahead of Matchday 5 in the Champions League.

But there was opportunity here as well as threat: beat Paris Saint-Germain and the Reds would be sailing into the round of 16; lose or draw and everything would hinge on the tricky visit of Napoli to Merseyside in December. As it stood after defeat in Belgrade, all four teams could still qualify.

Ahead of the game, PSG boss Thomas Tuchel reported that both Neymar and Kylian Mbappé were fit to play, having missed the weekend's league match against Toulouse having picked up minor injuries on international duty.

One other key difference from the teams' previous meeting was the availability of midfielder Marco Verratti, who missed out in September due to a suspension held over from last season.

ESPN's Jonathan Johnson previewed the tie for Liverpool's website and said the Italian international would make a big impact at Parc des Princes. "It is no understatement to say that [Verratti] is absolutely integral to this side and not only because the French capital outfit do not boast the greatest strength in depth," he wrote. "Verratti is metronomic, dictates play for PSG from the middle of the pitch and his quality was sorely missed at Anfield."

Jürgen Klopp was tight-lipped about his final selection in the pre-match press conference but he reveled that Sadio Mané would be fit, having been a doubt through illness. He stressed that Liverpool would have to be brave with and without the ball and that there would be few surprises in store, given PSG's well-known quality up front.

"How are we going to play? We are going to be brave in a very difficult game," he said. "It's difficult because in a game like this you need to be at your best in all departments. Especially with a tolerance that you are not annoyed by yourself or lose confidence when [PSG] pass you with the ball or with a run. It's a challenge but we enjoy these [big] games. We need to perform at our highest level."

"It's much more difficult to prepare a game when my players don't know an opponent," he said. "We give them videos, yes, but this generation probably watch 500,000 YouTube videos of Mbappé, Neymar and Cavani, and they know about their individual strengths more than I do. But [those players] can only shine with the ball, so that means we have to defend them. When they have the ball, with the speed of them, they are away if you are not compact."

It is one thing, however, to address this in theory – quite another in practice. Where Neymar was listless for large parts of the match at Anfield, here he was at his twinkle-toed best. His rapid link-up play with Mbappé – especially in the early exchanges – was dizzying. And with Verratti bossing the midfield, PSG quickly took a grip of the game.

They took the lead on 12 minutes, through Juan Bernat, the Spaniard profiting when Virgil van Dijk's half clearance from Mbappé cross fell kindly. Bernat wriggled into a shooting position and tucked the ball neatly past Alisson.

Mbappé was a nuisance all night, hugging the left touchline and exchanging intricacies with Neymar that frequently unlocked the space between Liverpool's defence and midfield. One such combination led to PSG's second, when Alisson was able to stop Cavani converting Mbappé's cross but was powerless to prevent Neymar calmly slotting in the rebound.

A penalty – earned by Sadio Mané and converted by James Milner on the stroke of half-time – gave the Reds hope at the break. But though Liverpool flickered occasionally on the counterattack, PSG also had good chances of their own to extend the lead and were worthy winners on the night.

Klopp was vexed by some of the referee's decisions – notably not sending off Marco Verratti when he caught Joe Gomez late and high, and also booking six Liverpool players for comparatively innocuous offences.

"The number of interruptions in the game was not cool," he said. "We won the fair play award two times in England and tonight we looked like butchers with the number of yellow cards.

"It was clever of PSG, especially Neymar, but a lot of other players went down like there was something serious. We were not that calm anymore, rather frustrated and negative frustration does not help.

"For me, [Verratti's tackle] is a red card. I had a very good view of it and it was for sure not just another yellow card. But then we have a story and it looks like I am a bad loser."

The upshot of the defeat – ranged alongside Napoli's 3-1 win over Red Star – was that Liverpool dropped to third in the table, but a win over the Italians (or least a certain flavour of win, more of that in the next chapter) would ensure progress to the knockout stage. For now, it was result to shake off, as mindsturned to Everton.

NOVEMBER MATCH REPORTS

SATURDAY 3 NOVEMBER 2018 | PREMIER LEAGUE | EMIRATES STADIUM
ATTENDANCE: 59,993

ARSENAL 1
(Lacazette 82)
LIVERPOOL 1
(Milner 61)

A glut of goals was widely predicted here and with good reason – under Jürgen Klopp the scores in this fixture to date read as follows: 3-3, 4-3, 3-1, 4-0, 3-3. And as the action unfolded, we could easily have had a similar weight of scoring and more. Quite how the game was goalless after an hour remains a mystery.

Three times inside the first three minutes Arsenal threatened down the left flank, with a clear plan to overload that area. Lacazette came close to converting at the near post from Aubameyang's cross, but Alisson was able to block.

Then Aubameyang fired in an angled shot from the left but Joe Gomez got a telling touch that diverted the ball into the side netting, and Henrikh Mkhitaryan was inches wide with a header as Alisson came racing out to try to punch but the Armenian beat him to the ball.

For all that pressure on the Liverpool goal in the first quarter of an hour, it was the visitors who could have taken the lead on 17 minutes. After some nimble footwork on the right from Trent Alexander-Arnold, the youngster clipped the ball into the run of Roberto Firmino, beating Arsenal's high defensive line. The Brazilian lifted the ball over Bernd Leno, it hit the top of the right-hand post and Sadio Mané was there to put in the rebound. The offside flag was raised, as Mané had been beyond the last defender from the initial through-ball.

Mo Salah then played a delicious lofted pass to van Dijk, as the defender raced through the centre. The Dutchman controlled superbly with his chest and looked certain to score but Leno made himself big and blocked with his chest.

Then the pendulum swing again and Arsenal enjoyed a good spell before the break. Lacazette fired narrowly wide from a tight angle and then had the ball in the net from Skhodran Mustafi's header across goal; but the Gunners, too, were denied by the assistant's flag.

In the last minute before half-time van Dijk struck the post with a header from James Milner's long-range free kick – this time it was Leno's turn to come haring out of goal and make no contact. Everyone in the ground needed to take a breath and a little time to digest the fact it was still 0-0.

The second period began with Arsenal back in control and this time enjoying success down their right side, with Mkhitaryan and pacy right-back Hector Bellerin testing Andy Robertson's defensive prowess.

But Liverpool finally broke the deadlock just after the hour. Sadio Mané's first-time cross from the left was pawed away by Leno but only to the edge of the box, where Milner was able to measure a firm, right-footed drive through a thicket of Arsenal bodies.

Midfielder Lucas Torreira might have responded almost instantly for the Gunners but with the whole of the goal to aim at from a central position, he shot straight at Alisson.

If the game was open before, now – with the home side hunting an equaliser – it went up a further notch. Mané narrowly failed to reach a cross from Salah after a rapid counterattack. Then Holding blocked a similar cross from Robertson to prevent it reaching Salah. From the subsequent corner, van Dijk's header was arrowing in but Leno threw up a hand to tip over. On another day, the Dutch defender might have had a hat-trick to celebrate.

Back came Arsenal, with substitutes Alex Iwobi firing a dangerous cross just out of the reach of Özil. But it was Lacazette – a menace throughout the match and still full of running – who would bring his team level in the 82nd minute.

The Frenchman seized on Iwobi's neat through ball and although the advancing Alisson did well to avoid bringing Lacazette down, the striker turned, made a yard of space bent a pinpoint effort round the keeper and Gomez into the far corner.

TEAMS

ARSENAL

Leno; Bellerin, Mustafi, Holding, Kolašinac (Welbeck 81); Torreira, Xhaka; Mkhitaryan (Iwobi 68), Özil, Aubameyang (Ramsey 73)

LIVERPOOL

Alisson; Alexander-Arnold, Gomez, van Dijk, Robertson; Wijnaldum, Fabinho, Milner; Salah (Matip 90+4), Firmino (Shaqiri 80), Mané

MATCH FACTS

- James Milner's goal was his 50th in the Premier League – 14 for Liverpool, more than in any of his other teams.
- Arsenal had not led at half-time in any of their 11 Premier League matches in 2018-19.
- Liverpool had still only conceded once in the first half of a Premier League match this season.

THEY SAID

Phil McNulty, BBC Sport: "With every passing game, Liverpool's lavish payout [on van Dijk] looks money well spent. [He] was the focal point as Arsenal's first half excellence put Liverpool's defence to the test, demonstrating not only his aerial prowess but also his uncanny knack of making vital interceptions and deflections at the vital moment. He has solved an obvious area of vulnerability in Liverpool's team and gives them an added dimension. He will be a central figure in their Premier League title pursuit."

TUESDAY 6 NOVEMBER 2018 | UEFA CHAMPIONS LEAGUE – GROUP C
STADION RAJKO MITIĆ | ATTENDANCE: 51,318

RED STAR BELGRADE 2
(Pavkov 22, 29)
LIVERPOOL 0

Liverpool fell to a second away defeat in Group C on a wild night in Belgrade, unable to profit from numerous chances and conceding two goals via hulking Red Star centre-forward Milan Pavkov.

Jürgen Klopp made three changes to the side that started against Arsenal: Joel Matip, Adam Lallana and Daniel Sturridge came in, while Joe Gomez, Fabinho and Roberto Firmino dropped to the bench.

Sturridge had the Reds' first clear sight of goal, when neat footwork from Adam Lallana released Sadio Mané on the left wing, his cross was met by Andy Robertson, bursting into the box, and though the Scot was well tackled, the ball broke to Sturridge, unmarked at the back post. He was unable to keep his volley down, however, and ball flew high over the bar.

It was a miss the visitors would soon have cause to regret. After Alisson turned El Fardou Ben Nabouhane's long-range shot behind for a corner, former Chelsea midfielder Marko Marin swung over a delicious delivery from the right. Pavkov lost his marker and planted a free header low into the left corner.

Only a few minutes later, Liverpool were loose in possession and again punished. Marin intercepted James Milner's inside pass to Gini Wijnaldum, fed Pavkov and the big striker set off down field. Nothing much looked on, but he shielded the ball well from Wijnaldum and, with Matip and Virgil van Dijk retreating, let fly right-footed from 25 yards. The strike sailed past Alisson's right hand and into the net. It had been noisy in the stands all evening; now it was utter bedlam.

Firmino and Gomez were introduced at half-time and the Brazilian carved out an opening almost immediately. A tricky run to the byline delivered a chance for Mané but his effort was blocked a yard from the line by Australian international Miloš Degenek.

Then Mané found Robertson in an acre of space at the left corner of the box. The Scot looked to measure a cross but it flicked off the head of Ben Nabouhane and floated onto the top of Red Star's crossbar, much to the relief of keeper Milan Borjan. Firmino cut the rebound back in but the defence scrambled the danger away.

Klopp was becoming increasingly animated on the touchline and his team responded, with Mo Salah twice going close. The first was a curling shot that deflected off the back of substitute Marko Gobeljić and wrong-footed Borjan. The keeper did well to adjust and flap the ball away from goal. And from the resultant corner Salah improvised a snap shot that pinged off the outside of the post.

Then Matip couldn't find the target with a close-range header from Gomez's long throw and the angle was too tight for Salah's follow-up. The ball just wouldn't go in.

A final opportunity fell to Salah in stoppage time, but again Borjan was equal to the task and gathered comfortably.

TEAMS

RED STAR BELGRADE

Borjan; Stojković (Gobeljić 59), Savić, Degenek, Rodić; Jovančić, Krstičić (Jovičić 73); Srnić, Marin (Causić 64), Ben Nabouhane, Pavkov

LIVERPOOL

Alisson; Alexander-Arnold (Gomez 45), Matip, Van Dijk, Robertson; Milner, Wijnaldum, Lallana (Origi 79); Salah, Sturridge (Firmino 45), Mané

MATCH FACTS

- This was Liverpool's 200th match in the European Cup/Champions League.
- Liverpool had lost three consecutive away games in the Champions League for the first time.
- In all, Liverpool had 72 per cent of possession and fired in 23 shots to Red Star's 10.

THEY SAID

James Milner: "We didn't start well [and] when you don't start in the Champions League, you get punished. I thought we did better in the second half and we had a few chances, we were patient and we kept plugging away but ultimately we weren't good enough."

SUNDAY 11 NOVEMBER 2018 | PREMIER LEAGUE | ANFIELD
ATTENDANCE: 53,128

LIVERPOOL 2
(Salah 41, Shaqiri 53)
FULHAM 0

The scoreline gives a routine look to this home win against the league's bottom side, but tells little of the story of a match in which Fulham impressed in all departments. They left Merseyside still without an away win in the league or even an away goal, but manager Slaviša Jokanović would have been cursing his luck on the way back to London.

The key passage of play that arguably decided the match came five minutes before half-time. From Tom Cairney's cross on the right, centre-forward Aleksandar Mitrović thought he had headed the visitors in front, only to be flagged offside. Replays showed him level or played marginally onside by Andy Robertson's heel a tight call either way. But as Fulham cut short their celebrations, quick thinking from Alisson sent Trent Alexander-Arnold racing down the right flank He played in Mo Salah and within 15 seconds of the ball being in Liverpool's net, it was in Fulham's, but for a legitimate goal.

It was tough on Jokanović's side, who had also created the clearest opportunity beforehand, with Ryan Sessegnon latching onto Mitrović's flick-on but pulling his shot wide when bearing down on Alisson's goal.

Liverpool's defenders might have been forgiven for wanting a break from burly Serbian centre-forwards after having to deal with Red Star's Milan Pavkov in midweek. And Mitrović was a handful all match, holding the ball up well for his team a role so critical to Fulham's heavily defensive set-up to allow them to venture further up the pitch and prevent a Red siege.

Meanwhile, in goal, Spaniard Sergio Rico performed superbly for the Cottagers, repelling multiple efforts from Mo Salah and Sadio Mané from both long and close range. There was nothing he could offer, though, to prevent Liverpool's second, seven minutes into the second half.

Virgil van Dijk found himself near Fulham's left-corner flag and played a one-two with Fabinho before laying the ball back to Andy Robertson. The Scot spotted Shaqiri unmarked at the far post and delivered a precision pass over the defence. The Swiss slotted in an accomplished, cultured close-range volley.

Trent Alexander-Arnold and van Dijk both had attempts from dead-ball situations but neither could clear the defensive wall, while Rico produced another flying stop from Robertson's crisp side-foot.

Fulham tried hard but as the match went on Mitrović became increasingly isolated up front. One wayward shot from outside the box summed up his frustrations. And, with no great urgency from Klopp's side to chase hard for a third, the game rather petered out towards the final whistle.

TEAMS

LIVERPOOL
Alisson; Alexander-Arnold, Gomez, van Dijk, Robertson; Wijnaldum (Henderson 69), Fabinho (Keïta 90+2); Shaqiri (Milner 81), Firmino, Mané; Salah

FULHAM
Rico; Christie, Odoi, Mawson, Le Marchand; Zambo Anguissa (Johansen 84), Chambers; Schürrle (Vietto 78), Cairney (Seri 63), Sessegnon; Mitrović

MATCH FACTS

- Xherdan Shaqiri's strike was his fifth direct involvement in a goal in his last six games (two goals, three assists).
- Liverpool had won all nine home Premier League games under Jürgen Klopp against newly promoted teams.
- Fulham's record at Anfield was now one win in their past 34 visits.

THEY SAID

Xherdan Shaqiri: "I want to help the team. When it's with a goal or assist, it's always good for the team. I came in the summer to help this team go forward and make the process better. I'm very happy with my performances; I just have to keep going like this and train hard every day. I hope we keep going until the end like this."

SATURDAY 24 NOVEMBER 2018 | PREMIER LEAGUE | VICARAGE ROAD
ATTENDANCE: 20,540

WATFORD 0
LIVERPOOL 3
(Salah 67, Alexander-Arnold 76, Firmino 89)

In an archetypal "game of two halves", Liverpool ran out comfortable winners against Watford with three goals after the hour mark, albeit finishing with 10 men after Jordan Henderson was sent off. As in the Reds' encounter with Fulham, though, Javi Gracia's team had cause to rue missed opportunities in the first period that might have given the scoreline a very different look.

Coming back from the international break, Jürgen Klopp had pretty much a full squad to choose from, with only Adam Lallana and Joe Gomez ruled out due to a minor knocks. Two changes meant Dejan Lovren coming in to partner Virgil van Dijk in defence and Henderson returning to take the armband and line up alongside Gini Wijnaldum in midfield.

Gracia selected a 4-4-2 with Troy Deeney and Gerard Deulofeu up front and plenty of steel centrally in the French pair of Étienne Capoue and Abdoulaye Doucouré.

Former Everton and Barcelona forward Deulofeu had the ball in the net inside two minutes but was flagged offside and later in the half he combined well with Argentinian teammate Roberto Pereyra, the latter testing Alisson with a stinging shot that was well saved.

Throughout the opening exchanges, Deulofeu and Deeney exerted pressure on Liverpool when out of possession and it took time for the visitors to grow into the match. Xherdan Shaqiri was frequently the Reds' best outlet, with a couple of perceptive passes narrowly missing their targets in Mo Salah and Roberto Firmino. Then, as half-time approached, the Swiss found Sadio Mané, whose volley was kept out by Hornets keeper Ben Foster.

After their initial burst, Watford appeared happy to concede the ball and stay in shape while looking for opportunities to counter, so at half-time Liverpool had enjoyed nearly 64 per cent of the ball and in the second 45 the visitors eventually made that dominance count.

But there was still plenty of threat from Gracia's team, who appealed loudly for a penalty when Will Hughes tumbled over Andy Robertson's challenge in the box. Referee Jon Moss was unmoved by the appeals.

Gracia introduced Isaac Success in place of Deulofeu and almost immediately Henderson picked up a yellow card for impeding the forward to stop a counter-attack.

Then on 66 minutes, the breakthrough: Firmino found one of Sadio Mané's trademark outside-to-in runs with a pass inside the full-back; and Mané's cross was converted by Mo Salah at the near post.

Andre Gray replaced Hughes for the home side as they sought an equaliser, but with 15 minutes left Liverpool extended the lead. From 25 yards, Trent Alexander-Arnold bent a wonderful free kick past a motionless Foster. Having opened his England account the previous week against the USA, this was becoming a purple patch for the youngster.

Henderson was dismissed after earning another yellow card, this time for a foul on Capoue, but the result was confirmed late on with a third Liverpool goal. A rapid break was initiated by Wijnaldum, who sent Robertson haring down the left wing. The Scot hurdled a sliding challenge from Capoue, powered into the box and cut the ball back for Mané. His shot was superbly saved by Foster but the rebound popped up for Firmino to nod home.

TEAMS

WATFORD
Foster; Femenia, Mariappa, Cathcart, Masina; Pereyra, Doucouré, Capoue, Hughes (Gray 75); Deulofeu (Success 57), Deeney

LIVERPOOL
Alisson, Alexander-Arnold, Lovren, van Dijk, Robertson; Henderson, Wijnaldum; Shaqiri (Milner 74), Firmino (Matip 90+2), Mané; Salah (Fabinho 86)

MATCH FACTS

- Mo Salah's goal was his sixth in only three meetings with Watford.
- Never before had the Reds conceded as few as five goals after 13 league games.
- Klopp recorded the 300th league win of his managerial career (101 with Mainz, 133 with Borussia Dortmund and 66 with Liverpool).

THEY SAID

Watford manager Javi Gracia: "The game was closer than the scoreline. We tried, we did a good defensive job for 66 minutes and after that the game changed. We had opportunities and didn't take them."

WEDNESDAY 28 NOVEMBER 2018 | UEFA CHAMPIONS LEAGUE – GROUP C
PARC DES PRINCES | ATTENDANCE: 46,880

PARIS SAINT-GERMAIN 2
(Bernat 13, Neymar 37)
LIVERPOOL 1
(Milner pen 45+1)

Paris Saint-Germain turned on the style at Parc des Princes to leave Liverpool's hopes of progression to the Champions League round of 16 in considerable jeopardy. Goals from wing-back Juan Bernat and Brazilian forward Neymar were enough to secure three points, despite James Milner's penalty on the stroke of half-time and a second-half rally from the Reds.

Jürgen Klopp was frustrated at the discipline meted out by referee Szymon Marciniak, who brandished six yellow cards to Liverpool players, yet allowed Marco Verratti to remain on the pitch after a dangerous, studs-up challenge on Joe Gomez in the first half. Klopp said the officiating had made his team "look like butchers".

Liverpool had won the European Cup on this very stage in 1981, but it was the modern pretenders to the crown – desperate this season to improve on their best effort to date of a quarter-final place – who made a lightning start.

With only two minutes gone, Mbappé raced onto Àngel Di María's pass but scuffed his shot wide. Then the young forward returned the favour to Di María with a chested lay-off on the edge of the area, and the Argentinian tested Reds keeper Alisson with a dipping left-footed drive. PSG looked dangerous every time they had the ball and Italian Marco Verratti was conducting midfield matters with guile and assurance.

On 12 minutes, the home side were deservedly ahead. Neat play from Verratti left Liverpool's midfield three trailing and the Italian played in Mbappé on the left. His cross was intercepted by Virgil van Dijk but the ball dropped kindly for wing-back Bernat, who took a touch then reversed a shot past Alisson into the left corner.

Mo Salah might have done better when played in by Milner but pulled his effort wide of Gianluigi Buffon's near post. And Sadio Mané appealed for handball when his dink inside hit Thilo Kehrer's hand – nothing given.

The French side had a huge slice of luck on 23 minutes when the influential Verratti caught Joe Gomez halfway up the shin with a reckless tackle. Nine times out of 10 you'd expect a straight red card but Marciniak only showed yellow.

PSG were enjoying good combination play on the left flank and were nearly two ahead on the half hour. Verratti dispossessed Milner on halfway – although there appeared to be a push – and Neymar played a one-two with Edinson Cavani, then found Mbappé's run into the box. His cross was reached by Alisson before Cavani could turn in a finish, but the warning was there. And five minutes later the home team did go two-up, with a near carbon copy of a move. This time Neymar and Mbappé exchanged passes and the latter's cross did find Cavani. Alisson saved but the rebound fell to Neymar, who stroked in first time.

Now the flicks and tricks were on show from PSG and Liverpool needed cool heads to stay in the match. It was much to the credit of Mané that he continued to pick up the ball and drive at the opposition; and he found his reward in first-half stoppage time as an injudicious challenge from Di María clipped the Senegalese on the corner of the box. After a long delay, during which the referee appeared to be taking instruction from his assistants, the penalty was awarded and Milner's spot kick sent Buffon the wrong way.

Early in the second half, Marquinhos had the ball in the net from Di María's curled free-kick delivery but the flag correctly went up for offside.

Just before the hour mark, Liverpool might have fashioned a clear chance, but with four against three in a break, Salah could not find a way past the covering defence. The ball found its way to Andy Robertson who, as so often, was able to plant a cross on the head of Roberto Firmino; but the Brazilian's header was wayward.

Shortly after, Firmino was replaced by Daniel Sturridge, but the Reds were unable to find another route to goal. In fact, it was PSG who came closest to making it 3-1, when Marquinhos's powerful header from a Neymar corner was directed straight at Alisson.

TEAMS

PARIS SAINT-GERMAIN

Buffon; Kehrer, Thiago Silva, Kimpembe, Bernat; Neymar, Verratti, Marquinhos, Di María (Choupo-Moting 65); Mbappé (Rabiot 85), Cavani (Alves 65)

LIVERPOOL

Alisson; Gomez, Lovren, van Dijk, Robertson; Wijnaldum (Keïta 66), Henderson, Milner (Shaqiri 77); Salah, Firmino (Sturridge 71), Mané

MATCH FACTS

- James Milner played his 150th match for the Reds.
- Neymar became the highest-scoring Brazilian in Champions League history with 31, overtaking Kaka (AC Milan, Real Madrid).
- PSG last lost a Champions League group stage match at home in December 2004 – a 3-1 defeat to CSKA Moscow.

THEY SAID

Jordan Henderson: "We thought we were good enough to come here and win. It wasn't our night but we kept going until the end. We didn't start particularly well and they started quickly, which they knew they would, so that's disappointing. But the reaction was good. We kept fighting right until the end and caused them problems. Now we've just got to keep it in our own hands by winning at Anfield."

PREMIER LEAGUE TABLE AT END OF NOVEMBER 2018

Pos	Team	Pld	W	D	L	GF	GA	GD	Pts
1	Manchester City	13	11	2	0	40	5	35	35
2	Liverpool	13	10	3	0	26	5	21	33
3	Tottenham Hotspur	13	10	0	3	23	11	12	30
4	Chelsea	13	8	4	1	28	11	17	28
5	Arsenal	13	8	3	2	28	16	12	27
6	Everton	13	6	4	3	20	15	5	22
7	Manchester United	13	6	3	4	20	21	-1	21
8	AFC Bournemouth	13	6	2	5	22	18	4	20
9	Watford	13	6	2	5	17	17	0	20
10	Leicester City	13	5	3	5	18	17	1	18
11	Wolverhampton Wanderers	14	4	4	6	13	17	-4	16
12	Brighton & Hove Albion	13	4	3	6	14	19	-5	15
13	Newcastle United	13	3	3	7	11	16	-5	12
14	West Ham United	13	3	3	7	14	22	-8	12
15	Cardiff City	14	3	2	9	13	27	-14	11
16	Huddersfield Town	13	2	4	7	8	22	-14	10
17	Crystal Palace	13	2	3	8	8	17	-9	9
18	Burnley	13	2	3	8	13	27	-14	9
19	Southampton	13	1	5	7	10	24	-14	8
20	Fulham	13	2	2	9	14	33	-19	8

UEFA CHAMPIONS LEAGUE GROUP C AT END OF NOVEMBER 2018

Pos	Team	Pld	W	D	L	GD	Pts
1	Napoli	5	2	3	0	3	9
2	Paris Saint-Germain	5	2	2	1	5	8
3	Liverpool	5	2	0	3	1	6
4	Red Star Belgrade	5	1	1	3	-9	4

CHAPTER FIVE

—

DECEMBER

"THE BOYS PLAYED WITH THEIR WHOLE HEART ON THE PITCH"

Goalkeepers can't win games on their own. But they can lay the foundation for a winning team. You won't find many examples in recent years of teams winning titles in top-level domestic or European competition without an unarguably first-rate goalie. So, when Liverpool paid Roma a record-breaking fee in the summer for Alisson Becker, it was product of sound logic from the scouting team, coaching group and club board.

A product of the youth set-up at Brazilian side Internacional, Alisson moved to Europe to join AS Roma in 2016, although he spent most of his first season in Italy as understudy to former Arsenal stopper Wojciech Szczesny. But he made his breakthrough the following year, after Szczesny moved to Juventus. His performances were vital to Roma's progression to the Champions League semi-final, where – of course – they lost to Liverpool, but prior to that goalfest, the Romans had been parsimonious in the competition, conceding no goals at all in five games at the Stadio Olimpico. Additionally, his 17 domestic shutouts helped Roma to third place in Serie A, attracted the attention of scouts across Europe's big leagues and cemented his starting berth for Brazil in the World Cup.

So, what are the ingredients that make up the ideal Liverpool goalkeeper? There's no one better to ask than Ray Clemence, winner of five league titles and three European Cups during his time at Anfield and by most people's measure, the greatest player to pull on the gloves in the club's illustrious history.

"There is no questioning that Alisson has done extremely well, and made a huge difference to Liverpool's defensive qualities," says Ray. "The club might have paid a lot of money for him, but that's not the issue. He had to prove his worth irrespective of the size of the fee, and he has done that to such an extent that you would have to say that it has been money well spent.

"The hallmark of a great goalkeeper is not just about making great saves, but making important saves, vital saves, and that is what marks Alisson out as an exceptional goalkeeper worthy of the price. When you are 1-0 up or 1-0 down, whether in a narrow winning position or narrowly behind but still in the game, that is when you need your goalkeeper to keep you in the game, and that is what Alisson has done consistently.

"Technically, he has all the attributes of an outstanding goalkeeper, he is a great size, quick on his feet, and – as the modern game has changed so much where keepers have the ball at their feet, more than they do in their hands – he is good with his feet. He commands his box and he commands the people around him. He has been a great signing and a great presence about him, to such an extent that even before the kick-off the opposition will look at him and think he will be difficult to beat, he just stands there and he looks big and strong and in control.

"When he did make a mistake against Leicester and got caught in possession – and you can't expect things to go your way 100 per cent as a keeper – he learned from that error, and he realised you cannot play too much or you might cost your side a goal.

"It's always a good sign when a goalkeeper, or any player for that matter, is prepared to learn, as nobody should think they've cracked it in this game, no one is going to have a perfect season, but he controls the back four and along with van Dijk has made such a big difference to the team."

Ray is loath to make comparisons with some of the Liverpool goalkeeping greats as he explained: "You judge goalkeepers these days by vastly different criteria from what the rest of us had. In fact, virtually everything about goalkeeping has changed; the ball is different, it's lighter, it moves differently, more quickly, swerves more, you need to use your feet more – all of that does make a huge difference.

"To do so well in his very first season is pretty impressive, but to be a so-called "legend" you really need to be doing it consistently for seven, eight, nine, even 10 years at the club, then you become a genuine true legend of Liverpool FC. Also, you really do need to win things and be part of a winning team over a number of years, and he is very much capable of doing just that. He is certainly a crowd-pleaser, and he has also settled in Merseyside very quickly and that's important sign that he will be there a long time and accomplish all that he is capable of doing."

You may by now be wondering what these extended observations on goalkeeping have to do with the story of Liverpool's December. Suffice to say the first game of the month – the Merseyside derby at Anfield – was one in which the ups and downs of being a keeper at the top end of professional football found dramatic expression.

Asked for his favourite Alisson save, Ray cites one in this match. "There have been a few, but saves are more important if they are meaningful to the result, and that is why I would pick out his save against Everton when the score was 0-0 and he made a save from point-blank range, a header about five yards out," he recalls. "From that distance, the first thing is to make yourself as big a target as possible, which he did; and, I am sure he'd be the first to admit, that you are taking a gamble that you are in the right place to make the save. It was such a vital time of the game, that is why I would mark that down as such an important, as well as exceptional, save."

The resultant clean sheet laid the platform for an extraordinary denouement at Anfield, with Everton keeper Jordan Pickford at the centre of the drama. With 95 minutes played and the game still goalless, Trent Alexander-Arnold pumped a long ball from near half-way into the Toffees' box, where it was comfortably cleared by Yerry Mina. The ball fell to Virgil van Dijk, who swung a leg at an ambitious volley, and the stadium groaned as the effort looped, in seemingly harmless flight, towards Pickford. Van Dijk himself spun away, kicking the air in frustration. But as the ball headed towards the angle of post and bar, Pickford seemed caught between catching it or tipping over and ended up doing neither. Substitute striker Divock Origi hadn't turned away. He sniffed a chance; and when the ball bounced down off the top of the bar, he was on hand to nudge it over the line for the latest of winners. Anfield erupted and Pickford – the hero of England's World Cup in Russia – was crestfallen.

Unable to contain his excitement, Jürgen Klopp sprinted onto the pitch to embrace Alisson who, even amid the uproar, may still have spared a thought for his unfortunate counterpart in the goalkeepers' union.

The result extended Everton's winless run at Anfield to 19, and kept Manchester City in check after the league leaders had extended the gap to five points the day before with a home win over Bournemouth.

"All my respect for Everton, they were really good," said Klopp afterwards. "Both teams delivered a proper fight, a proper derby from the first second."

The demands of three league games in six days prompted wholesale changes to the Liverpool starting XI for the trip to Burnley. Sean Dyche's side had endured a difficult run in October and November, losing five of their last six league games and conceding 17 goals in the process. That sequence had pulled the Clarets into the relegation zone – at kick-off, only Fulham were keeping them off the bottom of the table.

Jürgen Klopp made seven alterations in all, among them rewarding Divock Origi for his late efforts against Everton with a rare league start, and bringing Jordan Henderson back in midfield after suspension. Notably, it was the first time since May 2017, that Liverpool had started a match without any of Mo Salah, Roberto Firmino or Sadio Mané in the line-up.

"[Rotation] is absolutely normal in this period of the season," said Klopp pre-match. "I said to the boys in the meeting: I have done the job now for a while and if somebody would have told me 15 years ago I could change seven positions and have a line-up like that, I would have said it was not possible.

"We do it because we have to do it in two or three cases, and because we can do it because we have these boys. They train really hard.

"The midfielders played a lot of games already. We had to change the midfield, the most intense area of the pitch. Using Daniel [Sturridge] was clear; [Origi] after the last game makes sense, using the momentum. Alberto [Moreno] – [Andy Robertson] played pretty much all the games so far. Gini [Wijnaldum] played a lot of games.

"There's always a reason. But, in the end, you cannot only change; you have to make sure that it fits, that it's tuned. The two sessions we had where we could work a little bit on it, it looked really well, so I'm looking forward to this game."

Meanwhile, Dyche wrote in his programme notes that "nights under the lights here at the Turf are always a little bit special and it's important, from our point of view, that we put in a performance in front of our home fans."

Lashings of Lancashire rain were illuminated by those floodlights as Burnley set about their task with no sign of the hesitancy that might have been expected given their run of form. While Liverpool's new-look team took a little time to gel, the home side took advantage of the slippery conditions, sliding into tackles. One such from Ben Mee sent Joe Gomez off the pitch and into the perimeter. The defender was unable to continue and was replaced by Trent Alexander-Arnold. X-rays later revealed Gomez had fractured his leg and would be ruled out until well into the new year. It was tough luck on the youngster, who had forged a formidable centre-half partnership with Virgil van Dijk in recent months and also offered versatility and vital depth at full-back.

Klopp didn't know the extent of the injury but believed referee Stuart Atwell ought to have warned Burnley about their sliding tackles. "On wet ground the injury threat is massive and I know people like the first three or four challenges – it's part of football – but [if you say nothing] it leads to that situation and now Joe Gomez is injured."

For a time in the second half it seems as if the combination of selectorial changes, inclement weather and an aggressive approach from Burnley might swing the result for Dyche's team. Although both Daniel Sturridge and Naby

Keïta tested keeper Joe Hart in the early minutes of the second period, Jack Cork then stabbed home after a scramble in the box following a free-kick and the hosts led.

Just after the hour, Klopp was lining up his changes and readying Mo Salah and Roberto Firmino, when Liverpool equalised quite out of the blue. Origi had the ball in the box but couldn't find a space to shoot, so laid the ball off to James Milner on the edge of the 'D'. Milner fired in a low skimmer through Cork's legs that also caught Hart off guard and nestled in the corner.

The attacking substitutes came on and Firmino scored with his first touch to turn the game around. In frenetic scenes towards the end, Burnley could have snatched a point, but Alisson turned Ben Mee's header onto the post, then threw out to Sturridge on the right wing. The Englishman fed Mo Salah, whose first-time pass was converted by Xherdan Shaqiri for a classic counterattack clincher.

The *Liverpool Echo*'s James Pearce said this comeback was a genuine marker for Liverpool's title aspirations.

"Make no mistake, this was a gargantuan win for Liverpool," he wrote. "They showcased their powers of recovery en route to making history on a filthy night in Lancashire. With an hour gone in a Turf Moor monsoon, the Reds' Premier League title dream looked in serious danger of being washed away. They trailed to Jack Cork's controversial opener and had been roughed up by lowly Burnley.

"A debate would have raged about Klopp's selection gamble and a five-point gap to Manchester City would have felt like a chasm. But rather than meekly accept their fate, Liverpool dug deep and rallied.

"An outstanding second-half display turned a potential wake into another booming party on the back of Sunday's dramatic Merseyside derby triumph."

Bournemouth have been a quirky, curiously effective addition to the Premier League ranks since their ascent from the Championship in 2015. Working on a small budget, in a small stadium, manager Eddie Howe has assembled a group of players who know not only how to stay in the division, but thrive in it.

In their first season they finished 16th, but that position was mitigated by a tough run-in. During their last eight games, they lost to Tottenham, Man City, Liverpool, Chelsea, Everton and Manchester United. The fact was, they'd done the hard work early and all but secured their safety by the beginning of March.

They went on to finish 9th in 2016/17 and 12th in 2017/18, and what Howe and his side seemed to have perfected was the knack of putting in a little run of results when it really mattered. Their returns against the big hitters of the division were patchy, but they were always capable of pulling off a shock – for evidence, you may recall their 4-3 win over the Reds in December 2016, or the 4-0 drubbing of Chelsea that was to come in January 2019. More importantly – and the key for long-term survival in the top-flight – they are brilliant at beating the teams around them.

In 2018/19, they'd made a stunning start to the campaign. Six wins in 10 league games had them riding high in sixth and even after a dip in November, they still lay seventh ahead of Liverpool's visit.

Before the match Howe was asked for his assessment of Liverpool's progress this season. "They've definitely improved as a team," he said. "They are a lot more resolute and resilient. Their defensive record is excellent and that takes a lot of work on the training ground – a lot of discipline. I don't think you win the league without that, so I think they're definitely moving in the direction that they want to.

"They've also got players that can win a game in a moment and we're going to have to be good in all disciplines of our defending to have any chance of getting a result."

He was also asked if it might play in the Cherries' favour that their visitors had a huge upcoming Champions League meeting with Napoli on their minds, but he brushed off any speculation about distractions.

"I don't think I'd disrespect Liverpool in that way," said Howe. "You look at how they approached the Burnley game – yes, they made changes, but they were very professional in the job that they did. They will look at our game as a very important one in their Premier League season – they're not going to take us lightly in any way. We anticipate meeting a full-strength Liverpool team."

Jürgen Klopp's changes numbered five in all; and despite a reshuffle that meant using the ever-adaptable James Milner at right-back, it was a strong attacking line-up that ran out at the Vitality Stadium. Mo Salah and Roberto Firmino were back up front, while Sadio Mané was deemed fit enough for a spot on the bench.

It would be Salah's day to shine on the south coast. Back to his very best, the Egyptian was uncontainable and fired in a classy hat-trick as Liverpool eased to a 4-0 win.

This was also a lunchtime date to remember for Milner, who captained the side on the occasion of his 500th Premier League appearance, but one to forget for Bournemouth centre-half Steve Cook who just had "one of those days", his bad luck capped by an extraordinary back-heeled own goal.

Liverpool were too strong in all departments for a Cherries side missing their main striker in Callum Wilson – rested due to a hamstring problem – and influential young midfielder Lewis Cook – out with a long-term knee injury. Consequently, the hosts flickered only occasionally in attack.

Klopp was pleased with his players' endeavours post-match. "We had to keep the ball and win the ball back as quickly as possible," he said. "We did both very often; but not always as they had their moments too, of course.

"We improved in the second half and controlled the game. It was really nice. Mo Salah scored [the second goal] and I don't think many do in that situation. [His] third goal was again brilliant. We played nice football and the players we brought on did really well."

They included Mané, back from a foot injury, and Adam Lallana – who had begun his career as a youth-teamer at Bournemouth – coming on for the last 25 minutes to rest some legs before the visit of Napoli.

Later in the day, spirits were raised further by the news that Manchester City had lost at Chelsea, a first league defeat of the season for Pep's men and one that ensured Liverpool would keep top spot in the league after 16 games played and retain the only unbeaten record in the division.

We observed in an earlier chapter that winning your home games in the Champions League brings, if not a guarantee, then at least a high statistical probability of a place in the knockout stage of the competition. That remained the case as Matchday 6's crunch tie against Napoli approached; but in this instance, not all winning scorelines would be of equal value.

While progress to the round of 16 was still technically in Liverpool's hands, with Napoli three points ahead and the Italians having a goal difference advantage of +2, the permutations were fiendish. Now, pay attention at the back...

First, we must clarify the rule that if teams are tied on points in the group stage, they are ranked by head-to-head record. Napoli beat Liverpool 1-0 at home in the reverse game, so assuming Paris Saint-Germain were going to beat Red Star Belgrade in their final group game, the very least Liverpool needed was a 1-0 home win. That would take the Reds through on goals scored. A win by two or more goals with any scoreline would be enough, owing to a better head-to-head record. However, a one-goal win with any scoreline equal to or higher than 2-1 (eg 3-2, 4-3, 5-4) would mean Liverpool going out as Napoli would have scored an away goal or goals, so would progress on head-to-head record. But any one-goal win *would* be enough were PSG to fail to win in Belgrade, a task that had already proven beyond Liverpool and Napoli.

Still with us? Good.

Jürgen Klopp would have been in full command of the evening's possibilities but was keen to play them down in his pre-match remarks. "We should ignore all the rest around and try to get the best result we can get," he told the club website. "We always go for a clean sheet, we never want to concede goals – so that's not a big difference.

"We have to defend them with all we have, we have to defend them much better than we did in Naples. And we have to play better; that's easy because that was our worst game of the season. So, we will be better, I'm pretty sure – not only because of us but because of the atmosphere as well.

"We need Anfield – we need a special atmosphere. I really think the boys deserve that. Everybody here knows how big the influence can be and that could be an advantage. If it's enough, we'll know after the game."

And what a game it was. Packed with incident, tension, high quality, missed chances, a heart-stopping finish and, ultimately, a result that fell on the right side of the knockout equation.

There were three changes in Liverpool's starting XI from the win at Bournemouth: Trent Alexander-Arnold, Jordan Henderson and Sadio Mané replaced Fabinho, Naby Keïta and Xherdan Shaqiri, with James Milner moving into midfield.

The atmosphere inside Anfield was electrifying. Fully three-quarters of an hour before kick-off, Napoli's away section were singing their heads off as if their team were leading with five minutes to play. The visitors wouldn't lack for boisterous support but it was more than matched by vociferous backing from the Anfield stands. It proved to be another of *those* European nights.

Mo Salah made the difference with some sublime trickery to create a goal from nothing, and Liverpool might have run out comfortable winners but for some uncharacteristically wayward finishing from Sadio Mané. And the outcome – and post-match atmosphere – would have been markedly different if Alisson had not been on hand to save point-blank from Napoli substitute Arkadiusz Milik in the second minute of added-time.

The Brazilian commanded a world-record fee in the summer and paid back a big chunk of it here. As Ray Clemence said, it's all about "important saves".

Klopp's post-match comments reflected the breathless nature of the evening's events. "I'm still full of adrenaline," he gasped. "This game was just amazing, it was outstanding... unbelievable. The boys played with their whole heart on the pitch.

"I want to say thank you, Anfield. It was unbelievable what the people did tonight. The atmosphere they created was just so special. I couldn't be more proud of [everyone] involved."

With one more hurdle in the club's European journey negotiated, now came a domestic game that is annually circled in red by both sets of fans the moment the fixture list is released: Liverpool v Manchester United.

The rivalry between Liverpool and Manchester United transcends football. It speaks to the birth and growth of these two great northern cities through the industrial revolution and beyond, and to an ongoing battle for cultural and sporting pre-eminence that has arguably driven each to greater heights.

Each has had its own footballing dynasty in the last half-century, each of these delivering hauls of silverware beyond the imagining of most football clubs' fans. Each has suffered its own post-imperial decline and the agonies of trying to rediscover a consistent, winning formula.

Local rivalries are hugely important, of course – and in terms of current form and fortune, one is building with Manchester City – but in the grand sweep of footballing history, measured not in individual results or bragging rights but in volume of European and domestic titles, the benchmark of success for Manchester United is to be better than Liverpool and vice versa.

Approaching the teams' first meeting of 2018/19, the moods in the respective camps could not have been more contrasting. Liverpool were on cloud nine: through in Europe from the toughest group, top of the table and enjoying the club's best-ever start to a league campaign. Morale was high and momentum building through the busy December schedule.

Meanwhile, United had the winter blues. A stuttering campaign up to this point saw José Mourinho's side in sixth place, six points behind Arsenal in fifth and 16 behind second-placed Liverpool. A 4-1 success over struggling Fulham had stopped a run of four league matches without a win, but all was not well at Old Trafford.

Week upon week, fans were urging the team to attack more, and – two-and-a-half years into the Mourinho's reign at United – pragmatism about a defensive approach needed the support of results. Without those, the United board felt compelled to act and two days after this defeat to Liverpool, the "special one" was gone.

His final selection appeared set up to contain: three centre-halves, two wing-backs and two defensive midfielders ranged behind an attacking trio of Jesse Lingard, Marcus Rashford and Romelu Lukaku. And while they stayed in the game until the final quarter, Liverpool were deserved winners.

The stats for a Liverpool v United match made exceptional reading. The home side fired in 36 shots to United's six; 11 on target to United's two; thirteen Liverpool corners to United's two. There's always more to a game of football than the raw numbers, but these only bore out what was obvious to the naked eye. Liverpool were utterly dominant.

This game's matchday programme featured Xherdan Shaqiri on the cover, arms folded after scoring and looking pleased with life against a backdrop of delighted fans at Anfield. He may not have felt quite so buoyant when the manager left him on the bench but he probably has a copy of that programme stored somewhere now, after a two-goal supersub display that put the game to bed inside seven stirring second-half minutes.

Liverpool went ahead on 23 minutes as Fabinho found Sadio Mané cruising into the penalty area. The striker's chest control and finish were exemplary, although United fans might have wondered how he was allowed the freedom of the area. But the visitors hit back after a rare handling error from Alisson, who spilled Lukaku's cross on the greasy surface to the feet of Lingard. The England player made no mistake.

The second half was a virtual siege on the United area, with Mourinho's team packing the central spaces with bodies. But few clear chances were created until Shaqiri rose from the subs' bench to change the game. First, he clipped in de Gea's block from Mané – in off the bar after a ricochet from Young's knee. Then another deflection from Eric Bailly helped Shaqiri's shot fly past the Spanish stopper's reach. Anfield was in raptures.

Mourinho conceded that "the best team won" and declared himself "tired just watching Robertson". "[My] players gave everything," he added. "[But Liverpool] are fast, intense, aggressive and physical. They play 200 miles per hour with and without the ball."

Klopp was understandably delighted. "The first half an hour was outstanding," he said. "We scored only once but I don't think anyone expects to score three, four, five times or whatever. How we played was just perfect, really. We tried to pass in the right areas, we accelerated, we wanted the ball back, we played in behind the line.

"Then after half an hour we lost the momentum of the game a little bit, they scored and it was a bit more open. They changed and when Fellaini is on the pitch it is never a good sign for the other team, because these balls are really difficult to defend. We did even that really well tonight.

"So, we stayed in the game, got the dominance back step by step and then Shaq closed the game. I think [we] absolutely deserved tonight. You need [the] bit of luck, we needed for both goals with the deflections, but bringing the situations, having these moments, that's football!"

Meantime, Manchester City had bounced back from their disappointment against Chelsea and beaten Everton at the Etihad the day before, so the league lead changed hands yet again. Another three league games in seven days were on the way over the festive period and a huge twist in the title race in the offing.

Liverpool were up first in the final rounds of fixtures before Christmas with a Friday night date at Molineux before the majority of games took place the next day.

Wolves were enjoying an immensely impressive first season back in the top flight under the guidance of manager Nuno Espírito Santo. If their form wasn't exactly consistent – seven wins to date sandwiched a run in October and November of five defeats in six – they had shown they belonged in the Premier League. Draws against both Manchester clubs and Arsenal were followed by a 2-1 win over Chelsea, so this was an altogether different proposition to your average newly promoted side.

Before the game, the Wolves manager pointed to teamwork as the key to his side's success so far and to the test of playing the league leaders.

"It's a big challenge for us, [but] we're prepared," said Santo. "Liverpool are a fantastic team with a fantastic manager. We'll try to compete to the maximum of our efforts and belief, trying everything we can.

"Team spirit, the way we feel and think as a team, is what can push us forward and help us achieve the things we want as a team. It can never go away from us, the way we work and believe."

One person in the Wolves ranks who knew plenty about the visitors was captain Conor Coady. The 26-year-old came through Liverpool's academy alongside players such as Raheem Sterling, Jon Flanagan and Andre Wisdom and went on to captain England to success in the UEFA European Under-17 Championships in 2010.

He ultimately didn't make it as a first-teamer at Anfield but, having grown up on Merseyside as a Liverpool fan, he does have huge respect and admiration for his former club.

"The club helped me improve as a player and a person," he told the *Wolverhampton Express & Star* in an interview before the visit of Liverpool. "It was a good age group, we came through at a good time, but not many made it through to the first team, which shows how hard it was."

"It wasn't a difficult decision to leave. That's nothing against Liverpool. I grew up wanting to be a footballer – when I was young I wanted it to be for Liverpool, but after a few years I became more realistic. I had Steven Gerrard, Jordan Henderson, Joe Allen and Lucas Leiva ahead of me."

He went on loan to Sheffield United before signing for Huddersfield in 2014 and then moving again to Wolves in 2015. Kenny Jackett was then in charge but Coady has already seen four managers in his time at Molineux. Happily, stability has been achieved under Santo and Coady says he is revelling in the management style of his Portuguese boss.

"I've not been involved in something like [this before]," he says. "It becomes easy in that way – [the manager] explains something and it just makes sense. It all comes from him. It's hard to explain. The way he explains and talks to you, you can picture what he wants to happen.

"He speaks at great length in terms of playing our way and keeping our identity. We won't change, no matter who we're playing," Coady adds. "We'll have no fear and we'll play to win the game. Liverpool have got a brilliant team but we'll be ready for them. The whole club is high on confidence, supporters, players, everyone. We'll be fearless."

Wolves's attractive passing style and pace on the counter had given plenty of teams pause for thought over the first half of the campaign, but Santo knew better than to be gung-ho against the form team in the league. He was missing one key player in winger Diogo Jota and brought in defensive midfielder Romain Saïss to stiffen the midfield. The lightning-quick Adama Traore was also included to threaten in behind if Liverpool looked to play a high line.

The weather was appalling at Molineux and the match, in truth, wasn't a classic. Both sides gave the ball away frequently and it was a spectacle to be enjoyed for its hustle and bustle rather than the quality you might expect from two teams blessed with such skilful players. The two exceptions were those who ended up on the scoresheet.

Mo Salah was magnificent. As the rain lashed down, he kept his impish disposition all night, bagging the first goal, assisting van Dijk for the second and continuing to make a mockery of press suggestions earlier in the season that he was off colour in this campaign. The Egyptian's form in 2017/18 had been stratospheric: a career-defining masterpiece; an epic glut of goals. If this was a drop in form: to be leading the race for the Golden Boot and doing it, as they say, on a wet night in the Midlands, then Reds supporters would take it and plenty more. "The Egyptian King", as far as the travelling fans were concerned, was very much still on his throne.

The other regal presence was that of Virgil van Dijk, who scored his first league goal for the club, achieved 92 per cent in passing accuracy, won four aerial duels, made five clearances and generally bossed the defence like a man playing on another plane, one in which time moves at a different speed.

As the *Daily Telegraph*'s Sam Wallace put it: "In van Dijk they have the season's outstanding individual player so far and for all the times he blocked, tackled or headed the ball away, none matched the moment he was obliged to catch the rocket-speed Wolves winger Adama Traore. Klopp said that chasing Traore required a defender "to get on his motorbike" and if that was the case then van Dijk was Liverpool's easy rider, accelerating smoothly and putting himself between ball and man."

Another away win ensured Liverpool would top the Christmas table and the club's festive cheer was made yet brighter the following day when Crystal Palace confounded expectations by beating Manchester City. Andros Townsend's volley in a 3-2 win was a goal-of-the-season contender as Palace shocked the Etihad; and a gap opened for the first time between the Reds and the defending champions.

If Boxing Day is traditionally a time to entertain the extended family, who better to welcome to Anfield than the avuncular and much-cherished former Reds boss Rafa Benitez? The Newcastle United manager has a place in the Liverpool pantheon, of course, as a European Cup winner (alongside numerous other trophies), but he also retains a place in the hearts of ex-players and fans who remember his reign for its warmth and dignity. The Spaniard was a terrific fit for the club and the city.

The relationship was well understood by current Reds boss Jürgen Klopp, who paid tribute in his programme notes.

"I really love the affection and respect our club has for Rafa and the appreciation towards him for what he has given LFC," Klopp wrote. "The word 'legend' might be overused these days, particularly in sport, but for Rafa it's almost underselling him.

"When his name is mentioned at Melwood or Anfield or to any Liverpool supporter you see their face instantly fill with joy and love. They remember the amazing times and moments LFC enjoyed under his leadership and I think that is so cool.

"Of course, today friendship ceases on both sides for the 90-plus minutes our teams face each other. He remains, rightly, one of the most admired managers and coaches in Europe and his pedigree is simply outstanding."

Well said. However, the festive period is not necessarily the happiest time for managers juggling squad resources with travelling and Newcastle and their fans had been handed two away games straight after Christmas: a total of 880 miles in round trips, plenty of which would be shared by the squad as Liverpool Airport was closed.

"We have to travel [on Christmas Day] after lunch, but that's it, and the rest of the time we have to train, recover, and be ready," Rafa told *The Chronicle*.

"We will have to use the squad over the Christmas period. Obviously when you play two games in three days, physically you don't have time to recover. [So] it is important to have the squad available, it's important to have everybody concentrated and focused because maybe some will not play this game, but they may be needed for the next one. I have to be sure that everybody is ready because that is the key during these busy periods."

Benitez was a good as his word and, after failing to beat bottom side Fulham at home last game, he made six changes for the visit to Anfield. Out went Javier Manquillo, Fabien Schär, Christian Atsu, Ki Sung-yueng, Ayoze Perez and Salomon Rondon; in came DeAndre Yedlin, Federico Fernandez, Isaac Hayden, Kenedy, Yoshinori Muto and Joselu. It was a bold ploy to reshuffle the side so extensively; and one that ultimately came unstuck.

Klopp, meanwhile, made just three changes. Trent Alexander-Arnold was passed fit in timely fashion as James Milner had a hamstring problem, while Gini Wijnaldum and Xherdan Shaqiri also started.

Dejan Lovren was an unlikely scorer on 10 minutes, seizing on a clearance that dropped inside the area and firing a howitzer of a half-volley high into the net. And once ahead, the Reds never looked unduly troubled. Alisson enjoyed a quiet afternoon between the sticks with Joselu heading an early chance off-target and Isaac Hayden failing to wrap his foot around a decent chance in the second half.

By then Liverpool were two ahead, with Mo Salah surefooted from the spot after a pull on the Egyptian by Paul Dummett. Shaqiri plundered his fifth goal in five games at Anfield when converting Alexander-Arnold cross with just over 10 minutes to play, and Fabinho completed the rout with a near-post header from Salah's corner.

A delighted Lovren reflected on scoring his first of the season – only his seventh in four and a half years at the club.

"It was quite difficult to catch the ball, to be honest," he said. "Usually it's a ball [I'd] kick into the stand, like defending a set-piece! But luckily enough, I did it, I scored. It's always great to score for Liverpool and hopefully we can do it again in the next couple of games because we need everyone now. There are tough two games now: Arsenal and Man City. We need to keep this momentum."

Klopp concurred. The welcome news that Manchester City had lost a second successive league game meant the gap at the top of the table was six to Tottenham, seven to City, but the Liverpool boss refused to engage in speculation that his team were now favourites for the title.

"[The lead] means nothing," he insisted. "We play Arsenal and City [in our next two games], so it's good that we have six or seven points more than other teams. But that's pretty much all. What we wanted to do all the time [was] create a situation, a basis for the rest of the season and now the first part of the season is over.

"It's very difficult, there's a long way to go and we all know that. We have to win our games, we have to be focused, we need to be really in the mood, with tunnel vision. That's really important and then we will see where it leads us."

Just eight weeks on from having met at the Emirates, Liverpool and Arsenal rejoined battle for the final game of 2018. That fixture in north London had ended in a 1-1 draw; but, frankly, it could have been any score at all given the air-hockey, end-to-end nature of the match.

It also bore a tinge of sadness, being played soon after the untimely death of Leicester chairman Vichai Srivaddhanaprabha, and there was sad news before this game, too, as Arsenal announced the death of Peter Hill-Wood, a long-time chairman of the club, at the age of 82.

Hill-Wood brought both George Graham and Arsène Wenger to the club, oversaw the move from Highbury to the Emirates and saw 13 major trophies lifted before stepping down due to ill-health in 2013.

Wenger paid this tribute after his passing: "We all had huge respect for the way [Hill-Wood] carried the values of Arsenal through the generations. He guided the club with vision, courage and intelligence. We will miss him deeply."

A minute's silence was held before the match at Anfield.

Wenger's successor Unai Emery had difficult choices to make in his selection and, in fact, they weren't very different to those he'd faced on 1 November. Then, as now, he'd been short of defensive cover. Centre-half Konstantinos Mavropanos was unavailable, Hector Bellerin and Nacho Monreal were doubtful; and in addition Rob Holding had a knee problem and Shkodran Mustafi needed to pass a fitness test. Laurent Koscielny was deemed only fit enough for the subs' bench. It was a challenge to put out any sort of back four at all – let alone one able to take on the in-form team in the division.

In the end, Mustafi was passed fit and lined up with Sokratis in central defence, with Stefan Lichsteiner and Sean Kolašinac either side.

On the right-side of midfield, Emery selected England youth international Ainsley Maitland-Niles who, after recovering from a leg fracture in August, had impressed in the Europa League and was now getting regular game time in the top-flight. As a member of the England team that won the Under-20 World Cup in 2017, he was one to watch and had an instant impact on this game, stunning Anfield with the opening goal – his first for Arsenal – after 11 minutes. However, this merely seemed to have the effect of tweaking the tiger's tail.

While Arsenal looked patched up, Liverpool's squad was near its most potent strength. James Milner was still out with a hamstring problem and Joe Gomez and Joel Matip continued their recuperation, but given the rigours of December, Jürgen Klopp would have been pleased with a near-full squad from which to choose.

Crucially, all three of Liverpool's terrific trio of first-choice attackers were fit and in form and after conceding early – this being the first time in 364 days that the Reds had been behind in a league game at Anfield – the team's reaction was devastating. By half-time, all three forwards were on the scoresheet and the home side were 4-1 up and out of sight.

A second-half penalty for Firmino made it a hat-trick for the Brazilian and equalled Liverpool's best result against the Gunners in the Premier League era.

With Tottenham losing against Wolves and City yet to play against Southampton, the Reds opened a nine-point lead at the top of the table and now speculation about Liverpool's title chances was approaching fever pitch.

It was left to the manager, again, to try to manage expectations, in spite of his evident delight at the team's latest high-scoring performance.

"The reaction [to going behind] was absolutely brilliant," Klopp said. "We didn't concede a lot of goals this year so you never know exactly how the reaction will be [but it was] just outstanding. We increased the intensity again a little bit, immediately put them under pressure again.

"[But] tomorrow [our lead] could be seven and then we play against Man City and it could be four. So it's really nothing, it's absolutely not important how many points you are ahead in December."

Those predictions would prove correct, but there was no denying the spirit of optimism that was running through the club as Liverpool's annual fixture list was completed.

Unbeaten at Anfield in the Premier League and Champions League in 2018, Liverpool ended up recording 88 points from 37 league matches, a points-per-game ratio of 2.38 that bettered any calendar year in the club's history.

Virgil van Dijk – after another peerless performance at the back and celebrating a year in which he had transformed the club's defensive mettle – reflected the spirit of optimism suffusing the squad.

"Anything [is possible]," he told BT Sport. "That's how we should go out there and play. You still need to do it on the pitch but we feel good. It's a great time to be a Liverpool player – and also a fan, I think.

"We still need to improve a lot of things but obviously we're very happy with the situation at the moment. We want to keep going and keep working hard and keep the intensity high, to make sure we keep doing well. That's the only thing for it."

DECEMBER MATCH REPORTS

SUNDAY 2 DECEMBER 2018 | PREMIER LEAGUE | ANFIELD | ATTENDANCE: 51,756

LIVERPOOL 1
(Origi 90+6)
EVERTON 0

Liverpool won the 232rd Merseyside derby in sensational fashion with a last-gasp goal by Divock Origi, who profited from a bizarre error by Everton and England goalkeeper Jordan Pickford.

There appeared little danger when a final chance of a hard-fought but goalless game fell to Virgil van Dijk on the edge of the area and his attempted volley ballooned upwards. But backspin made the effort hang in the air and the keeper was unable to clear safely. The ball bounced down off the top of the bar and Origi nodded home, sparking wild scenes in the stands and on the touchline.

Jürgen Klopp was complimentary about his opposite number Marco Silva in the build-up and mindful of the threat Everton posed, despite the visitors' recent poor record at Anfield. "This is the best-tuned [Everton] squad I have faced," said the Reds boss. "They have good speed, creativity, organisation – in any other league in Europe this would be a team in European competition. It's difficult in England but the development and improvement is obvious."

Klopp made three changes from the side that started in Paris. Jordan Henderson was serving a one-match ban for his sending off against Watford, so Fabinho came into midfield; Trent Alexander-Arnold returned at right-back with Joe Gomez shuffling over to centre-half and Dejan Lovren dropping to the bench, while Xherdan Shaqiri came in for his first derby, replacing James Milner. Everton were unchanged from the previous week's win over Cardiff at Goodison.

The derby kicked off at a furious pace. Yerry Mina might have scored after only four minutes with a header from Lucas Digne's freekick that slid narrowly by the left-hand upright. Sadio Mané was in frisky mood early on, taking up good central positions and creating half a chance for Mo Salah, who couldn't quite pull down a lofted chip under challenge from Digne. Then Salah returned the favour with a sumptuous first-time pass playing in Mané, who held off Mina but fired high over the bar.

A twin effort in defence then repelled Everton after smart work by André Gomes released Bernard down the left. The Brazilian's cross was nodded back across goal by Theo Walcott and Gomes headed firmly towards goal from only a couple of yards out. Alisson blocked the effort but the ball hit Gomes on the floor and was about to trickle into net when near-namesake Joe Gomez slid in brilliantly to hook it away. Everton boss Silva held his head in disbelief that the hosts hadn't scored.

Then it was Pickford's turn to make a crucial intervention, denying Shaqiri, who was sent clear on right side of the box by Salah. The Swiss player's strike was firm but Pickford saved with his body, conceding only a corner. Alisson also thwarted Theo Walcott's attempt to round the keeper and though the half ended scoreless, it wasn't for lack of goalmouth incident.

The fun continued after the break, as Mané had another sight of goal when latching on to Firmino's pass. As challenges came in from Seamus Coleman and Pickford, he shot into the side-netting.

The Senegalese remained at the heart of most of Liverpool's attacking play, shooting just wide from distance with the hour approaching and nearly connecting with a cross from Andy Robertson but being put off-balance by a last-ditch challenge from Digne. Both sides made changes as the pressure of the occasion began to exert itself on players and fans alike. It was noticeably more edgy inside Anfield as the half wore on.

Mané was close to converting a cross from substitute Divock Origi on 87 minutes; then the Dutchman – making a first Premier League appearance since August 2017 – had a great chance from the subsequent corner when van Dijk won the first header from Alexander-Arnold's delivery. It fell awkwardly to Origi, but he conjured a shot with the outside of his foot that struck the bar and bounced clear. Fellow sub Daniel Sturridge fired the ball back in against Gylfi Sigurdsson's arm and claimed a penalty. Nothing was given.

Two Everton substitutions, plus an injury to Idrissa Gueye, extended added-time to six minutes – crucially so, as there was still time for one last attack from Liverpool and, thanks to Pickford's error and Origi's alertness, a derby finish for the ages.

TEAMS

LIVERPOOL

Alisson; Alexander-Arnold, Gomez, van Dijk, Robertson; Wijnaldum, Fabinho,

Shaqiri (Keïta 71), Firmino (Origi 74), Mané; Salah (Sturridge 75)

EVERTON

Pickford; Coleman, Keane, Mina, Digne; Gomes, Gueye; Walcott (Lookman 63), Sigurdsson (Zouma 90+1), Bernard (Calvert-Lewin 89); Richarlison

MATCH FACTS

- This was the 100th league meeting between Liverpool and Everton at Anfield.
- Divock Origi's winning goal was the 350th of Jürgen Klopp's reign at Liverpool.
- Liverpool extended the record for more Premier League winning goals in added time than any other team (31, with Arsenal next on 25 and Man United on 22).

THEY SAID

Divock Origi: "It's a special moment. I'm enjoying the moment, it's a special win for the club and the city. [The goal] was just instinct, I knew there would be some open balls like this, so had to be nice and sharp. In the end, Virgil gave me a nice assist!"

WEDNESDAY 5 DECEMBER 2018 | PREMIER LEAGUE | TURF MOOR
ATTENDANCE: 21,741

BURNLEY 1
(Cork 54)
LIVERPOOL 3
(Milner 62, Firmino 69, Shaqiri 90+2)

On a wet and wild night at Turf Moor, Liverpool fought back from a goal down with three strikes in the last half-hour to stay in touch with leaders Manchester City as the winter fixtures began to pile up.

Three days after the derby, and with dates against Bournemouth and Napoli looming, Jürgen Klopp made seven changes and would have been concerned when Jack Cork put the hosts ahead 10 minutes into the second half.

However, once James Milner had brought the sides level, the strength of the Reds' bench told, as Roberto Firmino came on to score with his first touch, and fellow sub Mo Salah set up an injury-time third to secure the points.

The early exchanges were scrappy, with both sides coming to terms with sodden grass and swirling winds, and the first incident of note came as a result of the playing conditions. Burnley defender Ben Mee dived in to tackle Joe Gomez and took the ball, but as Gomez slid off the pitch he collided with the boundary boards. The injury was later diagnosed as a leg fracture; for now, he was replaced at right-back by Trent Alexander-Arnold.

Burnley were in energetic mood and after Phil Bardsley sent a long-range shot narrowly wide, the hosts thought they were ahead through Ashley Barnes. From a free kick on the left, Robbie Brady sent in an inviting delivery that Barnes volleyed superbly past Alisson. Unfortunately for the home fans, the assistant's flag cut the celebrations short.

Early in the second half, Daniel Sturridge worked himself a shooting opportunity on the edge of the area and brought a fine save from Joe Hart to the keeper's right. Then Naby Keïta drew an even better stop from Hart, who tipped the midfielder's searing drive onto the post.

Soon after, though, Burnley were ahead. On such a difficult night for defenders, set pieces were always likely to be a profitable avenue for the home side to explore, and when Johan Gudmundsson swung a corner in on 53 minutes, James Tarkowski won the initial header. Alisson patted the ball down under pressure from Chris Wood and saved from Barnes's follow-up challenge but the ball rolled back to Cork, who poked it over the line.

With an hour gone, it was time for the cavalry. Sadio Mané had a minor injury so had been left out of the 18, but two-thirds of Liverpool's first-choice forward line – Salah and Firmino – were among the substitutes and itching to get involved. Before they were stripped, though, the Reds were on terms. Accepting Divock Origi's pass 15 yards out, Milner fizzed a shot across the slick surface and inside the right-hand post.

It didn't take long for Firmino to make an impact. By his standards the Brazilian had been short of goals in the league, with just one in six weeks since scoring at Wembley against Spurs, but here he netted with his first touch of the ball. Alexander-Arnold's free-kick was reached by Virgil van Dijk on the stretch and the Dutchman's centre laid the chance on a plate for Firmino to finish from a yard out.

The Clarets kept going, with Aaron Lennon and Sam Vokes replacing Brady and Wood, but were unable to summon a clear chance until stoppage time, when Alisson pushed Mee's header onto the woodwork. That was the cue for the keeper to find Sturridge with a long throw, and with Burnley heavily committed upfield the break was on. Sturridge found Salah, who looped a pass to Xherdan Shaqiri and the ball was past Hart in a flash.

TEAMS

BURNLEY

Hart; Bardsley, Tarkowski, Mee, Taylor; Gudmundsson, Westwood, Cork, Brady (Lennon 71); Wood (Vokes 71); Barnes (Vydra 83)

LIVERPOOL

Alisson; Gomez (Alexander-Arnold 23), Matip, van Dijk, Moreno (Salah 65); Shaqiri, Keïta, Henderson, Milner; Sturridge, Origi (Firmino 65)

MATCH STATS

- Jordan Henderson played the 300th league game of his career (with spells at Sunderland, Coventry City on loan and Liverpool).
- Alisson matched a club record by going unbeaten in his opening 15 league matches (level with Javier Mascherano in 2007).
- Liverpool's six goals conceded in 15 league matches equalled the all-time defensive record for the top flight (Man United 1985/86, Arsenal 1990/91, Chelsea 2004/05, 2008-09)

THEY SAID

Ian Doyle, *Liverpool Echo*: "Going to Burnley brings out the gambler in Liverpool boss Jürgen Klopp. [Last season], the Reds boss [also] made seven changes for his team's last visit to Turf Moor. A last-gasp Ragnar Klavan goal secured a dramatic 2-1 triumph that chilly afternoon, a result Klopp later admitted was a catalyst for the second half of the season. Whether this latest gutsy win proves the same, only time will tell. But this was arguably one of Liverpool's biggest wins of the season."

BOURNEMOUTH 0
LIVERPOOL 4
(Salah 25, 48, 77, Cook og 68)

Mo Salah's hat-trick secured a comparatively comfortable three points at Bournemouth as Liverpool overtook title rivals Manchester City at the top of the Premier League table.

The Egyptian was back to his imperious best, tormenting the hosts' defence on his way to the match ball, the reward for his second treble in Liverpool colours.

A sunny morning on the south coast had made way for low cloud and drizzle by kick-off, but the Reds made a bright enough start, an early free kick from Xherdan Shaqiri skimming off Charlie Daniels's head in the wall after a handball by Nathan Ake.

Bournemouth keeper Asmir Begović then had to be alert to clear danger at Salah's feet after Andy Robertson's centre before Naby Keïta's follow-up was blocked.

Shaqiri was in creative mood, reading Salah's runs well, and the striker was just unable to connect with a neat through-ball from the Swiss on his right foot.

The Cherries had their share of the play, though. Alisson was tested when Junior Stanislas slid in Welsh youngster David Brooks, his shot beaten away at the near post. Then Andrew Surman's long-ranger fizzed over the corner of post and bar.

On 24 minutes, though, the visitors were ahead. A quick one-two between Salah and Roberto Firmino led to a snap volley from distance from the Brazilian. Begović went down to block but the ball rebounded in front of him where Salah, ever the poacher, nipped in to finish. Replays showed Salah fractionally beyond left-back Daniels as Firmino shot, but the goal stood.

A stiff breeze began to whip around the stadium as half-time approached and Milner was grateful to his goalkeeper when a sliced clearance flew into the air near the edge of the box. Alisson sprinted out to meet the ball and showed he could put in a handy shift at centre-half with a towering header to clear the danger.

Shortly after the break, Salah made it 2-0. Firmino intercepted Steve

Cook's pass on halfway and immediately sent his forward partner running. Cook had a nibble at Salah's heels as he approached the box, but the striker stayed upright to guide the ball inside the right-hand post.

It got worse for the unfortunate Cook on 67 minutes, when in attempting to clear Robertson's cross from the left he only succeeded in backheeling the ball past Begović for Liverpool's third.

And the defender's misery was complete when substitute Adam Lallana's clever first-time ball left him in a foot race with Salah once more. Cook slid in to clear but Salah was away, beating Begović twice to earn a clear sight of goal and prodding home past Ake and Cook on the line.

TEAMS

BOURNEMOUTH

Begović; Francis, Cook, Aké, Daniels (Mings 83); Brooks (Mousset 65), Lerma, Surman, Stanislas (Rico 83); Fraser, King

LIVERPOOL

Alisson; Milner, Matip, van Dijk, Robertson; Wijnaldum, Fabinho, Keïta (Lallana 65); Shaqiri (Mané 65), Salah, Firmino (Henderson 81)

MATCH FACTS

- James Milner became only the 13th player to reach 500 Premier League games, the first since Steven Gerrard in 2015.
- Mo Salah's first goal was his 40th in 52 Premier League appearances (only Andy Cole and Alan Shearer – both 45 games – reached the mark quicker)
- Salah's hat-trick took him to 10 Premier League goals for the season, leading the race for the Golden Boot alongside Arsenal's Pierre-Emerick Aubameyang

THEY SAID

Martin Keown, *Match of the Day*: "[The first goal] is a gift for a player of [Salah's calibre]. He makes it look so easy in front of goal. He creates panic as well for defenders and credit to him for staying on his feet [for the second]. The third is sublime – calmness, confidence and he's back at the top of his game."

TUESDAY 11 DECEMBER 2018 | UEFA CHAMPIONS LEAGUE – GROUP C
ANFIELD | ATTENDANCE: 52,015

LIVERPOOL 1
(Salah 34)
NAPOLI 0

On a night of nerve-jangling tension at Anfield, Liverpool progressed to the round of 16 in the Champions League at the expense of Napoli, securing one of the scorelines that would guarantee qualification, regardless of the result between PSG and Red Star in Belgrade.

The Reds knew winning 1-0 or by two clear goals would definitely mean a successful navigation of an extremely difficult group, but as chances came and went to earn a cushion in the match, the atmosphere in the stadium was tumultuous.

Fortunately, the players kept cool enough heads to see the game out, but the joyous celebrations at the end proved just how tough an evening it had been for them, too.

Both sides began with plenty of attacking intent and either might have gone ahead inside the first 10 minutes. Andy Robertson clipped an inviting ball into Mo Salah, beating the offside trap. Salah decided to take a touch with his left foot rather than shoot first time with his right, but he miscontrolled and the ball dribbled harmlessly into goalkeeper David Ospina's arms.

At the other end, Allan picked out Dries Mertens with a perceptive pass and the Belgian teed up Napoli skipper Marek Hamsik, but the Slovak's first-time shot curled just over Alisson's bar. Then James Milner headed over from Trent Alexander-Arnold's long-range cross.

After those frantic opening minutes the game settled down, although Sadio Mané thought he had scored from Alexander-Arnold's centre before being flagged offside.

The goal, when it came, arrived seemingly from nowhere and was one of those pieces of Mo Salah magic that he seems to conjure like no one else. Milner's pass into the Egyptian on the right corner of the penalty area looked innocuous but then Salah eased Mario Rui aside with his body, faced up Kalidou Koulibaly and with a drop of the left hip and a blur of legs, scuttled past to make the shooting chance. The angle was still tight, but Salah nutmegged the keeper to find the far corner. It was a brilliant piece of improvisation that showcased the very best of the striker's skills.

Five minutes into the second half, he came close to bagging a second. Jordan Henderson dispossessed Hamsik and fed Roberto Firmino, who in turn found Salah – still prowling his favourite spot near the corner of the box. Again he was too strong for Mario Rui, who could only watch from a prone position as Salah dragged his shot narrowly wide.

Firmino then sent in a header from Alexander-Arnold's cross but it flew straight at Ospina, and the Spaniard was also equal to Henderson's long-range volley. Liverpool were in control but the match was still in the balance and Napoli's stopper was increasingly important to keeping his side in the tie.

Mané hit the keeper's legs when Robertson's cross fell to him eight yards out. And the Senegalese could have put the result beyond doubt with four minutes of normal time remaining but couldn't find the target from Salah's pull back. That miss might have proven costly in added time.

Napoli right-winger José Callejón swung in a cross and when both Virgil van Dijk and Fabinho failed to connect with headers, the ball dropped to substitute Arkadiusz Milik six yards out with the goal gaping. Alisson sprang forward and Milik's side-foot finish cannoned off the goalkeeper's body and out. A huge sigh of relief coursed around Anfield.

Mané had one final chance but it wasn't his night in front of goal. Clear through with Ospina to beat, he slid his effort a yard wide of the left post.

One was enough, though. At the final whistle, the bench hugged, red-and-white scarves twirled in the stands and Liverpool were in the hat for the knockout phase.

TEAMS

LIVERPOOL

Alisson; Alexander-Arnold, Matip, van Dijk, Robertson; Wijnaldum, Henderson, Milner (Fabinho 85); Salah, Firmino (Keïta 79), Mané

NAPOLI

Ospina; Maksimović, Albiol, Koulibaly, Mario Rui (Ghoulam 70); Callejón, Allan, Hamsik, Fabian (Zielinski 62); Insigne, Mertens (Milik 67)

MATCH FACTS

- Liverpool were now unbeaten in 19 straight European matches at Anfield (won 14, drawn 5).
- James Milner's nine Champions League assists since the start of the 2017/18 season were more than any other player.
- Napoli had failed to win any of their last seven away games in the Champions League, losing 5 and drawing 2.

THEY SAID

Virgil van Dijk: "[Alisson's] been fantastic for Liverpool. [He's a] great character, a great guy and he helps us all. He gives confidence to everyone. That's how it is and how it should be for the whole team. We should have made it a bit easier, I think, but the job is done and we're through."

SUNDAY 16 DECEMBER 2018 | PREMIER LEAGUE | ANFIELD
ATTENDANCE: 52,908

LIVERPOOL 3
(Mané 24, Shaqiri 73, 80)
MANCHESTER UNITED 1
(Lingard 33)

Xherdan Shaqiri's double from the bench saw off fierce rivals Manchester United in a result that also marked the end of José Mourinho's reign at Old Trafford.

Although Liverpool had bossed the match throughout, the scores were still level when Jürgen Klopp summoned Shaqiri on 70 minutes. Ten minutes later, the playmaker had put the game to bed with two deflected strikes past David de Gea.

The omission of Paul Pogba for such a crucial game in United's season raised eyebrows when the team sheets were handed out, and Mourinho opted for a 3-4-2-1 with wing-backs in Ashley Young and Diogo Dalot.

The eye-catching selection in Liverpool's team was Nathaniel Clyne at right-back. Clyne had been absent through injury since making his only appearance of the season against Chelsea in the League Cup in September, but was a welcome addition as Klopp revealed James Milner had a muscle problem that he preferred not to risk and Trent Alexander-Arnold was already ruled out with an ankle problem.

The opening period was a predictably high-octane affair and United had the ball in the net after only three minutes, but though Romelu Lukaku applied no touch to Ashley Young's free kick; his presence in an offside position was deemed sufficient to have distracted Alisson.

Then a mistake by Victor Lindelöf allowed Mo Salah to drive forward with only Eric Bailly covering, but the Egyptian overran the ball as United were able to get back in numbers. Fabinho's subsequent shot flew just wide. Next, a stabbed effort from a corner by Roberto Firmino was cleared off the line by Young as Liverpool tightened the screw.

All the play was in United's half and the rearguard action by the visitors could only last so long. A goal was coming and provided by Sadio Mané on 23 minutes. The Senegalese may have had his sights slightly askew in midweek against Napoli, but here he was clinical. One chance, one goal. A delicately chipped pass by Fabinho found Mané's run as he eased away from Young, the chest control was feather-light and the left-foot finish buried past de Gea.

It might have been the cue for an avalanche. United's Diogo Dalot was booked for halting Andy Robertson's dangerous run, then Dejan Lovren speared a chance over the bar after Firmino turned Robertson's free kick back into the danger area. But just after the half-hour, entirely against the run of play, United were level. Romelu Lukaku had been putting in a lonely shift up front but Jesse Lingard found his run into the left channel and when the Belgian's cross was spilled by Alisson – the ball and surface slicked by rain – Lingard was there to turn the rebound home.

At half-time United switched to a 4-3-3, with Marouane Fellaini coming on for Dalot and Young dropping to left-back, but Liverpool still held sway. Firmino was the first to threaten, wriggling through a crowd of players and toe-poking a shot that drew a flying, full-length save from de Gea.

United frequently had nine men behind the ball and Liverpool were unable to find a way through the congestion. With speculative shots from distance failing to trouble de Gea's goal, Klopp knew a change was needed – something different to prise apart the visitors' defence.

Naby Keïta made way for Shaqiri and within three minutes Liverpool were back in front. Sadio Mané skipped past Ander Herrera on the left edge of the box and his cross from the byline was cut out by de Gea's foot and rolled free. Clyne heard a shout to leave it and Shaqiri's right-footed effort bounced down off Young and up under the crossbar. There was a slice of luck in the pinball aspect of the move; but after knocking so hard on the door for so long, Liverpool thoroughly merited the lead.

On 80 minutes, the game was done. Shaqiri started the move with a ball to Firmino, whose scooped pass was intended for Mo Salah, but rolled through his legs back to the Swiss. His shot looped off Bailly's shin and out of de Gea's reach for an unassailable 3-1 lead.

TEAMS

LIVERPOOL

Alisson; Clyne, Lovren, van Dijk, Robertson; Wijnaldum, Fabinho, Keïta (Shaqiri 70); Salah, Firmino, Mané (Henderson 84)

MANCHESTER UNITED

De Gea; Darmian, Bailly, Lindelöf; Dalot (Fellaini 45), Herrera (Martial 79), Matić, Young; Lingard (Mata 85), Rashford; Lukaku

MATCH FACTS

- Xherdan Shaqiri became only the second player to score two goals in their first Premier League match for Liverpool against United. The only other to achieve the feat was Nigel Clough in January 1994.
- The Swiss had now scored four goals and given one assist in his last five games at Anfield.
- Liverpool were now 19 points ahead of United after 17 games – their biggest ever lead at this stage of an English top-flight season (adjusted for two or three points for a win).

THEY SAID

Sadio Mané: "We are very happy, we played great football today from the beginning and created many chances. We deserved to win. [Conceding the equaliser] is part of football, but we are Liverpool – we never give up. The ground was behind us and we focused more than ever."

FRIDAY 21 DECEMBER 2018 | PREMIER LEAGUE | MOLINEUX
ATTENDANCE: 31,358

WOLVERHAMPTON WANDERERS 0
LIVERPOOL 2
(Salah 18, van Dijk 68)

Liverpool ensured top spot at Christmas with hard-fought win on a foul night in the Black Country, with goals from Mo Salah and Virgil van Dijk seeing the Reds past a spirited Wolves side.

Amid the usual festive glut of fixtures, Jürgen Klopp made only two changes from the side that started against Manchester United, with James Milner returning at right-back in place of Nathanial Clyne and Jordan Henderson coming in for Gini Wijnaldum. Both he and Clyne were named among the substitutes.

Wolves named pacy winger Adama Traore in their front line and he was quickly into his stride in the opening minutes, twice feeding off a counterattack ball and shooting wide of Alisson's goal. Meanwhile, van Dijk had a sniff of a chance at a corner but his effort was blocked by a crowd of defensive bodies.

Midfielder Roman Saïss showed adventure by breaking into the Liverpool box and his shot rebounded from Alisson but Fabinho was nearby to tidy up.

On 17 minutes, Liverpool were ahead. Fabinho and Sadio Mané played a neat one-two on the right flank and the Brazilian's firm cross was planted into the net by Mo Salah with the outside of his left foot.

Wolves pressed for an equaliser and the game took on a frantic aspect up to half-time. Passes went astray and the play flowed end to end, but despite a couple of attempts on target, the hosts were unable to really test Alisson.

The second half was a scrappy affair until Liverpool finally took control after the hour. On 67 minutes, a rapid move featuring nimble footwork from Mo Salah switched to the left and, by way of Sadio Mané, to Adam Lallana. The Englishman took aim but was thwarted by keeper Rui Patricio.

Almost immediately, though, Liverpool went two clear. Wolves only half-cleared a short corner and Mo Salah lifted the ball back in, where van Dijk stretched to cushion a volley and record his first league goal for Liverpool.

Santo's team had chances to get back in the game. A loose ball in the box fell to Saïss, whose shot was directed straight at Alisson, while substitute Morgan

Gibbs-White hit the side netting late on after a cross hit Andy Robertson's heel. A goal then might have set up a nervy finish but it was the Reds who looked most threatening in added time and saw out time in some comfort.

TEAMS

WOLVERHAMPTON WANDERERS

Patricio; Bennett, Coady, Boly; Doherty, Saïss, Neves, Jonny (Vinagre 81); Moutinho (Gibbs-White 63); Jimenez, Traoré (Cavaleiro 63)

LIVERPOOL

Alisson; Milner, Lovren, van Dijk, Robertson; Henderson, Fabinho; Mané (Clyne 87), Firmino (Wijnaldum 76), Keïta (Lallana 58); Salah

MATCH FACTS

- Captain Jordan Henderson made his 300th appearance for Liverpool.
- Jürgen Klopp had now beaten all 32 of the British clubs he'd faced as Liverpool boss – Wolves were the only side he'd previously failed to beat, losing to them in the FA Cup in January 2017.
- In the last 27 league meetings between the sides, Liverpool had stopped Wolves from scoring on 16 occasions.

THEY SAID

Stuart James, *The Guardian*: "Klopp used the word 'mature' to describe Liverpool's performance and that captured it perfectly. They had a slightly difficult period towards the end of the first half, when Wolves started to take control of the game for the first time, but otherwise this was a highly professional Liverpool display, with van Dijk's commanding presence at the heart of the defence every bit as impressive as Salah's beautiful touches at the other end of the pitch."

WEDNESDAY 26 DECEMBER 2018 | PREMIER LEAGUE | ANFIELD | ATTENDANCE: 53,318

LIVERPOOL 4
(Lovren 11, Salah 47 pen, Shaqiri 79, Fabinho 85)
NEWCASTLE 0

Liverpool extended their lead at the top of the Premier League table with a comfortable win over a much-changed Newcastle side, while Manchester City lost again, this time at Leicester, to drop to third behind Tottenham.

Ex-Reds boss Rafa Benitez made wholesale changes to his starting XI – six in all – and his team were outclassed by a Reds side in a rich vein of form. This was an eighth successive league win for the first time in Jürgen Klopp's reign.

Both sides had presentable opportunities to take the lead in the first 10 minutes. The visitors threatened initially when Matt Ritchie's cross cleared Virgil van Dijk and Joselu was left with a free header at the back post. The Spaniard rose to meet the ball cleanly but nodded the chance down into the turf and wide.

At the other end, Sadio Mané found Xherdan Shaqiri unmarked 10 yards out but the Swiss scuffed his attempt off target.

The opener came only seconds later and bookmakers would have offered handsome odds on the first scorer. A short corner from Shaqiri was whipped in by Andy Robertson and when Jamaal Lascelles' clearing header dropped to Dejan Lovren, the Croatian spanked a half-volley high into the roof of the net for his first goal of the season.

Sadio Mané twice came close to extending the lead. First a penetrating through-ball from Trent Alexander-Arnold rolled just out of his reach. Then he was able to control a lovely dinked pass from Roberto Firmino on his chest but goalkeeper Martin Dúbravka was able to collect as the striker stretched to shoot.

As half-time neared, Dúbravka was called upon again when Shaqiri's free kick sailed in an arc over the wall towards the top corner. The Slovakian showed great agility to tip over.

Soon into the second half the Reds did go further in front. Salah picked up the ball on the right flank and as he jinked between Lascelles and Paul Dummett, the latter pulled the Liverpool man off-balance by the shoulder. The striker went down and referee Graham Scott pointed to the spot. Salah took the kick himself, tucking it low to the left.

Klopp made two changes after the hour, with Fabinho and Daniel Sturridge replacing Wijnaldum and Firmino. And Sturridge was involved in the build-up for Liverpool's third, starting a neat passing exchange on the edge of the box that went to Henderson, then to Alexander-Arnold; and the full-back's cross was a gift-wrapped present for Shaqiri, who couldn't miss.

And Fabinho then finished off a perfect Boxing Day feast with his first goal for the club, heading Salah's corner firmly past Dúbravka. News that City had lost to Leicester was the cherry on the festive cake.

TEAMS

LIVERPOOL

Alisson; Alexander-Arnold, Lovren, van Dijk, Robertson (Clyne 82); Wijnaldum (Fabinho 62) Henderson; Shaqiri, Firmino (Sturridge 69), Mané; Salah

NEWCASTLE UNITED

Dúbravka; Dummett, Lascelles, Fernandez, Yedlin; Hayden, Diamé, Ritchie (Murphy 81), Kenedy (Longstaff 73); Muto, Joselu

MATCH FACTS

- Mo Salah's penalty was the first awarded to the home side at Anfield in the league in 424 days.
- Jürgen Klopp achieved the 100th win of his Liverpool reign.
- The Reds were now unbeaten in the last 12 home fixtures on Boxing Day.

THEY SAID

Newcastle manager Rafa Benitez: "If you have little chances and you don't take them, or you make little mistakes and they make [something] from them, then it's quite difficult. I have to say "thank you" to the Newcastle fans and also the Liverpool fans [for their warm reception]. My relationship with the city, with the club and with the fans is fantastic and will be fantastic forever."

SATURDAY 29 DECEMBER 2018 | PREMIER LEAGUE | ANFIELD | ATTENDANCE: 53,326

LIVERPOOL 5
(Firmino 14, 16, 65 pen, Mané 32, Salah 45+2 pen)
ARSENAL 1
(Maitland-Niles 11)

The Reds opened up a nine-point lead at the summit of the Premier League, overwhelming Arsenal with a first-half blitz in which Roberto Firmino scored twice before bagging the match ball with a penalty past the hour.

With Tottenham losing against Wolves early in the afternoon and a suddenly vulnerable Manchester City due to visit Southampton on the Sunday, this was a chance to end the year on a high and Jürgen Klopp's men ran riot at Anfield.

The Gunners began brightly, as Alex Iwobi took advantage of a loose touch by Fabinho to sneak past Dejan Lovren and fire a low shot that Alisson had to turn behind at his near post. And on 10 minutes the visitors led. Iwobi again found space on the left and fizzed a cross behind Liverpool's back line. Ainsley Maitland-Niles, the England youth international playing on the right flank, had pulled away from Andy Robertson and slid in to convert at the back stick.

Anfield was startled at conceding a lead. The last time the Reds had been behind in the league was in the last game of 2017, when Vicente Iborra put Leicester City ahead. But this state of unaccustomed disquiet was brief. Two minutes later, Mo Salah's dancing run was halted by Granit Xhaka's covering tackle but as the ball squirted loose, Stefan Lichtsteiner's clearance cannoned into Shkodran Mustafi, wrongfooting goalkeeper Bernd Leno, and Roberto Firmino walked the ball into an empty net.

Ninety seconds later Firmino had his second and this one was all his own work. The ball broke to him as Sadio Mané dispossessed Lucas Torreira and the Brazilian set off on a slaloming run that left three defenders on their backsides. As more cover came in, he finished coolly past Leno.

Arsenal were still enjoying space on the left, though, and went straight up the other end through Sead Kolašinac, who made it to the byline and fed Aaron Ramsey, but Gini Wijnaldum was alert to the danger and timed his tackle perfectly. Then another Iwobi delivery from the left was just too high for Maitland-Niles. The match was pacy, energetic and terrific to watch.

Torreira speared in a ball from a deep free-kick that found the head of Mustafi – Alisson was equal to the header but the flag went up for offside anyway.

The opening for Liverpool's third came via some injudicious defending from Kolašinac, who over-hit a back pass and forced Leno into conceding a corner. The set piece was cleared but only as far as Andy Robertson, whose probing forward pass was turned square by Mo Salah for Mané to side-foot home. This was some of the very best of Liverpool in 2018, laid out in sequence – application of pressure to force a mistake, delivery of an early cross with real quality, the vision and selflessness to pick out a teammate in a better position to score, and icy execution in front of goal.

In first-half injury time, the result was effectively put beyond Arsenal's reach. Firmino rolled the ball into Salah's path on the left of the area and with a little dart past Sokratis the striker was in on goal. Trying to recover, Sokratis put a knee into Salah's back – a clear penalty, thumped down the middle with venom by the Egyptian.

Both Salah and Mané looked lively in the opening minutes of the second half, the latter stopped by a brilliant sliding challenge from Sokratis, the former by good anticipation from Leno.

Arsenal might have reduced the deficit when Xhaka played in Ramsey and his shot, drifting across goal, was somehow poked over from a yard by Pierre-Emerick Aubameyang.

Mané made way for Jordan Henderson on 61 minutes to a rousing ovation from the home crowd and then Fabinho tested Leno with a low drive after Salah's sleight of foot took three Arsenal defenders out of the game.

A minute later, Dejan Lovren was shoved in the back by Kolašinac as Henderson's swinging cross hung in the air and Michael Oliver again pointed to the spot. Salah allowed Firmino to take the kick, slotted to the right as Leno dived the other way.

TEAMS

LIVERPOOL

Alisson; Alexander-Arnold, Lovren, van Dijk, Robertson (Clyne 83); Wijnaldum, Fabinho; Shaqiri, Firmino, Mané (Henderson 62); Salah

ARSENAL

Leno; Kolašinac, Sokratis, Mustafi (Koscielny 45), Lichsteiner; Xhaka, Torreira; Maitland-Niles, Ramsey, Iwobi; Aubameyang (Lacazette 71)

MATCH FACTS

- Roberto Firmino had now scored more Premier League goals for Liverpool against Arsenal (8) than anyone except Robbie Fowler (9).
- The Reds had now gone unbeaten in 20 league matches – only the third time ever and the first time since 1988.
- Arsenal v Liverpool was now the highest-scoring fixture in Premier League history, with 155 goals.

Brazil and Roma's Alisson Becker signs to Liverpool on 19 July, becoming the world's most expensive goalkeeper at the time

Twelve months after signing, Naby Keïta finally makes his debut on the opening game of the season against West Ham, inheriting Steven Gerrard's number-eight shirt

Three days after an eye injury inflicted at Wembley by Tottenham's Jan Vertonghen, Firmino celebrates a goal against PSG in the UEFA Champions League by covering his damaged eye

A stunning 25-yard strike from Daniel Sturridge floors Chelsea keeper Kepa Arrizabalaga and rescues a point for Liverpool at Stamford Bridge on 29 September

Mo Salah scores a penalty against Red Star Belgrade in a UEFA Champions League group game at Anfield on 24 October

Jubilant team-mates pile on James Milner after he scores the opening goal against Arsenal at the Emirates Stadium on 3 November

Klopp is all a blur as he sprints across the pitch to celebrate a last-minute winner against Everton on 2 December

Salah dribbles the ball around Bournemouth keeper Asmir Begovic to complete his hat trick in a 4-0 victory at the Vitality Stadium on 8 December

Xherdan Shaqiri celebrates scoring Liverpool's third goal against Manchester United on 16 December, with Georginio Wijnaldum and Roberto Firmino

John Stones's goal-line clearance at the Etihad ensures a 2-1 victory for Manchester City on 3 January. It would be Liverpool's only league defeat of the entire season

Andy Robertson fends off Leicester City's Ricardo Pereira during a 1-1 draw
at Anfield on 30 January

Sadio Mané rises to score the opening goal in a 3-0 demolition of Bournemouth
at Anfield on 9 February

Van Dijk holds up two fingers to celebrate his brace of goals in an emphatic 5-0 victory against Watford on 27 February

Sadio Mane celebrates after scoring the opening goal against Fulham at Craven Cottage on 17 March

Mo Salah in a state of peace after scoring Liverpool's second goal against Chelsea on 14 April

Lionel Messi's stunning 35-yard free kick puts Barcelona 3-0 up after 82 minutes of the first leg of the semi-final on 1 May and looks to have ended Liverpool's UEFA Champions League hopes

Georginio Wijnaldum celebrates with Jordan Henderson and Trent Alexander-Arnold after scoring Liverpool's third goal during the second leg of the UEFA Champions League semi-final on 7 May

Trent Alexander-Arnold quickly sets up a corner kick in the 79th minute of the Champions League semi-final 2nd leg, from which Divock Origi will score the winning goal

Liverpool players and backroom staff unite in front of the Kop for a celebratory rendition of "You'll Never Walk Alone" after beating Barcelona in the UEFA Champions League semi-final

Mohamed Salah beats Tottenham keeper Hugo Lloris from the penalty spot in the second minute of the UEFA Champions League final

Divock Origi celebrates putting Liverpool 2-0 up against Tottenham during the UEFA Champions League final on 1 June

Jordan Henderson lifts the Champions League trophy to crown a glorious night in Madrid

Cheered on by Liverpool's travelling fans, Jürgen Klopp is thrown in the air as he celebrates with his players and staff

Players celebrate with the European Cup on board an open-top bus ride through Liverpool on Sunday 2 June

A triumphant Jürgen Klopp on the parade bus a day after the UEFA Champions League final

THEY SAID

Arsenal manager Unai Emery: "I think we started well with the first goal and then they had the difference with attacking moments, determination and quality. We know we need to get better defensively. Liverpool have progressed a lot and it is [a good] example for us. We need to [make] this progress."

PREMIER LEAGUE TABLE AT END OF DECEMBER 2018

Pos	Team	Pld	W	D	L	GF	GA	GD	Pts
1	Liverpool	20	17	3	0	48	8	40	54
2	Manchester City	20	15	2	3	54	16	38	47
3	Tottenham Hotspur	20	15	0	5	43	21	22	45
4	Chelsea	20	13	4	3	38	16	22	43
5	Arsenal	20	11	5	4	42	30	12	38
6	Manchester United	20	10	5	5	41	32	9	35
7	Wolverhampton Wanderers	20	8	5	7	23	23	0	29
8	Leicester City	20	8	4	8	24	23	1	28
9	Watford	20	8	4	8	27	28	-1	28
10	Everton	20	7	6	7	31	30	1	27
11	West Ham United	20	8	3	9	27	30	-3	27
12	AFC Bournemouth	20	8	2	10	28	37	-9	26
13	Brighton & Hove Albion	20	7	4	9	22	27	-5	25
14	Crystal Palace	20	5	4	11	17	26	-9	19
15	Newcastle United	20	4	6	10	15	27	-12	18
16	Cardiff City	20	5	3	12	19	38	-19	18
17	Southampton	20	3	6	11	21	38	-17	15
18	Burnley	20	4	3	13	19	41	-22	15
19	Fulham	20	3	5	12	18	43	-25	14
20	Huddersfield Town	20	2	4	14	12	35	-23	10

UEFA CHAMPIONS LEAGUE GROUP C FINAL STANDINGS

Pos	Team	Pld	W	D	L	GF	GA	GD	Pts
1	Liverpool	6	3	2	1	17	9	8	11
2	Napoli	6	3	0	3	9	7	2	9
3	Paris Saint-Germain	6	2	3	1	7	5	2	9
4	Red Star Belgrade	6	1	1	4	5	17	-12	4

CHAPTER SIX

—

JANUARY

"Every team has blips in a season.
It's about how you respond"

Footballing fortunes rise and fall but few have been as strongly ascendant over the past two decades as those of Manchester City. Twenty years past, as we rang in the final year of the last millennium, City lay seventh in the third tier of English football after successive relegations.

Back then, floating the idea that they would, in less than a generation, be winning multiple Premier League titles and mixing it among Europe's elite would have earned a brusque response from even the most die-hard Sky Blue.

Yet here they were. After beating Gillingham in 1999's Second Division play-off final – Paul Dickon and all that – through the Keegan years, the leaving of Maine Road, Thaksin and Sven, Robinho, the Abu Dhabi takeover, Carlos Tevez and the "Welcome to Manchester" billboard... Sergio Agüero's last-gasp winner in 2012 to seal a first title in 44 years proved City were back.

And now they had European football's most successful club coach in Pep Guardiola, one of the best playing squads in the world and were seeking to defend the Premier League title after a record-breaking points haul in 2017/18. It's fair to conclude these were worthy adversaries for a Liverpool side chasing its own return to glory.

City had wobbled considerably over Christmas, though. Three defeats – to Chelsea, Crystal Palace and Leicester – had allowed the Reds to open a seven-point gap at New Year. Many thought it would prove decisive. Yet the fixture list brought its own sense of drama to proceedings as the two main title rivals were due to meet in the first league game of 2019. A Liverpool win would mean a double-digit deficit for City to overcome; were City to prevail, the gap would be back to four.

In the teams' previous encounter Guardiola had set City up with a more defensive attitude than usual, mindful of the defeats inflicted by Liverpool the previous season. Now, playing catch-up, he was looking to be on the front foot. "You have to be aggressive," he said. "We cannot expect to be 12 or 13 points in front at Christmas like last season. This is a new season and the opponent is so strong. For me, that is an immense and huge motivation. If it is different pressure, we have to live it.'

Guardiola felt the Reds' history demanded success and that he could use some of that added burden to City's advantage. "When [Liverpool's] players put the shirt on, they know what they have to defend," said Pep. "We are trying to build that history. It is a question for Liverpool why they have not won it for so many years but I can feel what they feel. I understand it. It's difficult to handle. After 29 years not winning the Premier League to be there to win it, I understand. I said to the players, that's difficult to handle. Why don't we try it, to catch them up and pressure them?"

In the opposing dugout, Jürgen Klopp was playing it cool. For all the fist-pumping, player-hugging energy and gimlet-eyed scrutiny of the opposition, the German viewed himself as essentially calm.

"People don't see it but I'm a pretty calm person," he said pre-match. "Not during the 90 minutes, obviously, but in general. I don't get that easily excited about different things. If we lose a game, people will see it as slipping through our fingers again or whatever. We have to train, we have to work, we have to play, we have to fight, all these things and try to make the best of this season. All of the rest are stories. It's interesting because people read it – they like it. But for us, nothing changes."

All the other Premier League fixtures had been played by the time Klopp's men arrived in Manchester for an evening kick-off on the third of the month, with the headline news being that Chelsea had dropped points in a scoreless home draw with Southampton, while Spurs had edged back up to second with a 3-0 win at Cardiff on New Year's Day.

Now all eyes turned to the Etihad. City made two changes from the side that beat Southampton in their last game of 2018. John Stones came in for Oleksandr Zinchenko and Leroy Sané replaced Riyadh Mahrez. Fernandinho had been absent for the defeats to Palace and Leicester but returned at Southampton and retained his place. Klopp brought in Jordan Henderson and James Milner – the latter having missed the last two games – with Fabinho and Xherdan Shaqiri dropping to the bench.

Temperatures neared zero in Manchester but this time the contest between title rivals lived up to its billing. Fast-flowing football from two fully committed teams made for a gripping spectacle.

City came within just over a centimetre of conceding a bizarre own goal, when John Stones struck his own keeper with a clearance after Sadio Mané hit the post, then the centre-half had to hook the ball off the line.

Vincent Kompany was booked for a last-ditch challenge on Mo Salah that Klopp believed could have been red. "He is the last man and if he hits Mo more he is out for the season," said the boss. "He knows Mo is that quick so he takes the risk. I don't know if the ref saw it."

Two pieces of pinpoint finishing made the difference for City. Agüero appeared to have no angle at all to work with when he latched on to Bernardo Silva's cut-back, five minutes before the break. But the Blues striker has made a career of turning half-chances into goals. He lashed a shot high past Alisson before the keeper had time to react.

Then, after Roberto Firmino had levelled in the second half, Leroy Sané bagged the winner with a laser-accurate shot against the inside of the Alisson's left post.

As "Blue Moon" rang out after the final whistle, both teams' managers knew the result could have gone either way.

"We need Sergio in these games," said Guardiola. "He has special quality in these positions. He has done it all his career. His finish was incredible."

Klopp said: "[There] was big pressure on [this] game. It was very intense and we were unlucky in our finishing moments. A bit more unlucky than City. That was one of the main differences. They had periods where they dominated but we came back and had big chances. You have to score in those moments."

The Reds returned to Molineux in Wolverhampton just 17 days on from their last visit, but it was a very different-looking side that would turn out in this FA Cup third-round tie.

The stresses of the festive period upon the squad had to be taken into account in the context of Liverpool's push for the league title; and given the immense effort expended in defeat at the Etihad, Jürgen Klopp felt he had no choice but to make significant changes to his starting XI.

With the transfer window open, striker Dominic Solanke had signed for Bournemouth on a permanent deal, while Nathaniel Clyne also joined the Cherries on loan, and it was an unfamiliar-looking team that took to the pitch for this Monday evening tie, particularly in defence. Alberto Moreno and Dejan Lovren were accompanied by Fabinho, dropping in from midfield and debutant right-back Rafael Camacho, an 18-year-old Portuguese youth international who had been on the bench for December's matches against Burnley and Manchester United and now took his first-team bow.

The defensive picture was complicated further by the fact that Lovren sustained a hamstring injury after only three minutes and was replaced by 16-year-old Ki-Jana Hoever. In replacing Lovren, Hoever – a product of the Ajax youth system – became the youngest player ever to represent Liverpool in the FA Cup.

Simon Mignolet took the gloves in place of Alisson and in midfield James Milner and Naby Keïta would play alongside another debutant, local lad Curtis Jones, who had impressed in pre-season in the US and also caught the eye in Liverpool's UEFA Youth League group, scoring three times in five games. He lined up on the left wing, with Xherdan Shaqiri on the right, and Daniel Sturridge and Divock Origi playing as a strike pair.

Mo Salah – that morning awarded PFA player of the month for his performances in December – and Roberto Firmino were on the bench to provide extra firepower if needed.

Klopp said: "I had to make these changes. A few players were really ill and then in the last session yesterday we lost Adam Lallana with a minor thing... and [Jordan Henderson] had something from the Man City game.

"We had to make a few changes already, it was clear. Virgil cannot play; he is at home and hopefully it is nothing, but he has played all the games so far, so we had to try to find a solution for that – and we found it, hopefully, with Fabinho.

"[Curtis and Rafa] still have a lot to come. It's really nice having them around, but now it's time to show up – it's a situation where we need them 100 per cent, so let's try it."

Wolves made five changes themselves but looked to be much closer to full strength, with the highly skilled Portuguese trio of Ruben Neves, João Moutinho and Diogo Jota looking to supply – and profit from – the indefatigable work-rate of Mexican striker Raul Jimenez.

The alterations, added to windy conditions in the Black Country, made for a disjointed encounter and one decided in Wolves' favour by a couple of pieces of high quality – one from Ruben Neves, the other from keeper John Ruddy.

The match was evenly poised just before the hour, after Divock Origi had equalised Jimenez's first-half opener, but then Neves put the hosts back in front with a blast from 30 yards past Mignolet. The Belgian's opposite number then produced an outstanding stop from Shaqiri. The Swiss's free kick was flying into the top corner, but Ruddy flung himself high to the left and somehow applied a fingertip that diverted the ball on to the inside of the post, across the face of goal and away.

Wolves captain Conor Coady was delighted at the outcome against his . former side. "It was always going to be a nervy end, but we stood tall against a good team and it's a great victory for everybody," he said. "We had a game plan and we were outstanding – we moved the ball well and scored two outstanding goals."

A disappointing exit, then, at the first time of asking; but the bright spots were the assured performances of the youngsters, particularly Hoever, who was thrown in without even a regular centre-half to play alongside.

"I am not sure what you all would have said if immediately from the beginning our centre-half situation was Fabinho and Ki-Jana," said Klopp. "Of course... it doesn't make sense to bring in a 16-year-old boy from the start. You wait until he is completely ready, but he came on and did well. That's how it sometimes starts – when you are really needed then it is only about if you are good enough and not how old you are."

Despite kicking off 2019 with two defeats, there was still time before Liverpool's next assignment – away at Brighton in the league – to acknowledge what had been achieved in recent times.

In midweek, Mo Salah and Sadio Mané were awarded first and second place respectively in the CAF African Player of the Year standings, repeating their feat of 2017. Meanwhile, Jürgen Klopp was named Premier League manager of the month for December after the Reds eight wins out of eight in all competitions; and Virgil van Dijk was awarded PL player of the month.

Van Dijk gave an interview to *The Mirror*, in which he reflected on his manager's methods and attitude: "There is something about Klopp that makes him stand out," he said. "It's not just his energy, I think it's his man-management. He makes you feel great. He is genuinely pleased to see you in the morning and that has a big effect on the players who come in. Just look at the hugs he gives us all at the end of games. It is only a bit of affection, something very small, but it makes you feel great."

It's not all hugs and compliments, though, as the Dutchman added: "He can be stone-hard the next day and put you in your place when you have made mistakes. He will do that in front of the entire squad, but we all accept it because we know it is not something personal. [Klopp] has shown in so many moments that he cares about us – and that's why he is able to demand so much from us all."

Van Dijk returned to the centre of defence for the visit to the Amex Stadium, one of nine changes to restore the starting XI to something near full strength.

Chris Hughton's Seagulls had had a mixed December: three defeats in a row leading up to Christmas had seen them drop out of the top 10, but a battling Boxing Day draw with Arsenal was followed by a home win against Everton and a point away at West Ham.

Moreover, the Reds wouldn't have forgotten what a scrap it had been to prevail against Brighton at Anfield back in August. A lone Mo Salah goal earned that win, but Hughton's men had so nearly snatched a point at the death.

Again Salah made the difference, this time from the penalty spot, as Liverpool dominated in a performance Klopp described as "mature".

Clear chances were scarce on a grey afternoon in East Sussex but Salah was bright throughout – reunited with Roberto Firmino and Sadio Mané – and deadly from when it really mattered. Felled by Pascal Gross as he jinked inside the German five minutes into the second half, the Egyptian took the kick himself and sent it high into the top right of the goal.

Brighton's lone front men – first Glenn Murray and then replacement Florin Andone – barely had a kick, with Fabinho putting in another good shift in his new position at centre-half and partner van Dijk coolly patrolling, anticipating and shutting down threats with ease.

Hughton admitted his side had been second-best and later gave his thoughts on the opposition manager. "The most refreshing aspect of Jürgen's time at Liverpool is that he hasn't 'steamrolled' in an attempt to bring instant success, but instead has built something over a period of time. The result is that he has improved the team to the incredible level they are at the moment, especially with the two big signings last summer in the goalkeeper and van Dijk.

"He has my admiration for the way he has gone about the progression of the team, with backing from the club, he has set out to make improvements over a period of time rather than chase instant success, and in doing so has played a style of football that is very easy on the eye, very offensively orientated, and brought the level as close as he possibly could to achieve the success he has set out to do."

Hughton said he believes managerial passion can manifest itself in different ways and that Klopp's evidently emotional involvement with the game while on the sidelines was a clear window into the inner man.

"Jürgen is one of [those managers who] kick every ball, with a close relationship with his players, which he shows openly, so his emotions are visible for everyone to see. But he has the personality that allows him to show those emotions so publicly, because it is not put on, it is genuine, and it originates from an environment in Germany where managers do have a close association with the supporters and the players. He comes across as very genuine."

Manchester City held up their side of the title challenge with a comfortable 3-0 win over Wolves on Monday night to close the gap back to four points, while Tottenham's brief challenge over Christmas appeared to have faded as they lost at home to Manchester United. Spurs were now nine back. It was, by most observers' reckoning, a two-horse race and the form of the front runners would be pivotal in the coming weeks in deciding who would end in the winner's circle.

The mosaic of placards held up in the Kop read "Paisley 100". The home fixture against Crystal Palace – Liverpool's first of the new year after three away games – fell closest to the centenary of the birth of one of the club's true greats, Bob Paisley. The "quiet genius" led his team to three European Cups, six league titles, three League Cups and the UEFA Cup in nine seasons in charge, the culmination of more than 40 years' association with the Reds – as a post-war wing-half rising to captain, then assistant to Bill Shankly and eventually the top job.

Paisley remains one of only three managers to win the European Cup three times (alongside Carlo Ancelotti and Zinedine Zidane) and one of only five to win the English league title as player and manager of the same club (also Bill Nicholson at Spurs, Howard Kendall at Everton, George Graham at Arsenal and Kenny Dalglish at Liverpool). His legend – as overseer of the most dominant decade in the club's history – is powerful on Merseyside, as attested by the passionate minute's applause before kick-off, also in memory of Peter Thompson, the forward of the 1960s-vintage Reds and winner of two league titles and the FA Cup under Shankly.

Improbably, a Liverpool fan born four years *before* Bob Paisley was a guest of honour at the game. Bernard Sheridan from Great Crosby was celebrating his 104th birthday and, having received a personalised letter from Jürgen Klopp plus a birthday cake and signed shirt, was also given tickets to the Palace game. He told the *Liverpool Echo* in the week: "I've been a proud Liverpool supporter since I was a boy and have supported the club through thick and thin, so I'm absolutely thrilled to be off to the match on Saturday. Obviously, the icing on the cake will be when we beat Crystal Palace!"

Bernard met Jürgen and Kenny Dalglish after the game and was shown around the stadium, accompanied by his son, grandson and great-grandson. "All the happiness you've given me in the last few days has been marvellous," he beamed. "Exciting game, wasn't it?" Jürgen replied.

It certainly was. Having conceded only 10 goals in 22 league games to this point, Liverpool shipped three in one afternoon in a defensive performance that was thoroughly out of character. Thankfully for Klopp, Sheridan and everyone else of a Red persuasion, the forwards scored four.

This match kept the crowd guessing until the final whistle – at any point it seemed likely to take a lurch in another unexpected direction. The first half was dominated by Klopp's side, who contrived to be 1-0 down at the break courtesy of an Andros Townsend goal after good work by the tricky Wilf Zaha.

Liverpool then roared back into the match with goals from Mo Salah and Roberto Firmino and were pushing for more but pegged back when James Tomkins nodded in an equaliser from a corner.

Salah punished a handling error by veteran keeper Julian Spéroni to reinstate the lead; and in a frantic final few minutes James Milner was sent off for two bookings, Sadio Mané made it 4-2 and Palace pulled one back through Max Mayer to prompt a nervy few seconds before the final whistle.

A pumped-up Klopp bellowed his approval towards the Kop and expressed relief in his post-match thoughts.

"Crystal Palace traditionally do really well against Liverpool and in my experience, too, and what they're really good at is counter-attacks and set pieces and Zaha is a world-class player," he said. "But I loved our reaction after half-time, staying positive, that was the plan. We did what we needed to do."

He also paid tribute to the resilience of his players. "Nobody should be surprised about the character of the boys," he added. "That was here before I came in. The boys are ready to fight for all. It's not the first time that we've had to do it this season but today was pretty special.

"We were extremely dominant in the first half but we were 1-0 down, we created chances but not clear enough. We had not enough players in the decisive areas, we had a lot in the preparing areas. That can happen. At half-time it was clear we had to change, to be more decisive, more bodies in the box. Thank God it worked immediately!

"We needed more direction and to put more pressure on their last line. We created too much without having someone in a finishing position so we had to change that. We forced it a bit more, scored two really quick goals and then again we wanted to control the game more but it's difficult. The boys were not 100 per cent sure if we were still attacking or controlling and you could see that, so they could get their set pieces, which are brilliant. They equalised. We came back and everybody felt the atmosphere."

Palace and former Reds boss Roy Hodgson said he was extremely proud of his players for their performance. "I thought we tested Liverpool to the limits today," he said. "In the first-half our defensive organisation was such that they couldn't really create chances. They got two goals from deflections and I think we showed such character to come back to 2-2."

On Spéroni's error, he reflected that football can be a "cruel game" at times. "Julian's not had a chance to play in over a year and it was incredible misfortune to lose two goalkeepers in [our last] game. I feel sorry for [Julian] because it will grab the headlines but what he's done for this club over the years – it shouldn't happen to a man like him."

Salah's second of the game was his 50th league goal for Liverpool – which put the striker in rarified company as only Andy Cole, Alan Shearer and Ruud van Nistelrooy had reached the target in fewer Premier League games. "An exceptional achievement from a world-class player," was Klopp's assessment as his principal attacking weapon now topped the standings for the Golden Boot with 16.

One benefit of early exits from both cup competitions was a chance for the Reds to recuperate with warm-weather training in Dubai, while Manchester City were tasked with the second leg of the Carabao Cup semi-final against Burton Albion and a visit from Burnley in the fourth round of the FA Cup. Admittedly, these were negotiated with some ease – City led 9-0 from the first leg against Burton and so sauntered to a 10-0 aggregate win, while the Clarets were dispatched 5-0.

Whispers about City's prospects for "the quadruple" were getting louder: "Who is going to stop them winning everything if they're in that mood?" wondered Burnley boss Sean Dyche after a chastening afternoon at the Etihad. However, both City and Liverpool would have difficult questions to answer when the league programme resumed.

Twenty-four seconds and 121 seconds. That's how long it took for the two title challengers – courtesy of Sergio Agüero and Sadio Mané, respectively – to establish a lead in their respective matches in round 24 of the Premier League title race. At which point you'd have been hard-pressed to predict that between them they'd drop five points. But Rafa Benitez's Newcastle did not fold like Burton and Burnley before them and rallied to win 2-1, while Claude Puel's Leicester picked up on their Christmas form – when they'd beaten both Chelsea and Man City – and could have taken all the points from

Anfield with a little more accuracy in front of goal. A 1-1 draw represented a fair result but a missed opportunity for the Reds to re-establish a seven-point lead at the top of the table.

It was a jolt to both sides, particularly City, who had appeared to have rediscovered their most regal form after a brief stutter over the festive period. But the Blues travelling fans were stunned when, after Salomon Rondon had equalised in the second half, the usually dependable Fernandinho gave away a needless penalty, and Benitez's defensive organisation was such that goalkeeper Martin Dúbravka was rarely troubled after the early concession.

"The rhythm of the game was slow, we [lost] second balls and we were not aggressive enough," said a downbeat Pep Guardiola. "Sometimes it's not good [to score so early]. It didn't help us in the way we played afterwards. We have to be better."

With Liverpool playing a day later, this was an unexpected boost ahead of the Foxes' visit to Anfield. But Jürgen Klopp was clear about the danger posed by Leicester – a team whose results might have been patchy thus far but who had shown themselves at their most potent when faced by top-level opposition and reverting to the counter-attacking style that played to their strengths.

"They have a really good team, really interesting in defence, in midfield and in Jamie Vardy one of the best strikers in the league," said Klopp in his press conference at Melwood. "They like playing against the top sides and we expect a very dangerous opponent."

It's little wonder that Klopp made mention of Vardy. The English striker had been a thorn in Liverpool's side in recent years and scored seven times against the Reds in the Premier League, a record bettered only by Andy Cole (11) and Thierry Henry (8). He'd netted in the teams' last five encounters and, having missed the defeat at the King Power in September through suspension, would have been itching for this fixture.

It was a freezing day on Merseyside. Snow had been falling heavily before kick-off and it was a wintry scene at Anfield as a moment's silence was held for Argentinian striker Emiliano Sala and pilot David Ibbotson, whose plane had disappeared over the English Channel nine days previously as Sala was on his way from Nantes in France to join new side Cardiff City. Their deaths were confirmed when the wreckage was found 10 days later and it was a tragedy that touched the football community. For a player who wasn't well known to English fans, the tributes were widespread and heartfelt, and here applause gave way to a respectful hush, scrupulously observed.

Despite efforts to clear the pitch, one half was still covered in a film of slush, but that didn't prevent Liverpool pulling off a 30-pass move in the first two minutes that led to a goal for Sadio Mané: Liverpool's quickest in the league since April 2016. Leicester had touched the ball just once since kick-off.

Had Kasper Schmeichel not reacted quickly to Roberto Firmino's effort shortly after, this might have been a routine home win for the Reds, but what followed was an evening of toil against a well-organised and pacy Leicester side, who were happy to cede possession but typically threatening on the counter and at set pieces. One such led to Harry Maguire's equaliser on the stroke of half-time. The Reds defence failed to clear James Maddison's free kick adequately and Ben Chilwell's header over the advancing back-line found Maguire with the goal at his mercy. The centre-half showed his customary calm on the ball to stroke home.

Many of the crowd believed Maguire shouldn't have been on the pitch at all after a foul on Mané that prevented him running clear on to Andy Robertson's through-ball. The decision was a yellow card.

On this occasion, Vardy didn't bag his usual goal and the points were shared. Reds captain Jordan Henderson had been in the unfamiliar station of right-back and acknowledged his team hadn't been at their best.

"We are disappointed with the result because we wanted the win but Leicester are a good side," he told BT Sport. "It wasn't our best performance but we kept going and just couldn't find the winner. We'll take the point and move on to the next game. They defended well [and] we didn't really do enough. There's things we can improve on. The conditions were difficult, too, but that's the same for both teams."

Klopp explained his decision to deploy Henderson out of position, due to the unavailability of Trent Alexander-Arnold, Joe Gomez and James Milner: "We had to find a solution. We thought about Rafa Camacho [who debuted against Wolves]. He played there in training because Hendo couldn't train in the week. In the end, I made a decision for the [defensive] aspect and his experience… I didn't want to give Rafa in his first game such a big task. [Jordan] did really well."

And he took the long view on a frustrating night: "We have to accept the result, which is no problem because we [didn't] think we would go through the league winning every game. A difficult game on a difficult pitch and we got a point. Not perfect, but we accept it."

JANUARY MATCH REPORTS

WEDNESDAY 3 JANUARY 2019 | PREMIER LEAGUE | ETIHAD STADIUM | ATTENDANCE: 54,511

MANCHESTER CITY 2
(Agüero 40, Sané 72)
LIVERPOOL 1
(Firmino 64)

Champions Manchester City inflicted a first Premier League defeat of the season on the pretenders to their crown, cutting Liverpool's advantage to four points and setting the scene for a ding-dong title race in 2019.

Just how close the teams were to each other in terms of quality and endeavour was illustrated by the fine margins of goal line technology. Liverpool might have taken the lead after 18 minutes when Sadio Mané hit the post and chaos ensued. John Stones tried to clear but hit his own goalkeeper and had to clear again off the line as the ball looped up with Mo Salah closing in. To the naked eye it looked like a goal, but replays showed the ball had failed to cross the line by 1.12cm.

City were lively hosts, with ex-Red Raheem Sterling and Leroy Sané testing Liverpool's defence with probing runs into the channels. The former set up David Silva in the box but the Spaniard struck his effort straight at Virgil van Dijk.

The pace of the match and commitment in tackling led to four bookings before half-time – two apiece – but the key stat at the break was that City were ahead. For all their accurate build-up play in the first 40 minutes, Pep's men were yet to create a clear chance; but Sergio Agüero rarely needs more than a sniff. Bernardo Silva twisted his way down the left to the byline and Agüero reached his cut back before Dejan Lovren could react. The Argentinian's left-foot shot rocketed over Alisson's shoulder into the net. The goal extended Agüero's run of scoring against the Reds to seven straight home league games.

Five minutes after the hour, the visitors drew level through a superb combination from the full-backs. Trent Alexander-Arnold spotted Andy Robertson's unchecked run, swung a cross over with his left foot and the Scot lifted the ball across goal for Roberto Firmino to head into an empty net.

Alisson did well to thwart Agüero when a rapid City counter left Liverpool undermanned but the home side retook the lead from another break with Sané firing across the keeper and in off the far post.

Ederson pulled off a fine, fingertip save from Mo Salah when it seemed the striker was poised to level; and it might have been three for City, but Alisson blocked Bernardo Silva's shot and Sterling smacked an inviting rebound just wide.

An engrossing contest finished 2-1 and Liverpool's unbeaten league run was ended at 20.

TEAMS

MANCHESTER CITY
Ederson; Danilo, Kompany (Otamendi 88), Stones, Laporte (Walker 86); Fernandinho, David Silva (Gundogan 65), Bernardo Silva; Sterling, Agüero, Sané

LIVERPOOL
Alisson; Alexander-Arnold, Lovren, van Dijk, Robertson; Milner (Fabinho 57), Henderson Wijnaldum (Sturridge 86); Salah, Firmino, Mané (Shaqiri 77)

MATCH FACTS

- This was the first match in Pep Guardiola's reign at Manchester City during which the opposition enjoyed more of the ball. Liverpool had 51% of possession.
- Xherdan Shaqiri played in the Premier League for the 100th time; Daniel Sturridge made the 150th appearance of his LFC career.
- Roberto Firmino scored his 10th goal of the season in all competitions, recording double figures for the fourth consecutive term.

THEY SAID

Gini Wijnaldum: "I don't want to say it is a hammer blow. You are always disappointed to lose a game, especially when you come back and create chances. We would have been happy if we had a draw. We were unlucky with other chances not going in. One moment we didn't defend well and they scored.'

MONDAY 7 JANUARY 2019 | FA CUP THIRD ROUND | MOLINEUX | ATTENDANCE: 25,849

WOLVERHAMPTON WANDERERS 2
(Jimenez 38, Neves 55)
LIVERPOOL 1
(Origi 51)

Wolves put Liverpool out of the FA Cup for the second time in three years after Ruben Neves's long-range strike settled the tie at a blustery Molineux.

Jürgen Klopp made no excuses about nine changes to his starting line-up, with the XI featuring two teenage debutants in Curtis Jones and Rafa Camacho and nearly the whole game played by 16-year-old defender Ki-Jana Hoever after Dejan Lovren went down injured inside three minutes.

"[The young players] did really well. [They all] had good moments," said Klopp. "But it was chaotic football, nobody could really control the game. We couldn't get much rhythm and the boys can play much better."

Wolves produced the first decent move on the counter after 10 minutes, as Ruben Vinagre released Diogo Jota on the left flank. The Portuguese drove at the Liverpool defence then laid the ball off to Jonny Otto, whose shot from the edge of the area was blocked by Alberto Moreno.

It took half an hour for Liverpool to engineer a clear chance and in keeping with the scrappy nature of the first half, it came from a defensive mix-up. James Milner's lofted ball looked hopeful but indecision between Ryan Bennett and Jonny allowed it to drop to Xherdan Shaqiri. However, his left-footed effort was scuffed well wide.

Another mistake led to Wolves' opener. Milner lost possession to Jota near the centre-circle and Wolves broke at speed. Jota played in Raul Jimenez and while Milner tracked Jota's run, there was no covering defender to challenge the Mexican. He strode unhindered into the box and stroked a finish past Simon Mignolet.

Liverpool raised the tempo in the second half and were level after five minutes. Milner turned on the edge of the area and his blocked shot fell to Divock Origi, who powered the ball through Leander Dendoncker's legs and past John Ruddy's left hand.

The hosts' lead was restored shortly after by a rare moment of genuine quality in the game. Neves exchanged passes with Vinagre, then sized up his options and let fly a dipping drive from 30 yards that gave Mignolet no chance.

Jimenez came close to extending the lead after robbing Hoever and rounding Mignolet but he could only poke an effort with the outside of the foot into the side netting.

Shaqiri came within millimetres of equalising when his free kick was superbly tipped on to the inside of the post by Ruddy and Liverpool had further chances – notably when Hoever made an exciting forward dash from defence before setting up substitute Mo Salah – but the home side held out.

WOLVES

Ruddy; Bennett, Coady, Boly; Jonny (Doherty 75), Dendoncker, Neves, Vinagre; Moutinho; Jota (Cavaleiro 52), Jimenez (Costa 83)

LIVERPOOL

Mignolet; Camacho, Fabinho, Lovren (Hoever 6), Moreno; Shaqiri, Milner, Keïta, Jones (Salah 70); Sturridge (Firmino 70), Origi

MATCH FACTS

- At 16 years 354 days, Ki-Jana Hoever became Liverpool's youngest ever player in the FA Cup, and third youngest to debut for the Reds overall.
- Raul Jimenez's goal was Wolves' first at home against Liverpool in nearly 400 minutes of football at Molineux, since a Kenny Miller effort in January 2004.
- Wolves earned their first home win against Liverpool since August 1981.

THEY SAID

James Milner: "At the start of this season, we weren't playing our best but we were getting results. Back-to-back defeats… really isn't good enough for us, but every team has blips in a season. It's how you respond and how you bounce back. It's easy saying it in an interview, we have to do it on the pitch."

SATURDAY 12 JANUARY 2019 | PREMIER LEAGUE | AMEX STADIUM | ATTENDANCE: 30,682

BRIGHTON & HOVE ALBION 0
LIVERPOOL 1
(Salah pen 50)

For the second time in 2018/19, Liverpool edged out Brighton by a goal to nil, with Mo Salah the lone name on the scoresheet. The win reinstated – temporarily at least – a seven-point lead at the top of the Premier League table and righted the Reds ship in 2019 after two defeats since New Year's Day.

Jürgen Klopp's team had a more familiar look after the FA Cup exit to Wolves, with a raft of senior players returning – nine changes in all. One player who did keep his place and position was Fabinho, deployed again in central defence in the absence of Dejan Lovren, Joel Matip and Joe Gomez.

Also returning were Andy Robertson and Roberto Firmino, two of Klopp's men whose link-up play had been so profitable thus far in the campaign. And the pair came close to putting the Reds in front inside 10 minutes. The Scot's fizzing centre flew just behind Sadio Mané's run and tantalisingly in front of Firmino. The Brazilian stretched out a foot but could only direct the ball wide.

From the other side, Trent Alexander-Arnold – passed fit after turning his ankle in the warm-up – clipped in a cross for Xherdan Shaqiri, but the midfielder's header slid narrowly past the left-hand post.

Liverpool were dominating possession and territory and the hosts struggled to create in the final third, with Virgil van Dijk imperious as ever and Fabinho growing into his new role. Centre-forward Glenn Murray headed well over from Pascal Gross's cross in one rare moment of freedom; and stats revealed Murray only touched the ball seven times in the first half.

Salah came out after the break bursting with intent and forced a save from David Button after a strong run down the left channel. Then he twisted and turned on the right side of the area, edging goalwards until Gross grabbed a shoulder and then caught the Egyptian's leg. Penalty given. Salah slammed the spot kick to Button's left and though the keeper managed to get a hand on the ball, the net rippled.

With 15 minutes to play, Firmino fired a shot from a promising position straight at Button, then a lovely exchange between the Brazilian and Salah led to Gini Wijnaldum shooting just off-target.

Substitute striker Florin Andone caused brief concern for van Dijk and Alisson at the near post but the ball was scrambled clear. In the end, Brighton failed to record a single effort on target and the points were well deserved by a Reds side that enjoyed more than 70 per cent possession and all the best chances.

JANUARY

TEAMS

BRIGHTON
Button; Montoya, Dunk, Duffy, Bong; Stephens; March (Knockaert 66), Pröpper, Gross (Kayal 79), Locadia; Murray (Andone 66)

LIVERPOOL
Alisson; Alexander-Arnold, Fabinho, van Dijk, Robertson; Henderson, Wijnaldum; Shaqiri (Milner 72), Firmino, Mané (Keïta 90); Salah (Origi 90+4)

MATCH FACTS

- Sadio Mané reached 100 games for the Reds, while Virgil van Dijk reached 50.
- Only Chelsea in 2004/05 conceded fewer goals (8) after 22 matches in an English top-flight season than Liverpool's 10 this season.
- This was Liverpool's 50th clean sheet in 128 Premier League games under Jürgen Klopp.

THEY SAID

Paul Doyle, *The Observer*: "Defeats in their two previous matches led to this being billed as a particularly revealing interrogation of Liverpool, with a team aspiring to be champions required to give persuasive answers. Could Liverpool's confidence really be so brittle that a narrow loss at City and a practically invited one at Wolves in the FA Cup would cause it to crumble despite half a season of domestic invincibility prior to that? Answer: no."

SATURDAY 19 JANUARY 2019 | PREMIER LEAGUE | ANFIELD | ATTENDANCE: 53,171

LIVERPOOL 4
(Salah 46, 75, Firmino 53, Mané 90+3)
CRYSTAL PALACE 3
(Townsend 34, Tomkins 65, Meyer 90+5)

Crystal Palace gave their hosts a fright at Anfield before Liverpool ran out winners on a harum-scarum afternoon in the Premier League.

The visitors led at half-time, equalised in the final quarter after going behind, and even after going 4-2 behind caused some late panic with a third goal deep into stoppage time. It was an exhilarated but ultimately relieved crowd that welcomed referee Jonathan Moss's final whistle.

After a generous minute's applause in honour of the both the centenary of Bob Paisley's birth and the recent passing of former Reds winger Peter Thompson, the game kicked off with Liverpool in purposeful mood.

Centre-half Joel Matip nearly celebrated his return from injury with a goal, as James Milner found him with an elegant forward pass on eight minutes, but Palace keeper Julian Spéroni was quickly out of his goal to smother the chance. Third-choice glovesman Spéroni was back in the first team for the first time in over a year because of injuries to Wayne Hennessey and Vicente Guaita, and it would be a busy afternoon for the 39-year-old.

After some probing play around the box from the Reds, Sadio Mané headed a Milner corner straight at the keeper, then Spéroni could only watch as Matip's header from the same source drifted narrowly wide of the far post. Virgil van Dijk then nodded just over from Milner's free-kick delivery.

It was all Liverpool for the first half-hour, then suddenly Palace were ahead. Dangerous winger Wilfried Zaha had been a virtual spectator to this point, but he finally found himself in a position to run at Milner, scooted to the byline and pulled the ball back to Andros Townsend, the nemesis of Manchester City before Christmas. He buried the chance low under Alisson as Fabinho stretched in vain to block.

The second half was barely under way before the scores were level. Van Dijk advanced with Palace backing off and hit a long-range effort that ricocheted up into the air off James McArthur. Mo Salah reacted quickest to the dropping ball and stabbed an improvised finish past Spéroni.

Now the Reds pressed the accelerator. Andy Robertson zipped an effort beyond the right-hand post after a surging run, then Naby Keïta found Roberto Firmino in a pocket of space in the box and the striker swivelled and hit a shot that clipped Cheikhou Kouyaté and spun in for 2/1.

Palace hit back through centre-half James Tomkins, who rose unchallenged to meet Luka Milivojević's deep corner to plant a firm header back across Alisson and restore parity.

The key moment of the match came with 15 minutes to play. Fabinho found the overlapping run of Milner with a gorgeously weighted pass and the Englishman's first-time cross seemed to be within Spéroni's reach. Instead of catching the ball, though, he palmed it up one-handed and the trajectory looped back towards the goal. It was just crossing the line when Salah, alert to the opportunity, nudged it into the net.

Palace kept going, with Zaha a constant threat – so much so that Milner ended up earning two bookings in 10 minutes to be sent off as injury-time approached. And even when Sadio Mané thought he'd wrapped up the points with a clinical finish after Andy Robertson stretched to keep the ball in play on the left flank, there was still time for a twist.

Palace's substitute forwards Connor Wickham and Max Meyer combined in the box with the latter firing past Alisson for 4-3, then young substitute Rafa Camacho dispossessed Zaha in the box and from the rebound Patrick van Aanholt took aim with virtually the last kick of the match but fired well over.

TEAMS

LIVERPOOL

Alisson; Milner, Matip, van Dijk, Robertson; Fabinho (Lallana 87), Henderson, Keïta (Shaqiri 72); Mané, Firmino, Salah (Camacho 90+4)

CRYSTAL PALACE

Spéroni; Wan-Bissaka, Tomkins, Sakho, van Aanholt; McArthur (Mayer 81), Milivojević, Kouyaté (Schlupp 75); Townsend, Ayew (Wickham 81), Zaha

MATCH FACTS

- Mo Salah's second goal was his 50th in the Premier League in just 72 appearances.
- Sadio Mané had now scored in 22 games at Anfield in league and cup. Liverpool won them all.
- Roberto Firmino's goal was Liverpool 1,000th at Anfield in the Premier League.

THEY SAID

James Pearce, *Liverpool Echo*: "Talk about being put through the wringer. Much more of this and Liverpool will have to start issuing Valium with the match tickets. You could pick plenty of holes in such an erratic performance but all that matters is that Klopp's men found a way to win. When the pressure was cranked up, they refused to buckle. Instead they stood tall and showcased their powers of recovery. The character and hunger of this side is just as impressive as their quality and work ethic."

WEDNESDAY 30 JANUARY 2019 | PREMIER LEAGUE | ANFIELD | ATTENDANCE: 53,092

LIVERPOOL 1
(Mané 3)
LEICESTER 1
(Maguire 45+2)

The Reds failed to take full advantage of Manchester City's slip-up at St James's Park and had to settle for a point against Leicester on a wintry evening at Anfield.

Harry Maguire's leveller proved enough to earn a draw for the visitors, who might even have left victorious were it not for one splendid save from Alisson and a couple of wrong options taken in front of goal.

Temperatures plummeted on Merseyside and snow began to fall heavily before kick-off, leaving a layer of slush on the playing surface that made weight of pass and defensive anticipation exceedingly difficult.

But it didn't stop Sadio Mané opening the score with only two minutes and one second on the clock. At the end of a patient sequence of passes, Andy Robertson's ball into Roberto Firmino slid through into Mané's path and the Senegalese curved a controlled finish past Kasper Schmeichel, leaving a trail to the target through the icy surface.

The big Dane then pulled off a vital save from Firmino as the Brazilian took down Mo Salah's cross brilliantly on his chest, shifted the ball past Ricardo Pereira to make a shooting angle and fired across goal. Schmeichel plunged to his left to paw the ball away.

Salah almost slid in Xherdan Shaqiri, but on 24 minutes the visitors should have been level. Alisson was closed down by Jamie Vardy, and the deflection from the goalkeeper's attempted clearance fell to winger Marc Albrighton. His cross was perfectly weighted for James Maddison – unmarked at the back post – but instead of heading into the yawning net, he nodded back across the goalmouth and the chance was lost.

Another driving run forward from Robertson threatened to release Mané again, a danger that Harry Maguire spotted and stopped by bringing down the striker. Referee Martin Atkinson brandished a yellow card when arguably it could have been red. The incident was high in the Leicester half, but Maguire was the last defender between Mané and Schmeichel.

That decision proved vital as Maguire popped up to equalise in first-half stoppage time. Robertson conceded a free kick for a foul on Pereira near the right touchline and James Maddison's delivery was half-cleared to Wilfred Ndidi. The Nigerian's shot was blocked but Ben Chilwell then headed over the defence where Maguire was all alone to slide the ball past Alisson.

Early in the second half a Leicester free kick caused pandemonium in the Liverpool box. Vardy, Maguire and Jonny Evans all appeared to be offside at the point of delivery and when Maguire headed back across goal, Firmino's covering block was heading in until Alisson blocked with his right foot from close range.

Next, Anfield howled for a penalty when Naby Keïta's run in the box was halted by Pereira but the referee pointed only for a goal kick.

Jürgen Klopp brought on Fabinho and Adam Lallana for Keïta and Shaqiri but the visitors continued to threaten, with Chilwell flashing a dangerous centre across goal and Demarai Gray bringing a save from Alisson after a rapid counter. At the Kop end, Firmino again called Schmeichel into action, the keeper getting right behind a low, drilled shot.

Neither side could force a winner, though, and the Reds had to be content with inching one point further ahead of Pep's men.

TEAMS

LIVERPOOL
Alisson; Henderson, Matip, van Dijk, Robertson; Wijnaldum, Keïta (Fabinho 67); Shaqiri (Lallana 67), Firmino (Sturridge 82), Mané; Salah

LEICESTER CITY
Schmeichel; Pereira, Maguire, Evans, Chilwell; Mendy, Ndidi; Albrighton, Maddison (Choudhury 75), Gray (Okazaki 84); Vardy (Iheanacho 90)

MATCH FACTS

• Sadio Mané's opener was Liverpool's fastest league goal since April 2016, when Daniel Sturridge scored in 1 min 7 secs against Newcastle.

- It was also Liverpool's 100th goal against Leicester at Anfield.
- Substitute Adam Lallana made his 150th appearance for Liverpool.

THEY SAID

Jason Burt, *Daily Telegraph*: "This epic Premier League title race continues to twist and turn, brimming with drama and surprise and steadily rising tension, and so Liverpool extended their lead at the top to five points but will feel as if they suffered a shock defeat. A draw against Leicester was not what was expected, not what was demanded; and while Liverpool probably should have been awarded a second-half penalty, the bare fact... is that they simply did not do enough to win on an evening when they could have made such an emphatic statement of intent."

PREMIER LEAGUE TABLE AT END OF JANUARY 2019

Pos	Team	Pld	W	D	L	GF	GA	GD	Pts
1	Liverpool	24	19	4	1	55	14	41	61
2	Manchester City	24	18	2	4	63	19	44	56
3	Tottenham Hotspur	24	18	0	6	50	24	26	54
4	Arsenal	24	14	5	5	50	33	17	47
5	Chelsea	24	14	5	5	40	23	17	47
6	Manchester United	24	13	6	5	48	35	13	45
7	Wolverhampton Wanderers	24	10	5	9	30	31	-1	35
8	Everton	24	9	6	9	35	33	2	33
9	Watford	24	9	6	9	33	34	-1	33
10	AFC Bournemouth	24	10	3	11	37	42	-5	33
11	Leicester City	24	9	5	10	30	30	0	32
12	West Ham United	24	9	4	11	30	37	-7	31
13	Brighton & Hove Albion	24	7	5	12	27	36	-9	26
14	Newcastle United	24	6	6	12	21	32	-11	24
15	Crystal Palace	24	6	5	13	24	33	-9	23
16	Southampton	24	5	8	11	26	41	-15	23
17	Burnley	24	6	5	13	25	45	-20	23
18	Cardiff City	24	5	4	15	20	46	-26	19
19	Fulham	24	4	5	15	25	53	-28	17
20	Huddersfield Town	24	2	5	17	13	41	-28	11

CHAPTER SEVEN

—

FEBRUARY

"VERY FINE MARGINS CAN
MAKE THE DIFFERENCE"

Perhaps it's in the nature of a two-horse race to see the run-in from a distance. But firing the gun at the start of February seemed premature, even by modern media standards. And if some Reds were already dreaming of a league title in May, it was Jürgen Klopp's job to manage those expectations towards practical reality.

"I don't dream in the job. I am working, to be honest," said the Liverpool boss, before an important test away at West Ham. "My dream is to stay healthy until I am 96, 97, having no disease, can remember everything. I dream of that, together with my missus, having grandchildren. Our job [here] is to fulfil [others'] dreams, not our own ones."

Nevertheless, excitement at the potential for Liverpool to end a 29-year wait for the league championship was being amped up by the press and Klopp found himself frequently having to fend off questions about pressure and nerves around the club.

"I am not a nervous person, so I was never nervous before the first title [with Dortmund]," he said. "Yes, experience showed me that the way I did it in the past worked. So, I didn't change. Will there be nervous moments? Yes, for sure. But don't make them bigger than they are, because there were nervous situations last year, two years ago, three years ago. That is part of the game. People are in a little bit of doubt about this and that, and I understand – we were not champions for 29 years.

"[Liverpool fans] really want it, with all they have. But there are no guarantees. The only thing I always knew is to do the right thing as often as possible, stay focused on your own way and don't think about the other things around. Then, if you are good enough, it will happen. If not, it will not happen. That is pretty easy [to understand]."

Echoes of the club's last brush with title success were to be found at the London Stadium, where former Manchester City boss Manuel Pellegrini was now in the dugout. The urbane Chilean had led City to the title in 2013/14, edging out Brendan Rodgers's side on the last day. He admitted that while his priority was success in London, he still had a keen eye for events unfolding in the North West.

"If we win, I will be very happy for our club first," Pellegrini said. "We need a good performance against the leaders. After that, if we can give a hand to Manchester City, it's not our problem, but of course I am a fan of Manchester City also."

Injuries in Liverpool's defensive ranks had been an issue for some weeks and on the morning of the West Ham game came news that Joe Gomez – out since fracturing his leg at Burnley in early December – would need a further operation to aid his recovery.

"Obviously being out for longer than we'd first hoped for is hard to swallow but it's part and parcel of the industry," the young defender told the club website. "It was an injury caused by an impact, like nearly all the injuries I've had in my career, so I know it's just a case of when it's fully healed, I'm good to go again.

"The hardest part is not being able to help the team and contribute on the pitch at the moment, so it's important I come back ready to go and this procedure will help with that. My only focus is getting back for Liverpool as soon as possible and I can promise the supporters I'll be working hard every day to do that."

Meanwhile, Dejan Lovren and Trent Alexander-Arnold were also unavailable due to injury, meaning James Milner, back after a one-match suspension for his sending off against Crystal Palace, would again deputise at right-back.

After a shaky start to the season for Pellegrini – four straight defeats had been kicked off by a 4-0 defeat at Anfield – the Hammers steadied the ship with good wins over Everton and Manchester United in September, then enjoyed a sustained run of form in December with five victories lifting them comfortably into mid-table. Key to their success had been the form of mercurial forward Marko Arnautović and Felipe Anderson, a tricky Brazilian signed in the summer from Lazio. The Austrian hadn't recovered from a foot injury and would be absent but Anderson was a menace. His strong running with the ball and quality from dead-ball situations caused Liverpool problems all evening.

Defensive organisation at set pieces yielded numerous chances for West Ham, including the equalising goal from Michail Antonio after Sadio Mané had put Liverpool in front, and the visitors might easily have come away with nothing had the hosts been more clinical in front of goal.

"Our defending could have been a lot better, but it is what it is," said Virgil van Dijk. "We have to take our one point from tonight and keep going. Set pieces are their strength, they practice them a lot and it showed. For us, it would have been better to not give easy fouls away."

He also reflected on the challenge of having to constantly change the defensive line-up due to injuries: "All the players who come in have the quality to fill in, but when you have a back four that doesn't change, maybe it's a little easier. What can we do? We take it game by game. We're still top of the league, though we've made it hard for ourselves. But we're still in the title race, and some teams are not. We're disappointed, but we go again."

With Manchester City playing an extra game in midweek – and defeating Everton at Goodison – the Reds had been pushed down into second place on goal difference by the time of Bournemouth's visit to Anfield, so there was no room for error against Eddie Howe's men. A win to regain momentum was the only acceptable result.

The Cherries were in unpredictable form, having followed a stunning 4-0 home win over Chelsea with a 2-0 defeat against struggling Cardiff. And they had never won at Anfield, but the manager wasn't overawed by the task of trying to overcome a side unbeaten in 33 league games at home.

"These challenges have always faced us before and we tend to look at it as writing new history for the club," said Howe. "Winning at Anfield is something we would love to do. No team has done it for a long period of time in the Premier League, which goes to show how consistent Liverpool have been.

"The Chelsea result was where everything came together, and there have been other games where we have performed really well and just missed out. We want to put our last defeat at Cardiff to bed and really perform for our away fans."

Jürgen Klopp, meanwhile, showed his admiration for the work Howe and his staff had done in maintaining Bournemouth's steady presence in the top flight over four seasons since their ascent from the Championship.

"I don't watch, listen or read too much opinion on football outside of what I need to do the job, but when I do see things it feels to me that the work done by Eddie and his guys at Bournemouth is almost taken for granted now," Klopp wrote in his programme notes.

"These guys are benchmark coaches and leaders in the English game and what they have done at their club and how they continue to do it should be held up as an example of excellence.

"I love that Eddie has the courage to stick to his principles at all times and what is evident when you analyse them is that most importantly his team buys into it completely.

"I also know a number of their team, having worked with them here, and I'm sure they'll all receive a warm welcome back to Anfield, because when they were here they served the club really well."

One of those returning alumni was Dominic Solanke, who had left Merseyside for the south coast in January. The striker was on the bench but played the last half-hour in his return to Anfield.

"It's always a bit strange and scary if you play against a former player. Dom was here four weeks ago and we saw him every day," Klopp said, recognising the threat that always comes with a player keen to impress on their old ground.

"He's a wonderful guy and a big, big talent but we couldn't give him enough match time, so for his development it's unbelievably important that he gets these minutes. He had his first start last week. That's good."

By the time Solanke was introduced, however, Liverpool were 3-0 up and cruising. Plenty of attention during the 2018/19 campaign had been lavished upon the Reds' attacking trio, and much made of the transformative effect on the club's defensive record by the acquisition of Virgil van Dijk and Alisson. By contrast, the efforts of the midfield had flown somewhat under the radar, but this was a day to shine for a midfield three of Naby Keïta, Fabinho and Gini Wijnaldum.

Keïta had been in and out of the team in the early part of the season, but this was his fourth straight league start and he was becoming an increasingly influential presence for Jürgen Klopp. He was involved in the build-up for all three goals in this game, defending from the front and generally giving Bournemouth's midfield the hurry-up all afternoon.

Wijnaldum, meanwhile, showed an uncommon deftness of touch in his lob for the second goal. "Like Dennis Bergkamp!" was Sky Sports pundit Paul Merson's breathless assessment of the finish on *Soccer Saturday*.

But it was the less immediately eye-catching display of Fabinho that caught the eye of former Reds midfielder Danny Murphy on *Match of the Day*.

"I thought it was a superb performance from Fabinho," he enthused. "At times when there were a few nerves about, which is understandable after the last couple of games, he was tenacious, he was calm and at Anfield when it's a bit edgy you need someone who is brave enough to play forward passes and not worry about losing the ball.

"[Bournemouth] had a good shape and Liverpool were finding it difficult to break them down. Fabinho kept probing, giving Liverpool the impetus and wearing [them] down as time went by.

"He's shown the confidence and calmness... having that desire to get on the ball and break up play, getting Liverpool on the attack. He's settled into the role really well."

This was a welcome return to free-scoring form but the ante was promptly raised further by Manchester City, who clobbered Chelsea 6-0 at the Etihad the following day to leapfrog back to the top again, albeit having played a game more. Even at this stage it seemed likely these tit-for-tat exchanges would go right to the wire.

Back in December, Liverpool's reward for edging out Napoli in Champions League Group C was arguably the most attractive (to neutrals) and unarguably one of the toughest draws for the round of 16, against Bayern Munich. Each side boasted five European Cup wins – for a spell in the mid-1970s no one else got a look-in as Bayern won their first three and the Reds their first two – so this would be a clash of genuine European footballing royalty.

Extra spice, of course, was added in that Jürgen Klopp would once again lock horns with Bayern, the club whom he dethroned as domestic champions with Borussia Dortmund in 2011 and who in turn ended Klopp's quest for the biggest prize in European football in the all-German final at Wembley in 2013.

So there was plenty of back-story to this tie, although given the two clubs' regular participation in the Champions League over the years, it was something of an anomaly that they'd never met in its modern incarnation. The last time Liverpool played Bayern in the European Cup was in the semi-final in 1981, when Ray Kennedy's away goal in the Olympic Stadium took the Reds through to the final in Paris and a third lifting of the grand old trophy.

In terms of scheduling, the FA Cup fifth round fell on the weekend following the Bournemouth game, so Klopp was able to take his charges off to Marbella for warm-weather training. Although it proved not particularly balmy in southern Spain, there were important issues to address before the Bayern match, not least covering for Virgil van Dijk, who was suspended for the first leg after picking up three cautions in the group stage, the final one being on Matchday 6 against Napoli.

Dejan Lovren stayed behind at Melwood in a bid to regain fitness, but training had to proceed on the basis that Klopp would have only one senior centre-half available for selection in Joel Matip. Having played a couple of games there previously, Fabinho was earmarked for the role, with the proviso that playing against Bayern's front line of Robert Lewandowski and James Rodriguez would represent a considerable steepening of the Brazilian's defensive learning curve.

In attack, Roberto Firmino was passed fit after he, too, contracted the virus that had recently affected Gini Wijnaldum, while Jordan Henderson slipped neatly into the midfield space left by Fabinho dropping back.

The match, though, failed to live up to the pre-match hype and stirring atmosphere, as the two highly rated front lines were – for the most part – well marshalled by their defensive counterparts. Liverpool's only real moments of alarm were self-inflicted as Joel Matip cannoned a clearance against Alisson and shortly afterwards ceded possession on the edge of the box leading to a chance for Kingsley Coman. But no harm was done.

Matip also had a good opportunity just before half-time but couldn't steer Firmino's cross on target, while Sadio Mané had arguably the best chances of the night, one in each half. The first was scuffed wide as he turned on to a deflection from Naby Keïta, the second well saved by Manuel Neuer as Mané flicked Andy Robertson's cross towards the near post.

Bayern coach Niko Kovač said he was delighted by his team's defensive performance. "My glass is half-full," he said at the post-match press conference. "There aren't many clubs who haven't conceded at Anfield. Liverpool are a sensationally good team and we kept everything tight at the back and played to a high level technically, tactically and mentally. Over the two games, very fine margins can make the difference."

Klopp suggested he had been surprised by how defensive the German champions had been.

"You saw the respect both teams had for each other," he said. "A lot of situations I didn't see in all the games when we watched Munich, to be honest – like how the full-backs stayed in their own half protecting, how Gnabry defended on the wing in two-v-one situations. That made life uncomfortable. But in the first half we still had chances; if Sadio hits the ball a bit better, he strikes twice with a bicycle kick, which is obviously pretty rare. [It's] how it always is, a goal would have changed the game. The first half was… OK, we created. In the second half nobody created anymore."

Nor would there be a swift resolution to the tie: with the round-of-16 games on a split schedule, it would be mid-March before the Reds travelled to Germany. For now, the manager's priority was to prepare his team for another big Premier League test, at Old Trafford, where much had changed since the teams last met in December and an old foe of Bayern Munich was now installed as head coach.

Ole Gunnar Solskjær was always likely to become a manager when he hung up his boots. The Norwegian spent 11 seasons at Manchester United, and though he's rightly remembered as a supersub – notably for his late winner in the 1999 Champions League final – he also scored 97 of his 126 goals for United from the starting line-up. At his peak there were few deadlier finishers in English football.

But the time he did spend on the bench wasn't wasted. Solskjær studied the game, watched his manager in action and over time became one of Sir Alex Ferguson's most trusted senior professionals.

"His thought processes underpinned his skills. He had that analytical mind. As soon as he arrived in a shooting position, he had it all sized up. He had mental pictures everywhere," Ferguson wrote in his 2013 autobiography.

"In games, sitting on the bench, and in training sessions, he would make notes, always. So, by the time he came on he had analysed who the opponents were, what positions they were assuming. He had those images all worked out. The game was laid out for him like a diagram and he knew where to go and when."

The Norwegian retired in 2007 and immediately started working with the first-team strikers in training, then became reserve-team coach in 2008. He went home to his old club Molde FK for a first head coach job, winning two Norwegian league titles and a domestic cup before reappearing in the Premier League with Cardiff City in 2014.

But this was no happy return. The Bluebirds were a club in turmoil when they sacked Malky Mackay in December and Solskjær couldn't turn the ship around. They finished in last place, and a poor run at the start of the subsequent Championship season led to his departure in September.

He went back to Molde and to many it was a surprise when he was announced as interim manager after José Mourinho's departure. But the warmth of the United fans was evident, and the results instant. Beyond the initial "bounce" expected after a new managerial appointment – a 5-1 hammering of Cardiff in his first game would have given his former side pause for thought – United kept winning, and winning, and winning.

We know now that it didn't last long beyond that record-breaking opening burst but in early 2019, Manchester United had at least some of the old vibrancy that had been lost in the recent, post-Ferguson years. Before Liverpool's visit, they had won eight out of nine league games and risen into the top four for the first time all season.

This match, however, would principally be remembered for the bizarre spate of injuries that disrupted the first half more than any decisive action from either side. There was no lack of atmosphere inside Old Trafford and plenty of intent from the players, as you'd expect, but as against Bayern, the quality of attacking play in the final third didn't match the occasion. It wasn't a spectacle to rank among the more memorable in this fixture.

Most notable was the rare instance of United summoning all three substitutes before half-time as twanging hamstrings decimated the home midfield. Ander Herrera, Juan Mata and Jesse Lingard (who had come on for Mata) were all dispatched to the treatment room inside 42 minutes. Meanwhile, Roberto Firmino went over on his ankle and also departed. At one point it seemed as if the physios might have to send out for supplies.

Of the chances that accrued amid this chaos, United probably had the better. Lingard's injury was sustained in trying to nip the ball around Alisson – the Englishman seizing on an insightful pass from Romelu Lukaku – but the keeper was out in a flash to palm the ball out of harm's way.

The hosts then had a goal chalked off when Joel Matip diverted Chris Smalling's cross into his own net. The United defender was correctly given offside.

"Everything that could have gone wrong did go wrong in the first half," said Solskjær, reflecting ruefully on his side's injury woes. "We had to keep Rashford on [even though he was injured] and it seemed like it was going to be a tough afternoon but we worked hard. The atmosphere was bouncing."

Jürgen Klopp also cited the injuries as disruptive, when asked if his side could have made more of the situation.

"We lost Bobby [Firmino] in the first half as well, which doesn't help in general," he said. "But chipping the ball in behind, that's important with the high last line, but we didn't really do that. I would say if United played today with a full team like they played in the last couple of weeks or so then it's a completely different game, they know exactly [what to] do, know where to pass, and that means we know as well where they pass. Then it was completely different, the whole game changed and that obviously was not good for us today. I have no clue really why it happened, but it happened."

The point earned was enough for Liverpool to hit top spot again and stay there for a few days at least, as United's neighbours City were contesting the Carabao Cup final at Wembley against Chelsea, straight after this game in Manchester. It was a similarly featureless game – save for Chelsea goalkeeper Kepa Arrizabalaga's extraordinary show of defiance when manager Maurizio Sarri tried to substitute him for Willy Caballero before the penalty shoot-out.

Kepa refused to leave the pitch, Sarri was apoplectic and eventually City prevailed to lift the first silverware of the domestic season. However, injuries to Fernandinho and Aymeric Laporte tempered Pep Guardiola's joy at the win as the games started to pile up.

"[We played] extra time and… important players will be out for a while. But it's normal. [We play] a lot of games," said the Spaniard. "We demand a lot of these players. Look at United today. It's not exclusive with Manchester City. We demand a lot of the players. There are fewer games in other countries… but I trust our squad. We will find a solution."

A full midweek programme was scheduled for the final round of fixtures in February, with Liverpool welcoming Watford to Anfield while Man City had a home date against West Ham. Neither side was offered much preparation time.

Javi Gracia's Watford were up to seventh in the table after wins against Everton and Cardiff and posed a genuine threat, despite Liverpool's daunting home record, as Jürgen Klopp was happy to acknowledge in his pre-match remarks.

"They're on a good run and have different styles that they play," said the Reds boss. "We analyse them and [against the top six] they don't have a lot of possession, they are a proper counter-attacking team, good around set pieces, good around second balls. But then, when they play other teams, they are much more proactive. We prepare for both, but probably we will have [more of] the ball and we need to do something with it!"

And Klopp raised a laugh in the press room when asked about the return of Brendan Rodgers to the Premier League, as the ex-Liverpool and Celtic boss looked set to take the reins at Leicester City.

"As long as [Brendan] doesn't go to Everton then I'm fine with it," he said wryly, leaning back in his chair. "Because then he would want his house back!"

Roberto Firmino's injury at Old Trafford was not as bad as initially feared but Klopp preferred not to risk the striker in such a busy period, bringing in Divock Origi to play on the left of a front three with Sadio Mané, unusually, assuming the number 9 role. Trent Alexander-Arnold came back in at right-back, as James Milner moved into midfield to replace Jordan Henderson.

Watford were unchanged from the side that put five past Cardiff at the weekend. In fact there was only one change from the side that started against

Liverpool at Vicarage Road back in November – Darryl Janmaat played right-back instead of Kiko Femenía, who had been out with a thigh injury since mid-January.

Attacking pair Troy Deeney and Gerard Deulofeu brought their very different styles – the bludgeon and the switchblade – and in Roberto Pereyra, the Hornets boasted one of the most creative wingers in the division. So if the plan was, as predicted by Klopp, to contain and counter, the visitors would look to sit deep and then release the forward line through midfielders Abdoulaye Doucouré and Étienne Capoue.

But Liverpool were in scintillating form on a clear spring-like evening at Anfield and the visitors simply could not cope with the quality of delivery from wide areas; and the relish with which the Reds' forward line took to their task.

Sadio Mané was unstoppable in his newly minted role of centre-forward. He later revealed he was just as surprised as everyone else when Klopp told him of his plans for the line-up.

"I never played [there] before," he said. "For me, it was a little bit strange, but one day before the game, the coach called me, he said 'OK, we're going to make some changes and Sadio you have to play number 9'. I looked at my teammates, and we all looked like, ["What?!"]. I was laughing, and I said, "OK my boss, listen; we are a team so you have to trust me!' Almost everybody was laughing at me and I said, 'From today, call me Ronaldo, *Il Fenomono'*."

"The Phenomenon" is not too strong a description of Mané when he scored his second goal. He'd already risen high above the Watford defence to nod home Trent Alexander-Arnold's cross in the ninth minute, when he pulled in another centre from the right-back, 10 minutes later. The touch fell slightly behind him, so with his back to goal and Ben Foster rushing from his line, Mané improvised a back-heel, hard into the ground, that lobbed over the keeper's challenge and into the net. Digest that: a back-heeled lob. Try it 100 times yourself in the park and you won't get it right.

Origi celebrated his return to the side with a goal to effectively end the contest with 25 minutes to play and then Virgil van Dijk gleefully accepted two headed opportunities set up by either full-back to complete the rout.

"This was the perfect shot in the arm after those dour stalemates with Bayern Munich and Manchester United," wrote the *Liverpool Echo*'s James Pearce. "The swagger and attacking fluency returned.

"Slick passing, intelligent movement and a clinical edge in the final third was combined with real discipline and control as Liverpool kept a fourth successive clean sheet.

"Having stood accused of picking the wrong team and making ineffective substitutions at Old Trafford, this was a personal triumph for Klopp. All the big calls he made paid off handsomely."

The call to give Mané his debut as a no.9 was the biggest of all and the manager gave a glowing assessment of the striker's qualities.

"In that position you need someone who is able to play in the small space, who can give you as well offers in behind, who adapts to the defensive situation, who is football-smart, all that stuff," said Klopp. "We have other players who can play there but not in combination of the speed of Sadio, obviously. Sadio played different positions in his life and for us as well, so I was in no doubt that he would play [well] there."

On a day when all five assists were provided by the full-backs, one Red legend was hugely impressed by their contribution. Alan Kennedy won 11 major trophies in his time as Liverpool's left-back, scoring the winner in the 1981 European Cup final and the winning penalty in the final in 1984, so he's a keen judge of how attacking intent from defenders can make a huge difference to the side's effectiveness.

"The current team's general play is very similar to the way we did it back in the late 1970s and '80s, with the full-backs encouraged to go forward at every opportunity," said Kennedy. "It was one of Bob Paisley's mantras 'keep going forward', and whenever Ray Kennedy tucked inside I needed no excuse to go forward into the space down the left wing, to supply the ammunition for Kenny Dalglish and Dave Johnson. The simpler the instruction the better, as far as I was concerned, the better I understood it! I am not one for all this technical stuff of moving the ball across the midfield, or back to go forward. I enjoyed nothing more than getting round the back of defenders and trying to pick out a forward, and I see that in Andy Robertson. He is always in good positions."

Trent Alexander-Arnold won the headlines against Watford for his hat-trick of assists, but Kennedy was keen to focus on fellow left-back Robertson and his importance to the side.

"I like the timing of Andy's runs forward," he said. "They are always spot on, and he is exceptionally quick on his feet, striding out, unlike myself as my legs are a bit shorter – that's why they called me Barney Rubble, after the *Flintstones* character! But I'd like to see the space and get into it and have them chasing me, rather than me having to chase a winger. Andy is very similar and some of his play is quite exceptional, particularly his ability to find a player in the box – that is just uncanny, much better than mine. He has great interplay with all three forwards and is lovely to watch, whereas I'd be blasting it from 30 yards!"

Going into March, then, the Reds maintained the slenderest of leads over Manchester City – a single point after the Blues' narrow win over West Ham. Still there was nothing decisively to separate the sides as they pulled clear of the rest of the table. It was very much now a top two, with four sides chasing the two remaining Champions League places and – as 13 points separated Chelsea in sixth from Wolves in seventh – the rest a very long way back.

FEBRUARY MATCH REPORTS

MONDAY 4 FEBRUARY 2019 | PREMIER LEAGUE | LONDON STADIUM | ATTENDANCE: 59,903

WEST HAM UNITED 1
(Antonio 28)
LIVERPOOL 1
(Mané 22)

West Ham kept league leaders Liverpool at bay to share the points at the London Stadium, handing Manchester City the chance to return to the top of the table if they could beat Everton two days hence.

Michail Antonio's goal from a well-worked free-kick routine cancelled out Sadio Mané's opener and though both sides had good chances to secure the win, a draw felt like the right result; if not for the travelling fans then at least on the balance of play.

The Hammers began briskly, with Mexican striker Javier Hernandez latching on to Mark Noble's pass and spearing a shot wide of Alisson's left-hand post. Then Aaron Cresswell strode on to a loose defensive clearance and thumped a low drive past the same post and Hernandez fired in a long-range effort that drew a good stop from the keeper.

Liverpool were seeing plenty of the ball but couldn't find the right pass in the final third, or if they did were caught offside by West Ham's disciplined defensive line.

Eventually Klopp's men found a chink in the armour. After Roberto Firmino had scuffed a shot into Lukasz Fabianski's arms from an inviting position, Liverpool went ahead in the 22nd minute. A brilliant piece of skill from Adam Lallana – making a first league start since October – took out three Hammers defenders on the right flank and released James Milner. His centre was collected by Mané, who spun neatly inside Issa Diop and curled a finish into the far corner.

The lead lasted only six minutes, however. Fabinho was penalised for his challenge on Robert Snodgrass, some 35 yards from goal; and from the free kick Felipe Anderson sprang a surprise from the training ground. With everyone expecting a chip to the back post, Antonio made a run across the box to collect a pass from Anderson before Naby Keïta could react. The Hammers' forward sent the ball in off the far post and sprinted away in celebration.

Keïta looked to make amends with a penetrating run and shot, deflected wide with Fabianksi at full stretch, while Andy Robertson then drove a dangerous cross just out of the reach of Mané and Firmino, when any touch would have led to a second for the visitors.

West Ham, though, had the clearest opportunity to go ahead, when another Anderson free kick found Declan Rice, running free unmarked, but the youngster sent his header just over with Alisson a spectator.

In the second half, Mo Salah began to exert more influence, getting on the ball more but a couple of attempts were sent straight at Fabianski and one flew over the bar. Antonio then countered well for the home side but Hernandez couldn't sort his feet out to threaten the goal. It was still an open, entertaining game.

Mark Noble thrashed over after a dancing run from Anderson and one final chance fell to substitute Divock Origi from Keïta's lovely dink into the box in added time. The Dutchman could have won it but, under pressure from Ryan Fredericks, scooped the ball into the grateful gloves of the Hammers' keeper.

TEAMS

WEST HAM UNITED
Fabianski; Fredericks, Diop, Ogbonna Cresswell; Rice; Antonio, Snodgrass, Noble (Obiang 79), Anderson (Masuaku 90+1); Hernandez (Carroll 79)

LIVERPOOL
Alisson; Milner, Matip, van Dijk, Robertson; Keïta, Fabinho; Lallana (Shaqiri 69), Firmino (Origi 75), Mané; Salah

MATCH FACTS

- Sadio Mané scored away from Anfield for the first time since 1 September against Leicester.
- This was the second time Mané had scored in three consecutive Premier League games (also in August 2017)
- James Milner took his total of Premier League assists to 81, the seventh-highest in the competition.

THEY SAID

Mark Noble, West Ham captain: "As a neutral, it's going to be a fantastic end to the season to watch because there's going to be so many twists and turns. Especially when you're leading and you're top and everyone is chasing you and you know Man City are not going to rest for one game. You need to stick together. But [Liverpool] have got a fantastic squad of players and a world-class manager."

SATURDAY 9 FEBRUARY 2019 | PREMIER LEAGUE | ANFIELD | ATTENDANCE: 53,178

LIVERPOOL 3
(Mané 24, Wijnaldum 34, Salah 48)
BOURNEMOUTH 0

The Reds eased past Bournemouth to regain top spot in the Premier League table, with memorable goals from Gini Wijnaldum and Mo Salah capping an excellent all-round performance and a return to winning ways after two successive draws.

Wijnaldum had recovered from illness to be selected as the only change in Jürgen Klopp's starting line-up, replacing Adam Lallana in midfield. Returning striker Dominic Solanke had a place on the bench as Josh King was selected to play up front on his own and loanee Nathaniel Clyne was ineligible to play against his parent club.

Roberto Firmino didn't make it on to the scoresheet, but his vision and trickery illuminated this afternoon show of attacking strength at a blustery Anfield. His sublime back-heel for Mo Salah's goal was the pick of his interventions and the Brazilian could have had a hat-trick of assists in the second half but for Salah crashing an effort against the bar and Bournemouth keeper Artur Boruc saving well at the feet of Trent Alexander-Arnold.

This was damage limitation for the Cherries after Liverpool's dominance was rewarded by a two-goal lead after 34 minutes. An energetic start by the visitors earned a sight of goal for Ryan Fraser but his shot was beaten away by Alisson and thereafter the Reds took control.

Naby Keïta and Wijnaldum were superb in the centre of the park, the former benefiting from Klopp reverting to 4-3-3 system and playing a part in all three goals.

Mané opened the home side's account with a header from James Milner's swinging centre. The Englishman was allowed too much room to measure his delivery after accepting Keïta's pass on the right flank and Mané rose high above Dan Gosling to nod the ball down past Boruc.

Then another of Bournemouth's ex-Reds – Jordan Ibe – was robbed of possession on his right wing by Keïta and Andy Robertson floated a pass to Wijnaldum, alert to the space in behind. The midfielder was closed down by Nathan Aké but spotted Boruc fractionally off his line and lifted a delicate lob over the keeper that nestled in the far corner.

As half-time approached Salah nearly made it three with a stinging effort that Boruc was able to tip over; but he made no mistake after the break, sliding home from Firmino's cute reverse ball.

Mané headed wide from Wijnaldum's cross after more good work from Salah and it could have been a rout for the tiring Cherries' defence, but it ended 3-0 and the Reds' unbeaten home record in the league now extended to 34 games – the second-longest run in the club's history.

TEAMS

LIVERPOOL

Alisson; Milner, Matip, Van Dijk, Robertson; Wijnaldum
(Alexander-Arnold 77), Fabinho (Sturridge 90), Keïta; Mané, Firmino, Salah

BOURNEMOUTH

Boruc; Smith, Cook, Aké, Rico (Mepham 80); Gosling, Lerma (Mousset 73), Surman;
Ibe (Solanke 59), King, Fraser

MATCH FACTS

- Mo Salah's goal made him the first Liverpool player since Luis Suarez in 2013/14 to score 20 goals in all competitions in successive seasons.
- Salah had now scored more times against Bournemouth (six) than anyone in the Reds' history.
- Andy Robertson had now made 11 assists since making his Premier League debut, more than any other defender in the division during that time.

THEY SAID

Andy Robertson: "[The midfield] were [in a] different class. On my side, I thought that Naby was excellent. He has taken a wee bit of time to settle in but today was probably his best performance in a Liverpool shirt. Gini has been magnificent this season and he pops up with… a great finish. Fabinho just goes about his business and won the ball back for us so many times. [They] won their battles and that set us off and everyone followed suit."

TUESDAY 19 FEBRUARY 2019 | UEFA CHAMPIONS LEAGUE – ROUND OF 16 | ANFIELD
ATTENDANCE: 52,250

LIVERPOOL 0
BAYERN MUNICH 0

An eagerly anticipated clash of European heavyweights delivered something more like a bout of sparring as both sides failed to land a telling blow in the first leg of this round-of-16 tie.

And while both Liverpool and Bayern fans were able to take positives from the fact that the tie was still evenly poised, this felt like a missed opportunity for the Reds to take a lead to Germany, where Bayern had lost only two of their last 26 home matches in the Champions League.

On a wet night on Merseyside, Anfield was a sea of red and white: home scarves being held up during a rousing rendition of "You'll Never Walk Alone" as the teams entered the arena; the away section alive with red and white Bayern flags being vigorously waved.

After a low-key opening, Mo Salah had the first sniff of a chance on

11 minutes, squeezing himself between Joshua Kimmich and Niklas Süle to reach a long through-ball from Jordan Henderson, but unable to apply sufficient force to trouble Manuel Neuer in the Bayern net.

Liverpool survived a scare when former Arsenal winger Serge Gnabry burst past Andy Robertson and though his centre was beyond the reach of Robert Lewandowski, Joel Matip smacked his attempted clearance into the chest of keeper Alisson. Thankfully it rebounded forwards and away from the danger area.

Alisson and Matip found themselves in another uncomfortable tangle just seconds later when the keeper dwelled on a back pass and then gave it back to Matip on the edge of the area after pressure from Lewandowski. Bayern pinched possession and James Rodriguez touched the ball to Kingsley Coman; but the winger fired high into the side-netting.

A Trent Alexander-Arnold free kick – right on the byline – was only half cleared and the young full-back clipped a first-time cross from the rebound to the back post where Salah had a free header, but couldn't find the target.

Liverpool's best chance of the night fell to Sadio Mané, after Naby Keïta blocked shot appeared at the striker's feet near the penalty spot. He swivelled but didn't catch the shot cleanly on the turn and the ball bobbled wide. Another deflection from Keïta invited a more difficult opportunity for Mané and his acrobatic overhead sailed into the crowd.

Then Jordan Henderson broke up a Bayern counter from a Liverpool corner, Salah's back-heel put Firmino in on the left of the area but his centre was poked wide by Matip.

Fabinho displayed his increasing assuredness at the back with six minutes of the second half played. Coman found space to run into on the left and, after numerous step-overs, eked out some of the space to cross past Gini Wijnaldum, where Lewandowski had the ball under control just six yards out. Fabinho, though, slid in with a clean tackle to clear the danger.

Just before the hour, Gnabry's dipper from distance flew over the point of post and bar with Alisson in full flight but the last 30 minutes were scrappy and it took until only a few minutes before the end for either keeper to be tested again. Andy Robertson swung in a centre from the left and Mané's near-post header was scrambled behind by Neuer.

With a home leg to come, Bayern appeared to have marginally the upper hand; but with no away goal conceded, the Reds knew they could threaten in Bavaria. Game on.

TEAMS

LIVERPOOL
Alisson; Alexander-Arnold, Matip, Fabinho, Robertson; Keïta (Milner 76),
Henderson, Wijnaldum; Salah, Firmino (Origi 76), Mané

BAYERN MUNICH
Neuer; Kimmich, Süle, Hummels, Alaba; Thiago, Martinez; Gnabry (Rafinha 90 +1),
Rodriguez (Sanches 88), Coman (Ribery 81); Lewandowski

MATCH FACTS

- In four games, across 48 years, Bayern had never scored a goal against
Liverpool at Anfield (March 1971, 3-0 Liverpool; Oct 1971, 0-0; April 1981,
0-0; February 2019, 0-0).
- This was the first scoreless draw for Jürgen Klopp in 30 managerial
encounters with Bayern.
- Liverpool extended the unbeaten run in European competition at Anfield
to 20 games (W14, D6).

THEY SAID

Jordan Henderson: "We're disappointed not to score, but we kept a clean sheet
and defended well. We had enough chances, especially in the first half. It's
not the worst result in the world and the performance level was good but we
lacked that bit in the final third. It's still alive. We can go there and hurt them."

SUNDAY 24 FEBRUARY 2019 | PREMIER LEAGUE | OLD TRAFFORD
ATTENDANCE: 74,519

MANCHESTER UNITED 0
LIVERPOOL 0

Manchester United and Liverpool shared the points in a bizarre, injury-
strewn encounter at Old Trafford that ended goalless and ultimately did
neither side any favours in their respective quests for a top-four finish and
the title deeds.

The home side were obliged to use all their substitutes before half-time as Ander Herrera, Juan Mata and Jesse Lingard (himself a substitute) were all unable to continue because of hamstring injuries, and Marcus Rashford spent the afternoon limping around pitch after an early contact with Jordan Henderson.

It was T-shirt weather on a gloriously sunny day in Manchester, but in the first half the pitch frequently resembled a battlefield, with both teams of physios tending to their players. Roberto Firmino joined the departing wounded, having turned his ankle, and was replaced by Daniel Sturridge.

In the first minute, Ashley Young left a back-pass to David de Gea short and Firmino and Sadio Mané nearly capitalised; only quick reactions from the keeper prevented a clear opening. Shortly after, Joel Matip embarked on a mazy run and was barged to floor by Herrera on the edge of the area; but Mo Salah's free kick flew high into the Stretford End.

Then came the spate of injuries, which appeared to hamper both sides in the fluency of their play. The last of these came when Lingard – who had been a doubt anyway due to a previous hamstring problem – was brilliantly denied by Alisson when the Englishman looked to be rounding the keeper for a tap-in after a lovely disguised pass from Romelu Lukaku. His injury clearly aggravated again, Lingard was replaced by Alexis Sanchez.

Paul Pogba should have tested Alisson when unmarked from Young's free kick, but he was flagged offside anyway and this became something of a pattern, with good deliveries from set pieces by United not being matched by the positioning or control of the target players.

When, with 15 minutes left, they did finally get the ball past Alisson – Joel Matip turning Chris Smalling's cross into his own net – the result was the same. Smalling was fractionally beyond the last defender.

A point was enough to take Liverpool back above City and the away fans – who had given vigorous backing all game – continued with choruses of "Top of the League" and "Allez, Allez, Allez" long after the final whistle.

Jürgen Klopp reflected on a curious game: "The boys didn't feel okay. I could see it in their faces. It was strange. I was thinking, 'What is going on here today?'. They lost momentum and rhythm and couldn't really get it back. The performance was good enough for a draw at United. We'll take a point – it's more than a lot of people probably expected [given United's form]. The injuries cost us our rhythm. I'm not saying it should happen, but it did."

TEAMS

MANCHESTER UNITED
De Gea; Young, Smalling, Lindelöf, Shaw; Herrera (Pereira 21), McTominay, Pogba; Rashford Lukaku, Mata (Lingard 25 (Sanchez 43))

LIVERPOOL
Alisson: Milner, Matip, van Dijk, Robertson; Fabinho, Henderson (Shaqiri 72), Wijnaldum; Salah (Origi 79), Firmino (Sturridge 31), Mané

MATCH FACTS

- Jordan Henderson made his 300th Premier League appearance and his 400th in all club competitions.
- Liverpool played out back-to-back goalless draws for the first time since April 2013 (v West Ham and Reading).
- United were the first team to make all three substitutions in the first half of a Premier League game since Burnley in January 2015.

THEY SAID

James Milner: "A clean sheet is pleasing because it's not an easy place to come. We didn't get as many chances as we would have liked and we're disappointed not to win the game. Hopefully it's a good point come the end of the season."

WEDNESDAY 27 FEBRUARY 2019 | PREMIER LEAGUE | ANFIELD | ATTENDANCE: 53,316

LIVERPOOL 5
(Mané 9, 20, Origi 66, van Dijk 79, 82)
WATFORD 0

The Reds enjoyed a bumper return to goal-scoring form after two stalemates in a week, putting five past previously in-form Watford in a thrilling display of pace, power and pinpoint delivery.

He may not appear on the scoresheet but the star of the evening was Trent Alexander-Arnold, with three assists and countless contributions to Liverpool's attacking play.

His first creative intervention came on nine minutes. Shifting the ball to find a gap between two Watford defenders, his cross arrowed on to the head of Sadio Mané, who guided the ball into the top-left corner.

Mané – selected for the first time as a central striker by Jürgen Klopp – was determined to make the most of his outing and the next time he brought an Alexander-Arnold pass under control, his finish left Anfield purring with delight. As Watford keeper Ben Foster approached to narrow the angle, Mané – with his back to goal – snapped the ball into the turf with his heel and it lifted, like a perfect chip on a golf green, over Foster and into the net.

Mo Salah then took his turn for a little of the limelight. Soon after Foster gathered well from his low, fizzing shot from 20 yards, the Egyptian gathered in another inviting pass from Alexander-Arnold, rolled past Craig Cathcart and slipped the ball through the goalkeeper's legs. A rebound from Foster's right knee sent the ball against the inside of the post and only a timely intervention from Daryl Janmaat prevented Mané from having a tap-in for a hat-trick inside half an hour.

Watford enjoyed a little counter-play with half-time nearing – Joel Matip had to be on his toes to stop Gerard Deulofeu's cross from reaching strike partner Troy Deeney, then the Watford skipper did reach another pass from the Spaniard but his flick slid wide. Home keeper Alisson had been untroubled, though, and Liverpool looked fully in control of the match at the break.

Divock Origi – handed a rare start in the absence of Roberto Firmino – came to the party in the second half. The Belgian was deployed on the left and nearly set up Andy Robertson before having a couple of shots blocked, and then eased the Reds further ahead on 65 minutes. A quick shift of the ball sideways – via Fabinho, James Milner and Robertson – found Origi on the right flank. Janmaat looked to usher him inside and the striker accepted the invitation. Three touches opened up a shooting angle and a fourth powered the ball past Foster at the near post.

Watford boss Javi Gracia threw on Andre Gray for Deeney and he came closest to beating Alisson, but his effort from close range after Adam Masina's knock-down smacked into the keeper's shoulder and flew over the bar.

Finally, Virgil van Dijk profited from two more gorgeously measured crosses to treble his tally of Liverpool league goals in a matter of three minutes. Alexander-Arnold swung in a free kick from the right and the Dutchman climbed highest to head back across goal and in. Then he found the same corner from Robertson's lofted pass and peeled away in front of the Kop with two fingers raised to celebrate a rare double.

After his own salute to the Kop, the manager left the field with an arm round – and in deep conversation with – Alexander-Arnold, the youngster who was becoming an increasingly important cog in the Reds machine.

TEAMS

LIVERPOOL

Alisson; Alexander-Arnold, Matip, Van Dijk, Robertson; Fabinho, Wijnaldum (Keïta), Milner (Henderson 70); Salah, Mané (Lallana 78), Origi

WATFORD

Foster; Janmaat, Mariappa, Cathcart, Masina; Hughes, Capoue, Doucouré, Pereyra (Sema 84); Deulofeu (Cleverley 73), Deeney (Gray 73)

MATCH FACTS

- With a brace of goals, Sadio Mané achieved his best ever tally in a Premier League campaign (14).
- Mané had now scored in each of his last five home league matches.
- Divock Origi had direct involvement in 11 goals in his last 18 Premier League starts for Liverpool (seven goals, four assists).

THEY SAID

Javi Gracia: "We knew it would be a very demanding game. After conceding the first goal it was very difficult for us to compete. They dominated the game, I think they played really well and deserved the victory."

PREMIER LEAGUE TABLE AT END OF FEBRUARY 2019

Pos	Team	Pld	W	D	L	GF	GA	GD	Pts
1	Liverpool	28	21	6	1	64	15	49	69
2	Manchester City	28	22	2	4	75	20	55	68
3	Tottenham Hotspur	28	20	0	8	55	29	26	60
4	Arsenal	28	17	5	6	60	38	22	56
5	Manchester United	28	16	7	5	55	36	19	55
6	Chelsea	27	16	5	6	47	29	18	53
7	Wolverhampton Wanderers	28	11	7	10	35	35	0	40
8	Watford	28	11	7	10	39	40	-1	40
9	Everton	28	10	6	12	39	39	0	36
10	West Ham United	28	10	6	12	35	41	-6	36
11	Leicester City	28	10	5	13	34	39	-5	35
12	AFC Bournemouth	28	10	4	14	39	53	-14	34
13	Newcastle United	28	8	7	13	26	34	-8	31
14	Crystal Palace	28	8	6	14	32	38	-6	30
15	Burnley	28	8	6	14	31	50	-19	30
16	Brighton & Hove Albion	27	7	6	14	29	41	-12	27
17	Southampton	28	6	9	13	30	46	-16	27
18	Cardiff City	28	7	4	17	25	55	-30	25
19	Fulham	28	4	5	19	26	63	-37	17
20	Huddersfield Town	28	3	5	20	15	50	-35	14

UEFA CHAMPIONS LEAGUE ROUND OF 16 FIRST LEGS

Tuesday 12 February
Manchester United 0 Paris Saint-Germain 2
Roma 2 Porto 1

Wednesday 13 February
Tottenham Hotspur 3 Borussia Dortmund 0
Ajax 1 Real Madrid 2

Tuesday 19 February
Lyon 0 Barcelona 0
Liverpool 0 Bayern Munich 0

Wednesday 20 February
Schalke 2 Manchester City 3
Atletico Madrid 2 Juventus 0

CHAPTER EIGHT

—

MARCH

"DIG IN AND STAY IN.
THAT'S IT"

The "friendly derby"? Not so much, these days. But while there is plenty of competitive spikiness and banter surrounding fixtures between Liverpool and Everton, the two clubs still share more than separates them.

The proximity of geographical location is rare. In the league table of professional football neighbours in the UK, only Tannadice and Dens Park in Dundee are closer (for absolute accuracy, the City Ground and Meadow Lane in Nottingham are nearer than Anfield and Goodison as the crow flies, but you have to walk further to get across the River Trent). So a shared location, with fans of both clubs drawn from the same streets, same families – plus the fierce sense of community across Merseyside – lends a very different feel to the relationship of the clubs than that between, say, Tottenham and Arsenal.

That collective strength is telling from a historical perspective, too. Manchester may have been closing fast domestically over the past 25 years, but the city of Liverpool still boasts the highest number of English league titles (27) and the UK's most European trophies (12).

The lion's share of silverware resides, of course, in the Anfield trophy cabinet and the on-field battle has been lop-sided for some time now. At time of writing, another four months would make it 20 years since the Toffees came away from Anfield with a win, while their last win of any kind came in October 2010. But if there was no prospect for Everton of catching Liverpool this season, or adding to the overall Merseyside silverware haul, there was plenty of appetite to spoil the party, especially after the dramatic end to the sides' previous encounter at Goodison and Divock Origi's bizarre 96th-minute winner.

So there was much to ponder for visiting manager Jürgen Klopp as he assessed his options for the first game in March, a short hop across Stanley Park. "The Everton fans don't want us to win anything and probably for our fans it's the same," he mused pre-match. "In the game it's very emotional and passionate, and I hope it's like that again. That's how football should be. At Goodison, they really support their team so let's go there and use the atmosphere because it will be loud, it will be wild, and we have to deliver on the pitch."

Marco Silva's team were relying on that continued passion from the stands as these had been testing times in recent months. That late defeat at Anfield – after one of their best performances in years – seemed to put the skids under Everton's season. Thus a team that had won five of seven league games previously and was looking to consolidate a top-six spot went on to lose eight of the next 14 to sink into mid-table, and went out in the FA Cup fourth round to Millwall, at that time placed 19th in the Championship.

It was put to Silva whether the Liverpool result had an effect on his side in their subsequent run, a notion to which he played a straight bat. "It had an effect in that moment because we deserved more from the game," he said. "But if you're asking me if what we did in January or February is because of what we did in December, the answer is no. Maybe the week after, but after that, no. Each game is a new challenge. In the good moments and in the bad moments you have to react and show character and personality as a team. We have to work really hard – the players [on] the pitch, us [staff] and fans also."

But he was happy to counter when asked about Klopp's suggestion that the fixture was "like Everton's World Cup final". Rubbing his chin and smiling, Silva said: "For us, it's a special game, for both teams and for the city. But I didn't see a big difference [between the importance for either side]. They celebrated their lucky goal in the last second like it was the World Cup final for them."

Everton v Liverpool wasn't a fixture blessed with goals in recent years. You had to go back to 2013 for a game featuring more than two, and back three-and-a-half years even to find one with a goal inside normal time. As the rain tipped down on Merseyside, the scene wasn't exactly set for a feast of football but Toffees fans were looking for guts, passion and a result and they got what they wanted.

It had the customary fury-over-finesse derby opening, as Goodison roared its team on and the "travelling" fans roared back, with the only shape to the game emerging as Liverpool looked to work in tight spaces on the right flank. One such combination caused a moment of alarm as Jordan Henderson's cross nearly fell to Gini Wijnaldum, and another brought Jordan Pickford into play as Mo Salah twisted and turned but he hit his shot too straight to trouble the keeper.

Salah's best chance – the best of the whole match – came from a turnover in midfield as Fabinho closed down Morgan Schneiderlin to set the Egyptian through on goal. It was a chance he'd usually gobble up, but Pickford thrust out a hand to save.

Everton had fleeting moments in attack but nothing that really extended Alisson and though the Reds threatened – principally in a 15-minute spell either side of the hour – Michael Keane and Lucas Digne stepped in to thwart attempts from Salah and Fabinho respectively and you sensed it wasn't to be Liverpool's day. This time there was no late drama, no injury-time hero or villain.

Virgil van Dijk was a standout performer for Klopp's side, cruising effortlessly around the pitch, but cut a frustrated figure after the final whistle. "Of course [we are disappointed]," said the Dutchman. "We deserved the three points and it says a lot that they are celebrating. We had chances to win the game and did not finish them off. It is time to recover and be ready for the next game. Everyone wants to be top of the league and we cannot change the situation at the moment."

Understandably, writers on the red and blue sports desks at the *Liverpool Echo* took different perspectives on the outcome. Everton reporter Phil Kirkbride wrote: "This 0-0 was packed with the type of full-blooded and lung-bursting performances that meant Goodison barked like it hasn't for some time. Only a few weeks ago, [Everton fans] were questioning whether this type of performance could be summoned by this group of players and if the manager was able to motivate them to produce it. There were no such worries today. A growling Goodison fittingly erupted in defiance at the end, not only because their team had fought for a well-earned point but, no doubt, because of the dent it made in Liverpool's title chances."

Liverpool correspondent James Pearce was more downbeat: "Rather than show why they are 33 points better off than their neighbours, [Liverpool] slipped down to Everton's level. Predictably, Marco Silva's side raised their game – inspired by a raucous atmosphere [and] desperate to salvage something from a season of massive underachievement. But Everton were there for the taking, especially in the second half when they started to take more risks and left themselves exposed on the counter-attack. Nothing was decided at Goodison. This title race remains very much alive but the margin for error is now incredibly small."

Press attention in the wake of the derby stalemate inevitably focused on the difference between Liverpool's scoring prowess at Anfield and comparative struggles away from home. The stats made for a stark comparison: since the turn of the year Jürgen Klopp's men were averaging 2.6 goals per game at home (13 in 5) and 0.6 away (4 in 6). The tightness of the defence – leaking only four goals itself in those six away games – mitigated the potential losses to Manchester City in the title race, but the message was clear: the Reds needed more edge on the road.

With the benefit of hindsight, we can see that whatever Klopp decided to change and however it was implemented by his players – it worked. In the seven away games to the end of the season in all competitions, Liverpool scored 19 goals: 2.7 per game, a four-and-a-half-fold increase. Camp Nou aside, it was the key to keeping the Reds in the hunt for silverware right to the end of the season.

A home date with Burnley was next on the schedule, though, and given a rare full week to prepare, Klopp was keen to assess his midfield options from a near-full complement of players. Adam Lallana was fully fit and, having played late cameos in the last two games against Watford and Everton, was granted a starting berth, only his fourth league start of the season.

"Adam was the standout player in training," said Klopp. "Every player has to know that we watch and judge training. And if possible we show that. We saw it. A player with the ability and skills of Adam Lallana is a pure joy to watch when the fitness level is increasing and he is back on the pitch. It is clicking for him again. Adam is in a wonderful age group and when he is fit he is a fantastic player. That is the only thing I was waiting for. You cannot force that. You can only appreciate it when he is back."

Lallana's career at Anfield had been punctuated by injuries that, while not career-threatening, were often the kind of niggling muscular issues that prevented him from gaining momentum through a long run of games. But Klopp had always rated the England international highly for his quality and creativity on the ball. When the German first arrived at Anfield, Lallana started 15 of Klopp's first 17 games in charge before a calf strain intervened. When fit, he was always in the frame for selection.

Meanwhile, Alex Oxlade-Chamberlain had made a long-awaited comeback in an under-23s game against Derby on the Friday. The plan was to give him match time, as he had also impressed in training. However, excitement at the England international's recovery from knee surgery was tempered by the fact he was taken off "as a precaution", after motioning towards his right hamstring just a few minutes before his scheduled departure at half-time. The good news: there was no reaction from the repaired knee.

Klopp observed: "We were smart enough to take him off, even if it was only five minutes earlier than we thought. Maybe I'm a bit guilty for being too excited about it; if nobody asked me I wouldn't start talking about Ox, to be honest, but they ask me and I say the truth – and the truth was it looked so exciting in training. But it's only small-sided games, shooting situations and all that. It's Ox, we all know and love him, that's cool, but, at the end of the day, we all need to make sure we are ready."

The Ox wasn't ready yet. It would be exactly one year and a day since his knee injury that he would appear back in the first team, to a rapturous welcome against Huddersfield in late April and again on the final day against Wolves. This was a campaign of convalescence only for the midfielder.

For now, Lallana would make up a midfield three with Gini Wijnaldum and Fabinho – who adorned the matchday programme cover and was now looking every bit the thoroughbred central player Reds had hoped for after his signing from Monaco. Roberto Firmino was also match fit and came in for Divock Origi, reuniting the "MFS" front three.

Following the burst of springtime warmth in February, March was doing its best impression of winter, with freezing rain and a swirling wind on the Sunday morning of the match. The sun had broken through as the teams made their way out for a noon kick-off, but the weather still held a bit of everything in store: sleet, showers of hail, intermittent rain and all the while a blustering breeze around the stadium that made life difficult for attack and defence alike.

The conditions played a role in Burnley's opener, as Ashley Westwood's corner whipped in on the breeze, Alisson was hampered by the attentions of James Tarkowski and the ball flew untouched into the net.

All the goals except Mané's clincher at the death had an element of farce about them. Tarkowski and Burnley keeper Tom Heaton got in tangle to allow Mo Salah's cross to reach Roberto Firmino for a tap-in. Phil Bardsley dwelt on a clearance long enough for Lallana to block, the ball squirting via Charlie Taylor's tackle on Salah to Sadio Mané, who finished gratefully. And Heaton was again at fault for the third, hitting his clearance straight at Salah, who drew another superb tackle from the luckless Taylor, as a straightforward chance fell again to Firmino.

Sean Dyche's side capitalised on a freakish bounce off substitute Naby Keïta to close to 3-2 through Johann Berg Gudmundsson, but the outcome was settled via a classy through ball from Keïta's fellow sub Daniel Sturridge. The striker released Mané as Burnley pushed up and the Senegalese rounded Heaton to bag his second, Liverpool's fourth and his 50th goal in all competitions for the club.

Lallana was given the man-of-the-match award, not just for his feints and trickery – although there was much of that to admire – but for his tenacity and vigour in breaking up Burnley's play when out of possession. It was a superb all-round performance in midfield.

"It's good for the neutral and we're just going to enjoy it," he said post-match when asked about the title race. "City won yesterday and it was our job to put in a professional performance. I thought we showed great character after going one goal down and thoroughly deserved the win in the end. It has been a difficult 18 months, two years for me with injuries and I just want to contribute what will hopefully be an exciting end to the season. I enjoyed being out there."

Lallana wasn't the only Red relishing the limelight. Sadio Mané was in the form of his life in 2019 and being seen more and more by Liverpool fans as the key man in front of goal. With Mo Salah having a quiet time thus far in February and March, Mané seized his chance to make a difference. By now, he'd already sailed past his two previous totals for league goals under Jürgen Klopp (13 in 2016/17, 10 in 2017/18), and since the 4-3 win over Palace in mid-January, he'd only failed to score when everyone else had – against Man Utd, Bayern and Everton. Where he hadn't hit his straps in quite such style as in the last campaign was in the Champions League.

Mané terrorised Liverpool's opposition on the way to Kiev. While all three of Firmino, Salah and Mané hit double figures (a first for the competition from a single club), Mané played two games fewer and netted seven in the knockout stage alone. He bagged a hat-trick in Porto, scored in the decisive first half-hour against Man City, then registered in each leg of the semi-final against Roma and equalised in the final. It was a remarkable effort at the sharp end of the tournament.

But this season's competition to date had a very different edge to the gleeful romp of 2017/18. No thumpings of Maribor or Spartak Moscow, this time. Progression was hard-earned against Napoli, PSG and Red Star and now Bayern lay in wait, obdurate at Anfield and boasting an intimidating home record in Europe. Jürgen Klopp needed his big players to come to the party.

One of those key men – missing from the first leg through suspension but now available – was Virgil van Dijk, the defensive pack leader. Fabinho had deputised well in recording a clean sheet in the first leg, but it was still reassuring to see the Dutchman return to the Reds back-line.

"It is going to be an exciting tie," said van Dijk before leaving for Germany. "They played very well here, kept it tight especially at the back and obviously showed us a lot of respect. They changed a bit the way they played I think, so we need to be up for a big fight because they are probably going to come all-in, especially at the beginning."

He acknowledged that Liverpool had been below par in their away games in the group stage and would need to raise the level against Bayern.

"We need to do better," he said. "The group stage games were not as good as we wanted but we got through to the knockout phase. Now we have a 0-0 and we want to do everything that is possible to get through. We know it is going to be a very hard game."

There were some notable reunions in Bavaria: Jürgen Klopp was returning to the stage of some great duels during his time at Borussia Dortmund and to face some of the players who were pivotal in his success with *Der BVB*. The cornerstones of his two title triumphs were striker Robert Lewandowski and centre-half Mats Hummels, although this had been a tough week for Hummels, digesting the news that he – alongside Bayern teammates Thomas Müller and Jerome Boateng – would no longer be considered for selection by national coach Joachim Löw.

German football was going through a rare crisis of confidence. After a calamitous World Cup in Russia during which Löw's side exited at the group stage, *Die Mannschaft* then came bottom of their Nations League group, relegated to tier B by the Netherlands in Gelsenkirchen and a goal from a certain Virgil van Dijk. Now Schalke and Dortmund had been comfortably eliminated by Man City and Spurs in their round-of-16 ties, so Bayern were the last German team standing. By the end of the night, they'd be gone too; and the grim face of Löw in the Allianz stands told a tale of slipping standards at home, while one of their own was excelling overseas.

Klopp had been notably upbeat in the days before the match. "[I've loved coming] to the Allianz in the past," he said. "We celebrate the goals we scored and duels we won like winning the German Cup with Dortmund – we played great matches here. I'm [always] happy to pass by and see the red light of the Allianz [Arena]. It's always a sign a great match is ahead and I'm happy to be part of it."

Not everything went to plan – Jordan Henderson's influence in midfield was curtailed as early as six minutes in due to ankle trouble and though he hobbled around for a while trying to shake it off, he had to come off for Fabinho. But overall this was a princely showing from the Reds and – given the standard of the opposition – the best away performance of the season by a country mile.

The pick of the three goals was Mané's opener – a touch, turn and lob that defied understanding on first view. Watch it again and you'll see how he sends Rafinha and Niklas Süle one way, Manuel Neuer the other and then chips in, the whole move executed within the space of yard. Simply brilliant.

Van Dijk's header was a study in brute athleticism, as he towered above Hummels and Javi Martinez to convert James Milner's corner, while Mo Salah capped a night of quiet effectiveness by landing the ball cannily on Mané's head for the third.

A huge banner behind Alisson's goal read "Kampfen Bayern", urging the home team to fight, but there was no way back for the hosts.

High above the pitch, the travelling fans enjoyed the final stages, running through a selection of songs and unfurling a banner for van Dijk, drinking in the moment and echoes of 1981 in the same city, when Liverpool needed a result in the semi-final and got the job done then, too.

"We are back on the international map as a football club," enthused Klopp post-match. "I knew we had a chance – I didn't expect it – but the boys made it happen and it was really brilliant.

"It's massive – a big step for us. We will see what we can do with it but it's still fantastic for us that LFC as a club, we really are back for the last games of top international football. We all feel that's where this club belongs and we proved it at least a little bit."

Steve McManaman knows a thing or two about the Champions League, having won it twice during his time at Real Madrid, scoring in the 2000 final against Valencia with a superb volley. The former Red believes Mané's first goal was the catalyst for Liverpool's run to the final in the city he called home for four years.

"Liverpool have scored some great goals this season but that one was very classy and would be up there with the very best," said Macca. "And it was also a hugely important goal – it kick-started [the knockout stage]. It had, not just one, but three pieces of skill: the perfect touch and control under pressure from the defender; the awareness of the positions of keeper and defender and the way he turned away from them; and then the clever chip – cool as you like – left-footed into the open goal. It was more than an instinctive finish; it was actually very clever.

"Away from home the performances and results had been distinctly average," he added. "They lost in Napoli, at Red Star when everybody was beating them, and they were poor in Paris against PSG. So to go to Munich and win the game looked nigh on impossible [on the basis of form]. It was a huge test and they overcame a good Bayern team with an amazing history and unbelievable atmosphere inside the Allianz Arena, so all things considered it was an amazing result."

For the first time in a decade, four English teams were through to the quarter-finals, and this was also the first time since 2009 that neither Bayern nor Real would be in the semis. The last eight was wide open.

Back in Blighty, the fixture list threw up another convolution in the title race. With one pot already in the bag, Manchester City were still chasing an unprecedented quadruple and their FA Cup quarter-final clash with Swansea City fell on the weekend before the international break. That meant Liverpool could return to the top of the table with a win at Fulham on the Sunday, as the second Manchester derby of the season was bumped back to late April. But meantime the Sky Blues came oh-so close to going out against the Championship Swans. Pep's side were 2-0 down with 68 minutes gone before a late rally saw them through.

While we're on the subject of the FA Cup, Liverpool Women had lasted longer than the men in the 2018/19 edition, beating MK Dons and Millwall Lionesses to earn a spot in their own quarter-final, played on the same day as the men's visit to Fulham. No prizes for guessing who they ran into, though. In a season in which the two clubs seemed magnetically attracted to one another, the Reds were knocked out by Man City, 3-0 the scoreline at the Etihad Campus. And back at Anfield the U18s were taking on Watford in the FA Youth Cup semi-finals, enjoying a better outcome and running out 2-1 winners, thanks to a brace from hotly tipped young striker Paul Glatzel. They would, naturally, meet Manchester City in the final. But more of that in April.

To Craven Cottage, first, and a Fulham side looking squarely at the Premier League trapdoor. Scott Parker had been installed some three weeks previously, replacing Claudio Ranieri to become the Cottagers' third manager of the season. Down in 19th place in the table, they were 13 points from safety with eight games left – a near-impossible task. But that didn't mean they were going lie down and let the Reds enjoy a stroll by the Thames. Fulham had been much-improved in Parker's first game in charge, losing only narrowly to west London rivals Chelsea, and the players had much to prove to their new boss, not least ex-Red Ryan Babel who would have been anxious to impress against his old side.

Parker had no illusions about the scale of the task in this and subsequent matches, but he urged his team to play without fear. "It's a massive challenge [against] a team that are fighting at the right end of the table in terms of going for the championship, one full of individual quality that is up there with the world's best," he said. "But it's one we're looking forward to."

Five years previously, Steven Gerrard had memorably clinched a three points at the Cottage with a stoppage-time spot kick. Now Jürgen Klopp's men faced a similar predicament, needing a goal to stay in the title hunt, but with minds and legs tired after exertions in Munich and 80 further minutes of graft against a stubbornly resistant Fulham side.

Sadio Mané – who else? – had prised open the well-drilled Londoners' defence in the first half after a neat combination with Roberto Firmino, but the second goal wouldn't come and the precariousness of the lead was underlined with 15 minutes left when substitute James Milner's sliced clearance induced a mix-up between Virgil van Dijk and Alisson. Babel – following the classic "law of the ex" – nipped in to equalise.

Milner, though, soon atoned after Mané was tugged back in the box by Fulham keeper Sergio Rico. The Englishman struck his penalty down the middle as Rico dived to his right.

Van Dijk took responsibility for a rare but ultimately incidental error: "It's one of those situations where you try to head it back. The ball was a little too short and it was a difficult ball to get. Ryan was good to intercept the ball and score the goal," he told liverpoolfc.com.

"It gave them some belief but obviously that happens sometimes in games. Mistakes are a part of football, you have to take it and I will as well."

As the Reds completed their league fixtures in the capital – unbeaten in six in 2018/19 – the *London Evening Standard*'s David Lynch gave credit to Milner for his mental fortitude. "If ever there was any doubt, today proved it: there aren't many players in the Premier League as mentally strong as James Milner," wrote Lynch. "How easy it would have been for the Reds vice-captain to retreat into his shell after teeing up a Fulham equaliser with his very first touch after coming on. But when the chance to win the game came just minutes later, Milner stepped up to pass the ball in and collect all three points for his side. It was the perfect way to make amends for his mistake and said everything about the Englishman's character."

For a couple of weeks at least, Liverpool would be top, before Fulham hosted Manchester City on the Saturday after the international break and the Reds welcomed Tottenham to Anfield on the Sunday.

Among the headlines as national teams convened for Euro 2020 qualifiers and friendlies were Gini Wijnaldum and Virgil van Dijk both scoring in a 4-0 win over Belarus (Virgil's late effort was his fourth goal in six games), although both were then on the losing side against Germany in Amsterdam.

Young Reds were also in action, notably for Wales, for whom Ben Woodburn scored an injury-time winner against Trinidad & Tobago, while Harry Wilson, on loan at Derby, played 87 minutes of the 1-0 win over Slovakia in the first qualifier for Ryan Giggs' side.

Trent Alexander-Arnold withdrew from the England squad with a back problem and returned to Melwood for treatment, but Jordan Henderson was fully recovered from the ankle injury he sustained in Munich and earned his 49th and 50th caps for England in comfortable wins over the Czech Republic and Montenegro.

He reflected on how he had adapted his game to meet the demands of both club and country.

"Football always changes," he said. "There are always new players coming in at your club or with England. You have to be ready, given 100 per cent, improve and get better. It's about moving forward and going in the right direction and you don't want to be left behind, by any means. I want to improve every season, every training session. I'll continue that until I finish my career.

"My role has changed within the Liverpool team," he added. "I've adapted and improved. I can do that [holding] role, but prior to that I was a more offensive, box to box. I can do both roles.

"I can contribute in the final third a lot more than I did. But I can do the defensive role, the number 6, and be disciplined and protect. It's about what the manager asks me to do."

Looking forward, he said Liverpool's improvements under Jürgen Klopp – and near misses in two European finals – would drive him to extra effort in search of silverware.

"It gives you even more motivation to then keep going, keep wanting to be in that position again to make it right, and go that final step, really," he said. "Maybe I had a little taste of it playing in finals but I haven't really managed to win the big trophies, and that's the next step.

"That's what us as players want to do, for us as a team and for the fans as well, for the whole club. But when you play for Liverpool there's always pressure, pressure to perform, expectation. Of course, that's the reason why you want to go there. We've put ourselves in a great position to compete. And now it's down to us to just keep going."

Keep going. The mantra for a campaign against a relentless title rival – a campaign in which no one scored more injury-time goals than the Reds. So it was again versus Tottenham, who had been challengers themselves around Christmas but who had slumped alarmingly since mid-February with defeats to Burnley, Chelsea and Southampton, picking up only one point from a possible 12 with a draw in the north London derby at Wembley.

Crystal Palace's FA Cup quarter-final against Watford meant their scheduled game against Tottenham on 17 March was postponed (and would now be the first played at Spurs' new stadium). The relevance to this game against Liverpool was that the visitors hadn't taken the field for three weeks since losing to Southampton at St Mary's. They were itching to get back in the fray.

This was Anfield's designated "Kick It Out" match, with the players warming up in T-shirts emblazoned with the logo of the organisation that for 25 years has been dedicated to combating discrimination in football. The timing was particularly acute, as England's game in Montenegro six days before had been marred by racist chanting aimed towards Raheem Sterling and Danny Rose.

"[Danny] is okay," said Spurs boss Mauricio Pochettino when asked about his full-back pre-match. "We wanted to show support to him but also to Sterling and not only to players. We need to talk about the abuse that people [suffer] every day, all over the world." Rose had previously gone on record about his distress at racism in football and, five days after this game, would claim he "couldn't wait to see the back of [football]" due to racism's malign influence.

"People don't deserve to be abused and we need to fight against it," Pochettino added. "That these situations are still happening in 2019 – I can't believe it. It's in our hands to stop it."

Reds captain Jordan Henderson had been on the pitch as matters turned ugly at the end of the match in Podgorica and made his point in the matchday programme that there was no place for abuse in football.

"The atmosphere… today will no doubt be raucous and passionate, but I'm sure for both supporters of Liverpool and Spurs it will be about supporting their own team and not targeting hate at the opposition," he wrote. "It's one of the things I most love about playing at Anfield – the vast majority of the songs you hear are in support of Liverpool and that's how it should always be."

The Reds faithful didn't disappoint. This was one of the loudest afternoons of the entire season, with most of the songbook getting an airing on the Kop. Roberto Firmino received a rapturous serenade of "Si, Señor" after his first-half opener, and "Mo Salah, Mo Salah" (to the tune of James's "Sit Down") echoed around the arena on the Egyptian's eventual substitution in stoppage time.

In between times there was the small matter of trying to beat a top-level Premier League opponent and it came down to fractions. Either side could have won it after Lucas Moura equalised on 70 minutes, following quick thinking from Harry Kane at a free kick and a smart shift of the ball from Kieran Trippier to Christian Eriksen to create the chance.

Jürgen Klopp urged his players forwards and Spurs' Moussa Sissoko had a wonderful chance on the break, surging forwards with Son Heung-Min in support and only Virgil van Dijk to defend the two-on-one situation. The Dutchman did brilliantly, though, blocking the pass to Son and inviting Sissoko to shoot with his left foot. The effort sailed over Alisson's bar.

Still Liverpool pressed and as the game ticked into overtime Salah – aided by an error from Hugo Lloris – secured the points. A Trent Alexander-Arnold corner was headed powerfully away by Harry Kane, but Andy Robertson returned the ball straight to his fellow full-back. A looping first-time cross found Salah at the back post and his header was dropped by Lloris on to the shin of Toby Alderweireld, from where it dribbled gently over the line. Anfield erupted.

"The whole stadium... it was the best performance of a Liverpool crowd after an equaliser since I arrived," Klopp said, after emerging from the dressing room. "The crowd was outstanding – incredible atmosphere. They were really here to push us and at the end it helped. I said to the lads there are 500 ways to win a football game and today was slightly ugly. Who cares in the end? Who cares?"

Although Mo Salah wasn't credited with the winning goal, his key contribution was lauded by the fans, as were his efforts throughout the match. He said the vocal support played a huge part in Liverpool's habit of late wins.

"It's a big difference, especially if you see the fans after the game – it was crazy," Salah told Sky Sports. "They just really want to win the Premier League and we'll do everything to make that happen. They help us a lot during the game, the atmosphere and they push you hard to create chances and play better.

"Big teams always find a way to get the points. Maybe in the second half we didn't play at the top of our game but we won the game and that's the most important thing. That's a big team – you always have to find a way to win and that's what we did."

The match-up on the flanks between Liverpool's full-backs and Tottenham's wing-backs had been fascinating – a high-risk strategic ploy in the first half by Pochettino to deploy Danny Rose and Kieran Trippier high up the pitch allowed space behind in which Alexander-Arnold and Robertson could roam. And although the Spurs boss limited those avenues after the break, the pair still combined to lay on the winner.

The development of the two full-backs this season has been marvelled at by a former occupant of the right-back berth at Anfield, one who was there the last time Liverpool lifted the league title in 1990. Barry Venison now resides in Los Angeles, working as a coach at USL Championship team Orange County Blues, and he believes the quality of the current Liverpool side's wide defenders is on a par with any that he's seen.

"The full-backs have stood out all season the way Klopp has them set up, producing more assists than anyone else," says Barry, who was the same age, 20, as Trent Alexander-Arnold when he captained Sunderland in the 1985 League Cup final. "What is simply staggering is that it has not compromised their defending, which means they have to have such incredible physical qualities as well as technical abilities. Their understanding with Salah and Mané, the way the attacking players can dovetail by going wide is a testimony to how they have gelled on the pitch and it looks very much as if they have a good relationship off the pitch as well.

"When I was the full-back at the club I had certain gifts but my main priority was defending first and then attacking when I could," he adds. "These fellows are different. They do both without compromising either the supply of chances of their defensive duties, which means they have a great understanding with their centre-halves; and I cannot overstate how this has worked this season, it has been a stand out feature of the season."

MARCH MATCH REPORTS

SUNDAY 3 MARCH 2019 | PREMIER LEAGUE | GOODISON PARK | ATTENDANCE: 39,335

EVERTON 0
LIVERPOOL 0

Everton and Liverpool fought to a standstill at Goodison, allowing Manchester City to keep top position in the league for the first time since 7 December with both sides having played the same number of games.

On a dank late afternoon on Merseyside, the home crowd summoned a broiling, pulsating atmosphere but neither side was able to supply the vital touch whenever the goal beckoned.

Jordan Pickford, the unfortunate fall guy of the piece when the sides met at Anfield, redeemed himself here with a crucial stop from Mo Salah in the first half, while two pieces of last-ditch defending from the Toffees kept Liverpool out after the break.

Both managers made one change from their previous line-ups: Marco Silva brought in Bernard for Richarlison to play on the left of an attacking midfield three; Jürgen Klopp swapped Jordan Henderson in for James Milner in central midfield. Roberto Firmino was deemed fit enough for the bench, so Sadio Mané continued at centre-forward, with Divock Origi on the left.

Amid typically high-speed derby exchanges early on, the lavishly bearded Theo Walcott picked up a booking on six minutes for dragging back Origi, as the Reds looked to break after a long Everton throw in the box. Then Virgil van Dijk scooped a dangerous ball from Gylfi Sigurdsson behind after the Icelander was played in by Dominic Calvert-Lewin.

Liverpool's first sniff of goal came shortly afterwards, when Jordan Henderson found space to lift a cross towards Origi. Seamus Coleman managed to hold up the bigger man and the rebound fell on to Gini Wijnaldum's foot with no time to react, so Pickford was able to claim.

The England goalkeeper might then have been made to work harder by Salah, but after a jink left, right and left again, the Egyptian's strike flew down the centre of the goal. And Pickford was also alert to Michael Keane's back header, which narrowly evaded the attentions of Mané.

But the best of the stopper's work came with half an hour approaching. Morgan Schneiderlin's loose touch in centre-field allowed Fabinho to play in Salah first time and the forward bore down on goal with the covering defence nowhere near. Salah aimed for the far post but at a height where the goalkeeper was able to stick out a palm and push the ball away. Henderson's follow-up was blocked by a convergence of three Everton defenders and Coleman whacked his clearance upfield.

Walcott managed to get goalside of Andy Robertson from a long ball forward from Keane, but fired high into the stands with better options inside.

In the second period, Calvert-Lewin drew a good save from Alisson after connecting well with a header from Lucas Digne's corner and on the hour came the first of those two aforementioned tackles. Joel Matip strode into midfield and released Salah into the box where he appeared odds-on to score, but his first touch was fractionally heavy and allowed Keane to leap into a brilliant saving challenge, nipping the ball off the striker's toe.

Milner replaced Wijnaldum and Firmino came on for Origi and the latter came close to an assist for Mané, but the Brazilian's cross was just too high to head goalwards. On 69 minutes came the second crucial clearance. A wonderfully flighted pass from Robertson found van Dijk, who held off the attentions of Sigurdsson to nod back across goal. Fabinho brought the ball down on his thigh, but just far enough to the right that Digne was able to hook his foot around it and concede only a corner.

No further clear chances accrued, although Firmino had a shot blocked after a scramble in the box, while Trent Alexander-Arnold brought down Digne centimetres outside the area at the other end. The Frenchman's free kick drifted harmlessly out of play.

At the final whistle it was another stalemate – three now in four games in all competitions – and the Reds were playing catch-up.

TEAMS

EVERTON

Pickford; Coleman, Keane, Zouma, Digne; Gueye, Schneiderlin (Gomes 76); Walcott (Richarlison 59), Sigurdsson, Bernard; Calvert-Lewin (Tosun 74)

LIVERPOOL

Alisson; Alexander-Arnold, Matip, van Dijk, Robertson; Henderson, Fabinho, Wijnaldum (Milner 63); Mané (Lallana 84), Salah, Origi (Firmino 63)

MATCH FACTS

- This was the 100th Merseyside derby to be held at Goodison.
- Thirty-four of the 200 league meetings between Liverpool and Everton had now finished goalless, 15 more than any other English league fixture.
- Mo Salah had gone three games without a league goal for the first time since joining Liverpool.

THEY SAID

Jordan Henderson: "We are disappointed because we wanted to come here and get three points, but we knew it would be tough and frantic. I felt we created enough chances to win. We just need to be a bit more clinical."

SUNDAY 10 MARCH 2019 | PREMIER LEAGUE | ANFIELD | ATTENDANCE: 53,310

LIVERPOOL 4
(Firmino 19, 67, Mané 29, 90+3)
BURNLEY 2
(Westwood 6, Berg Gudmundsson 90+1)

A brace apiece from Roberto Firmino and Sadio Mané helped Liverpool dispatch a spirited Burnley side, who led early at Anfield but were masters of their own downfall as three defensive lapses were ruthlessly punished by the Reds.

On Saturday, Raheem Sterling's 13-minute hat-trick against Watford had extended Manchester City's lead at the top of the table to four points, so only a win would do for Jürgen Klopp's men, the task made that bit harder when the visitors opened the scoring with just five minutes played.

Despite losses against Newcastle and Crystal Palace in their last two league games, Burnley were unchanged on Merseyside. In fact, manager Sean Dyche had made only three changes to his team in the league since new year. Centre-half Ben Mee had played every minute in 2019, and the team's last nine goals had come from the strike pair of Chris Wood and Ashley Barnes. This was Dyche's first XI and they knew their jobs.

So it was something of a surprise to see midfielder Ashley Westwood on the scoresheet, his first Burnley goal sailing in directly from a corner. Reds keeper

Alisson was furious with the referee, believing himself to have been impeded, unable to punch clear while sandwiched between Jack Cork and James Tarkowski. The swirling wind around Anfield didn't help, either, and – despite sunshine at kick-off after a morning of freezing rain – as the players reconvened for the restart, sleet began to fall. It was a day to be well covered up.

Thankfully for Liverpool, if the officials were generous in the award of Burnley's goal, the visiting defence was also in the mood for handing out gifts. There seemed little danger from Mo Salah's centre after a one-two with Gini Wijnaldum; but keeper Tom Heaton and Tarkowski somehow allowed the ball to slide between them to Firmino, who was standing one foot in front of an empty net.

Adam Lallana – starting only his fourth league game of the season – had been tidy in possession but it was his lesser-heralded combative qualities that led to Liverpool's second. Burnley right-back Phil Bardsley was lining up a routine clearance from the edge of his own box when Lallana sensed an opportunity to close down and threw himself in front of the defender. The ball pinged back into the box, where Salah reacted first; and despite Charlie Taylor nipping the ball away from the Egyptian, it landed perfectly for Mané to sweep first time into the far corner. Although there was some luck in where the initial ricochet fell, as Lallana punched the air you could see how much it meant on his return to have conjured a goal from nothing.

The conditions – hailstones and a howling gale – continued to affect the play, meaning a scrappy end to the half, but Liverpool broadly in control as the players sought sanctuary in the dressing rooms.

Burnley began the second half brighter, giving Joel Matip and Virgil van Dijk some uncomfortable moments, but Salah soon sparked into life again. One shot curled just wide of the far post, then Firmino's cross-shot bisected Salah and the same post, with Heaton scrambling urgently across goal.

The front three were linking dangerously but it was another error that allowed the hosts to open a two-goal cushion. Heaton's scuffed clearance went straight to Salah and though Taylor again put in a brilliant, last-ditch tackle, he could only look on in dismay as the ball rolled out for Firmino to nudge in with the outside of his right boot.

Jordan Henderson came on for Wijnaldum, while Naby Keïta replaced Lallana, and Peter Crouch was afforded a warm welcome on his introduction from the bench for Chris Wood, but the former Red couldn't find a route to goal.

The game appeared to be winding down until Mané struck the bar in trying to convert Trent Alexander-Arnold's wicked delivery and then, in added time, Burnley's two other subs – Matěj Vydra and Johann Berg Gudmundsson – combined after a deflection off Keïta for the latter to halve the deficit from close range.

A few nerves were jangling with four minutes still to play, but Mané sealed the points, accepting a Daniel Sturridge pass through the middle to round Heaton and calmly slide his finish home.

TEAMS

LIVERPOOL
Alisson; Alexander-Arnold (Sturridge 86), Matip, Van Dijk, Robertson; Fabinho, Wijnaldum (Henderson 69), Lallana (Keïta 76); Mané, Firmino, Salah

BURNLEY
Heaton; Bardsley, Tarkowski, Mee, Taylor; McNeil, Westwood, Cork, Hendrick (Gudmundsson 79); Wood (Crouch 79), Barnes (Vydra 86)

MATCH FACTS

- Sadio Mané became the fifth Liverpool player to score in six consecutive home Premier League appearances (also Michael Owen, Fernando Torres, Luis Suarez and Mo Salah).
- Roberto Firmino had now contributed to 100 goals under Jürgen Klopp (63 goals, 37 assists), more than any other player in that time.
- Ashley Westwood scored his first goal since April 2016, when he had scored twice for Aston Villa against Southampton.

THEY SAID

Burnley manager Sean Dyche: "It was tricky. The wind was swirling. We wanted to ask questions and get the ball forward which I thought we did in spells. You cannot give a team like Liverpool four goals – we certainly gave them three. You can question the errors but we made a game of it. In the first half I don't think they had too many golden chances yet we were

2-1 down. Even at 3-1, the mentality of the group was good and we got a goal back."

WEDNESDAY 13 MARCH 2019 | UEFA CHAMPIONS LEAGUE ROUND OF 16
ALLIANZ ARENA | ATTENDANCE: 68,145

BAYERN MUNICH 1
(Matip og 39)
LIVERPOOL 3
(Mané 26, 84, van Dijk 69)
(1-3 aggregate)

Liverpool stunned the Allianz Arena with a display of power and precision to advance to the Champions League quarter-finals. Two goals from Sadio Mané and one from Virgil van Dijk earned a 3-1 aggregate success, inflicting a rare home defeat upon German champions Bayern.

In the Bündesliga, Niko Kovač's team had lost once at home all season, and in the five and a half years since Manuel Pellegrini's Man City beat Pep Guardiola's Bayern in December 2013, the Germans had only lost on home soil in the Champions League to Real Madrid. Each of those three times was in the semi-final and each time Real went on to win the cup. Only the very best prosper in Munich.

Added to that, the (English) Reds had only scored once in three previous away games and had lacked sparkle on their travels in Group C, so Bayern had reasonable grounds for confidence. But fellow Premier League teams had already shown the way in this season's round of 16. Manchester United had improbably – and with a little help from VAR – overcome a 2-0 deficit to win 3-1 away and knock out Paris Saint-Germain, while Man City and Tottenham had both disposed of German opposition in Schalke and Borussia Dortmund respectively. Plus, Real Madrid were already gone, stunned by Ajax in the Bernabéu.

Jürgen Klopp made two changes to his starting XI, bringing in James Milner, who had shaken off a muscle strain, and Jordan Henderson to captain the side, but the plan in midfield was disrupted early when Henderson went down early with an ankle problem after a collision with James Rodriguez. The Englishman struggled on for several minutes but eventually accepted he could not continue and was replaced by Fabinho.

Meanwhile, the anticipated clash between Virgil van Dijk and Robert Lewandowski was shaping up nicely. The Pole went down in the box after being muscled off the ball by the Dutchman, but despite Lewandowski's protests and howls from the stands, referee Daniele Orsato saw nothing wrong with the challenge.

Liverpool's first half-chance came when Mo Salah hooked a ball forward on 24 minutes and Roberto Firmino – playing up against a former teammate from his Hoffenheim days in Niklas Süle – took an early shot that hummed past Manuel Neuer's near post. Just over a minute later, though, the visitors were ahead.

Virgil van Dijk's long ball forward looked more hopeful than penetrative, but three surgical touches from Sadio Mané turned it into a goal of the highest class. His first to collect the ball wrongfooted the defence and alarmed Neuer so much the keeper came rushing out of his goal, the second took Mané on the spin past Neuer and the third lobbed the covering defence to land a finish gently in the far corner. It was moment of chilling precision and an away goal for the Reds to cherish.

Mané threatened again in combination with Andy Robertson, the Scot skating into the box on to a well-weighted pass and testing Neuer at his near post with a firm rap from his left foot. The German extended a big forearm to clear for a corner.

Robertson had his hands full at the other end, though, with pacy winger Serge Gnabry, and six minutes before half-time Bayern were level after excellent work from the former Arsenal man. Another long ball – in this instance from Süle – caused the problem, as Gnabry snuck goalside of Robertson, and his cross would have been a tap-in for Lewandowksi but for Joel Matip, who could only toe-end the ball into his own net.

With the tie poised only marginally in Liverpool's favour, the second half began scrappily, as if neither side quite knew whether to press or be patient. Mo Salah drove forward in a counter-attack and belted a shot at Neuer that the keeper punched clear, while Gnabry again teased a dangerous ball into the six-yard box after being played in by Franck Ribéry. This time there was no touch and the ball flew across goal and away.

On 67 minutes, Trent Alexander-Arnold swung in a corner that Neuer had to claw behind under pressure from Matip, and from James Milner's delivery from the other side, van Dijk rose above Mats Hummels and Javi Martínez to thump a header down into the bottom left corner.

Salah might have finished the job but Süle nipped the ball off his toe as he was about to shoot after a mazy run, but the Egyptian then supplied a perfect lofted pass – flipped with the outside of the boot – for Mané to nod home and seal the win.

TEAMS

BAYERN MUNICH

Neuer; Rafinha, Süle, Hummels, Alaba; Thiago, Martínez (Goretzka 72); Gnabry, Rodriguez (Sanches 79), Ribéry (Coman 61); Lewandowski

LIVERPOOL

Alisson; Alexander-Arnold, Matip, Van Dijk, Robertson; Milner (Lallana 87), Wijnaldum, Henderson (Fabinho 13); Mané, Firmino (Origi 83), Salah

MATCH FACTS

• Liverpool were now unbeaten in 10 clashes with German teams and had lost just one of 19 games since 1977 (4-2 to Bayer Leverkusen in 2002).
• No Liverpool player had scored more away goals in European Cup/Champions League history than Sadio Mané (7).
• No one had more assists in this year's competition than James Milner (10).

THEY SAID

Bayern centre-half Mats Hummels: "I know Jürgen Klopp [from when I played under him at Dortmund]. He is very good at eliminating the opponents' strengths and he showed that again today. The [second goal] took away our belief. After that, Liverpool was the better team."

SUNDAY 17 MARCH | PREMIER LEAGUE | CRAVEN COTTAGE | ATTENDANCE: 25,043

FULHAM 1
(Babel 74)
LIVERPOOL 2
(Mané 26, Milner pen 81)

The Reds were made to battle on St Patrick's Day by a gutsy Fulham side who may be doomed to relegation but weren't going quietly. A late penalty converted by James Milner secured the points, but it was a nervy final quarter-hour by the Thames, after former Red Ryan Babel drew the home side level courtesy of a rare mix-up between Alisson and Virgil van Dijk.

Two changes for Liverpool brought Fabinho in for the injured Jordan Henderson and Adam Lallana – again in the Premier League starting XI – for James Milner. Scott Parker was still searching for the right blend in defence and pulled Arsenal loanee Calum Chambers back from midfield to centre-half and introduced Timothy Fosu-Mensah at right back, replacing Denis Odoi.

Clear chances were few in a scruffy opening 20 minutes. Home midfielder Jean Michaël Seri curled a long-ranger towards goal but it dipped too late, while Mo Salah and Trent Alexander-Arnold were combining well on the right flank but prevented from threatening Sergio Rico's goal by good defensive organisation. The disjointedness of the match was rather summed up by Lallana and Salah running into one another as Roberto Firmino tried to play a cute pass on the left edge of the box.

Better was to follow shortly. Sadio Mané played a one-two with Firmino and the Brazilian cut the ball back from the byline to the Senegalese, who finished crisply, Lallana hopping out of the way at the last second to avoid another collision.

Andy Robertson explored the same avenue but, with a route for a cutback blocked, he shot for the far corner and Rico blocked with his knee. Former Red Ryan Babel then went on a jinking run to set up Tom Cairney at the other end; but Cairney's effort was wastefully high.

Firmino tried a cheeky back-heel from Gini Wijnaldum's driven cross early in the second half, then Wijnaldum himself had half an opportunity but couldn't get over a header from Robertson's cross. Virgil van Dijk hit the target with his head from Fabinho's cross but the effort was pushed away by Rico. Despite plenty of pressure and the vast majority of possession, a settling second goal wouldn't arrive.

Fulham thought they'd equalised when André Zambo Anguissa's deflected shot was nodded home by Floyd Ayité but the latter was given offside. Then Anguissa tested Alisson with a low shot saved to the keeper's left. The warnings were there.

Milner was brought on for Lallana, but his first act was to slice a clearance high in the air leading to confusion between van Dijk and Alisson. The defender urged the keeper to come, eventually headed it back but left it short and Babel picked up the deflection off Alisson's clearance to walk the ball into an unguarded net.

Soon, though, Milner had a chance to redeem himself. Salah stung the palms of Rico with a shot from the right edge of the area and, as Mané seized on the rebound, the goalkeeper hooked out an arm to pull him back. Penalty. Milner thumped his spot kick down the middle in front of the gleeful travelling support.

TEAMS

FULHAM
Rico; Fosu-Mensah (Christie 73), Chambers, Ream, Bryan; Seri (Sessegnon 65), Anguissa, Babel, Cairney (Kebano 82), Ayité; Mitrović

LIVERPOOL
Alisson; Alexander-Arnold, Matip, van Dijk, Robertson; Wijnaldum, Fabinho (Origi 72), Lallana (Milner 72); Mané, Firmino, Salah (Sturridge 90+2)

MATCH FACTS

- Sadio Mané reached 20 goals in all competitions for the season – 11 in his last 11 games.
- James Milner extended his record to 51 of never losing a Premier League game in which he had scored.
- Virgil van Dijk had now captained Liverpool in eight matches and won all eight.

THEY SAID

James Milner: "The gaffer told me to come on and calm it down and the first thing I do is slice it and put Virgil under pressure, which wasn't ideal. [But] the goal was important to put away. You have to go back to what you practise, be calm and do what you do."

SUNDAY 31 MARCH 2019 | PREMIER LEAGUE | ANFIELD | ATTENDANCE: 53,322

LIVERPOOL 2
(Firmino 16, Alderweireld og 90)
TOTTENHAM HOTSPUR 1
(Moura 70)

Another late goal decided a thrilling encounter between second and third in the league, with Liverpool leapfrogging Manchester City back to the top of the table having played one game more. An injury-time error from Hugo Lloris was the decisive moment, his spill from Mo Salah's header rebounding off the luckless Toby Alderweireld and into the net at the Kop end.

The match could have gone either way, with both teams having chances at 1-1, and Spurs were left to rue the missed opportunity with five minutes left when Moussa Sissoko broke clear late on but couldn't hit the target.

Visiting manager Mauricio Pochettino had three fitness concerns, two stemming from the international break as both Eric Dier and Serge Aurier were now unfit for selection, joining Harry Winks on the treatment table. And he also had to watch the match from the stands, serving the second of a two-match ban for his confrontation with referee Mike Dean after the defeat to Burnley.

For the hosts, Trent Alexander-Arnold had recovered from his back problem to start and Xherdan Shaqiri was back from a groin strain, so earned a place on the bench. Jordan Henderson and James Milner both started in place of Fabinho and Adam Lallana.

Lucas Moura – selected ahead of Son Heung-Min in a front three for Spurs – was lively early on, twice twisting to gain a yard of space on the edge of the area but both times crowded out.

The opener came on 16 minutes through a sumptuous cross from Andy Robertson, the Scot tirelessly working the left channel and finding Roberto Firmino in between the centre-halves. Unmarked, the striker nodded firmly down past Hugh Lloris.

Firmino then turned provider, dropping deep to measure an inch-perfect pass for Mo Salah, but Davidson Sanchez slid in with a well-timed tackle.

After the half-hour the two teams traded long-range efforts, Dele Alli catching a sweet volley that dipped over Alisson's bar and Sadio Mané curling an effort narrowly wide of the right-hand post.

Spurs needed a change to disrupt Liverpool's first-half dominance and it came not with personnel but in rearranging their shape, with Jan Vertonghen moving over to left-back in a back four, and Rose pushing up to the left of an attacking three behind Harry Kane.

It worked, and though the Reds forged a good chance from a well-worked corner routine through Alexander-Arnold and Milner – Virgil van Dijk heading over at the far post – the visitors grew much more into the game.

Harry Kane swerved past van Dijk to power in a shot that Alisson beat away and Robertson threw himself in front of Christian Eriksen as the Dane seemed certain to convert the rebound. Then Kane, having been fouled on halfway, was alert to the space on the right for Trippier. His quick diagonal was slid on by the full-back to Eriksen and on again to Moura, who fired past Alisson for a deserved leveller.

Son was now on for Tottenham, while Origi and Fabinho were the attacking introductions for Klopp, Henderson and Milner making way in the frantic push for a winner.

Spaces were opening up all over the pitch and Anfield held its breath as Sissoko galloped towards goal with Son alongside and lone defender van Dijk hedging his bets between the two. It proved an inspired piece of defending. Judging Son the greater threat, the Dutchman kept the Korean in his vision until Sissoko ran out of choices. Forced to shoot with his weaker, left foot, the midfielder struck his effort high into the Anfield Road End.

In the first minute of injury time, Alexander-Arnold's corner was cleared by Kane but found its way back to him via Robertson. Given a second chance, he floated the ball over the crowd scene to where Salah was prowling at the far post. Lloris dropped the Egyptian's header and Toby Alderweireld was powerless to stop the ball hitting his shin and rolling gently into the net.

As the crowd went wild, Klopp's celebrations were surprisingly muted. He turned to the main stand and held a hand over the club crest, a picture of exhausted relief amid the tumult.

TEAMS

LIVERPOOL

Alisson; Alexander-Arnold, Van Dijk, Matip, Robertson; Milner (Fabinho 77),
Wijnaldum, Henderson (Origi 77); Mané, Firmino, Salah (Lovren 90+4)

TOTTENHAM

Lloris; Vertonghen, Sanchez (Son 69), Alderweireld; Trippier, Sissoko, Eriksen (Llorente 90+1), Alli, Rose; Lucas (Davies 82), Kane

MATCH FACTS

- The Reds' two goals in this match made it 400 in all competitions under Jürgen Klopp.
- Roberto Firmino had now scored seven goals in his last six Premier League games at Anfield, as many as in his previous 25.
- Liverpool's total of 79 points was their best tally after 32 matches of a top-flight season (adjusting to three points for a win), surpassing the 76 they had in 1987/88.

THEY SAID

Trent Alexander-Arnold: "They're a top side, Tottenham. I think we wanted it maybe more than them and that showed at the end. Virgil did very well when it was two against one [with Sissoko and Son] – he's probably the best defender in the world – and that gave us the confidence to go on and win the game. The cross [for the winner] was a bit floaty, but when it's a second ball you look to stand one up to the far post, so I tried to put it in an area. We got a bit fortunate but you need that to win these types of games."

PREMIER LEAGUE TABLE AT END OF MARCH 2019

Pos	Team	Pld	W	D	L	GF	GA	GD	Pts
1	Liverpool	32	24	7	1	72	19	53	79
2	Manchester City	31	25	2	4	81	21	60	77
3	Tottenham Hotspur	31	20	1	10	58	34	24	61
4	Manchester United	31	18	7	6	60	41	19	61
5	Arsenal	30	18	6	6	63	39	24	60
6	Chelsea	31	18	6	7	52	34	18	60
7	Wolverhampton Wanderers	31	12	8	11	38	38	0	44
8	Leicester City	32	13	5	14	42	43	-1	44
9	Everton	32	12	7	13	45	42	3	43
10	Watford	31	12	7	12	43	46	-3	43
11	West Ham United	32	12	6	14	41	48	-7	42
12	AFC Bournemouth	32	11	5	16	43	58	-15	38
13	Crystal Palace	31	10	6	15	38	41	-3	36
14	Newcastle United	31	9	8	14	31	40	-9	35
15	Brighton & Hove Albion	30	9	6	15	32	43	-11	33
16	Southampton	31	8	9	14	35	50	-15	33
17	Burnley	32	9	6	17	37	59	-22	33
18	Cardiff City	31	8	4	19	28	59	-31	28
19	Fulham	32	4	5	23	29	72	-43	17
20	Huddersfield Town	32	3	5	24	18	59	-41	14

UEFA CHAMPIONS LEAGUE ROUND OF 16 SECOND LEGS

Tuesday 5 March

Borussia Dortmund 0 Tottenham Hotspur 1 *(aggregate 0-4)*

Real Madrid 1 Ajax 4 *(aggregate 3-5)*

Wednesday 6 March

Paris Saint Germain 1 Manchester United 3 *(aggregate 3-3, Man Utd win on away goals)*

Porto 3 Roma 1 *(aet, aggregate 4-3)*

Tuesday 12 March

Juventus 3 Atletico Madrid 0 *(aggregate 3-2)*

Manchester City 7 Schalke 0 *(aggregate 10-2)*

Wednesday 13 March

Barcelona 5 Lyon 1 *(aggregate 5-1)*

Bayern Munich 1 Liverpool 3 *(aggregate 1-3)*

CHAPTER NINE

—

APRIL

"WE WANT TO WRITE OUR OWN HISTORY"

The family tree of Liverpool's squad has branches to clubs across Western Europe and throughout the UK, but nowhere has supplied more players to the Reds' current first-team enterprise than Southampton.

Adam Lallana, Dejan Lovren, Nathaniel Clyne, Sadio Mané and Virgil van Dijk all wore the Saints' red-and-white immediately before arriving at Anfield, while Alex Oxlade-Chamberlain made the journey from the south-coast side's academy via Arsenal.

The relationship has been fruitful for both parties, not least in the last two signings, Mané and van Dijk, who were both crucial to Jürgen Klopp as his side hit the home straight in April.

Both were automatic choices in the manager's strongest XI and both were selected to start in the first game of the month, back at St Mary's. Lovren was on the bench again as he continued a phased return from the hamstring injury he suffered against Wolves in January. Lallana, though, was absent from the squad after another minor muscle issue interrupted his encouraging return to the action ("Ox" was still in recovery training at Melwood and Clyne on loan a few miles across the New Forest at Bournemouth).

Since the teams last met in September, Mark Hughes had been sacked as manager. When Saints dipped into the bottom three after a draw with Manchester United in December, the board acted to appoint Ralph Hasenhüttl, who had gained prominence after taking newly promoted RB Leipzig to a shock second-place finish in their first ever season in the Bündesliga in 2017. The Austrian's brief at St Mary's was nothing so lofty. Premier League survival, pure and simple, was the aim.

Southampton were still in a dogfight as this Friday-night clash approached, but three wins in four had edged them up to 16th, five points clear of the drop-line. In the Premier League form table since the change of management, Saints lay eighth. There had been no transfer business in January and it was broadly felt across the media that Hasenhüttl – nicknamed the "Alpine Klopp" for his similar high-pressing style – was simply getting a better tune out of the same group of players.

Sky pundit Jamie Carragher said: "The energy in the team has massively improved. James Ward-Prowse has been a huge part of that. He's playing a lot more now than he did under Mark Hughes and the energy... has completely changed."

Ward-Prowse had long shown promise at St Mary's but, having made only one league start during Hughes's reign, he was now playing a leading role, enjoying his most productive season in the Premier League, gaining a call-up to the England squad, and earning glowing reports from Hasenhüttl.

"I think he shows in every game that he's not only a hard-working guy, but he can also come into positions where he has the chance to score," the manager told southamptonfc.com. "Maybe he's in a position that's a little bit more offensive-orientated that allows him to score a little bit more. He's the complete package at the moment that fits perfectly in our game."

In turn, Ward-Prowse hailed Hasenhüttl for turning his Southampton career around. "He's saved my career here," he said. "Before he came in I wasn't really in the picture and I was a bit down in terms of confidence. But we had a meeting together and he told me what my strengths and weaknesses were.

"He was brutally honest with me and told me what he wanted, showing me clips of what he needed from me as one of his players. I respected him straight away for that and I made sure when I got on the training pitch the next day that I showed him I could play for his team."

Jürgen Klopp was in no doubt about the challenge ahead and had warm words for a coach with whom he'd shared a UEFA course in Cologne nearly 20 years ago.

"They have a really clear style and have made some really good decisions. The job [Hasenhüttl] is doing since his arrival is just incredible," said Klopp. "He's brought young academy players in, which is good but also brave in the situation they are in. They look confident, they do what they do and they stick to it.

"Do they have any weaknesses? Not so many, to be honest. How they play is a perfect example of a physically strong team combined with technical qualities, speed and good organisation."

Rickie Lambert played centre-forward for both teams – although his loyalties are deepest Red, having been born and brought up in Kirkby – and he offered his thoughts on the game ahead on LFCTV's *Premier League Preview Show*.

"It's a huge game for both teams, absolutely huge," Lambert said. "Liverpool are getting results at the minute. I think if they pass the ball through the lines they will cause Southampton a lot of problems. They're going to need to do it quickly, because once Southampton get in their shape, they're very hard to break down. If you can get it to the front three though, they will cause Southampton problems, so I do fancy Liverpool."

Mindful of the intensity needed to combat Hasenhüttl's side, Klopp opted for fresh legs in midfield, selecting Fabinho and Naby Keïta, the latter having been a key component in that Leipzig side's run in the German league and to the Europa League quarter-finals before joining Liverpool in the summer.

Keïta played a major part in this match, too, scoring for a first time in a Liverpool shirt in the opening period to level after Shane Long's early opener, but the headlines belonged to Mo Salah, who netted a brilliant solo effort as time ticked away – running from inside his own half and ending a run of eight games in all competitions without a goal.

In an entertaining game, Saints were a vibrant match for their visitors. As much as Hasenhüttl is believed not to care for comparisons with Klopp, from the way his team's forward press nearly led to a second goal for Long that would have changed the complexion of the match, the similarities in approach were inescapable. This team was flexible, dynamic and utterly transformed from the lacklustre showing at Anfield seven months previously.

"Outstanding," was Klopp's assessment. "I said it before when we did the analysis, we thought they [would] be really tough. This team is now brilliantly organised – they are really, really difficult to play against. They have good players in all positions. I am really happy for [Ralph], because he did it [success in management] the hard way."

And on Mo Salah, the Reds boss insisted he'd never doubted the goals would start to flow again.

"As a striker, you have chances and each striker is a human being – maybe you have better moments and less good moments," said Klopp. "But he is pretty consistent, his physical things are always there. It's normal, you have to adapt to the situation. He always stayed calm to deal with the situation. It's only [for people outside the club] that [lack of goals is] a big thing, we don't really care about it. But it's a nice moment for the first goal after a while, a really good moment."

The Reds had known since the quarter-final draw in mid-March that they would be reunited with Porto, last season's Champions League round-of-16 opponents. That tie in February of 2018 had effectively been dead at half time, when a 5-0 away win in Portugal – featuring a Sadio Mané hat-trick – rendered the second leg an impossible task at Anfield.

This new challenge, then, required some delicate management. The first task was to counter the assumption the Reds had been handed an "easy" draw – because there was no escaping the fact that avoiding Barcelona, Juventus and Manchester City, or indeed the resurgent Manchester United and dark horses Ajax or Tottenham, looked more straightforward on paper. However, since that last meeting Porto had become league champions again for the first time since 2013 and were considered a much better side than the one that had subsided in the Dragão the previous season.

The second trick was to avoid the temptation to look too far ahead. The draw split meant the prize for victory was a semi-final meeting with the winner of Man Utd v Barcelona – a mouthwatering prospect either way.

So while the players were throwing their heart and soul into the Premier League title race in the last few weeks, over the same period backroom staff at Melwood had been poring over hours of analysis into Porto, who were involved in a two-horse title race of their own with Benfica.

One member of the coaching team well placed to judge the merits of Porto is assistant manager Pepijn Lijnders, who spent seven years at the club between 2007 and 2014 learning his trade as a coach with the academy.

Lijnders missed out on the equivalent clash last season because he had accepted the senior coaching role at NEC Nijmegen in the Netherlands, but rejoined Liverpool in the summer after NEC missed out on promotion from the Dutch second tier. He spoke before the first leg about how his spell at Porto affected his approach to football.

"Porto made an impact on me as a coach, but even more as a person," Lijnders explained.

"I changed from a coach who had, as a starting point, individual development to a coach who started looking differently at the game itself. I never changed the essence – high-intensity, attacking football – I changed my way of thinking about [it], and especially the way to train it. I got more structure in my ideas, a better hierarchy of my principles.

"It was a beautiful time. I delivered three sessions a day. These boys gave us energy, they gave us joy – it made the longest session too short. We wanted our players to be able to survive at any situation, to be able to hide the ball by protecting it and to take players on non-stop.

"Above that, we focused on their self-confidence, their willingness to invest in themselves and their self-critical attitude. My Portuguese sentiment will never disappear. I really have the feeling I got everything out of my seven years at the club."

Meanwhile, José Mourinho – who lifted the Champions League with Porto in 2004 and was involved in numerous big clashes with the Reds during his time at Chelsea – said he believed the memory of last season and the embarrassment of a record-equalling home defeat would spur his former team on.

"FC Porto have a chance," Mourinho told Portuguese newspaper *Record*. "Compared with last season, I think [manager] Sergio Conceição will ask himself questions about what happened in order to do something different this time around. The tie is open and what happened last year, I believe, can [inspire] Porto in both games."

On a gloriously sunny afternoon on Merseyside, visiting supporters mingled in the town centre, bedecked in royal blue and white, but it was classic British spring weather – summer in the sun; winter in the shade. As temperatures dropped before kick-off, a biting wind was blowing around Anfield, the good-natured Porto fans in fine voice on their march to the stadium.

The evening's outcome – a 2-0 win for the Reds – looks straightforward on initial inspection but doesn't tell the whole story of a match in which Porto had clear chances to score at least one away goal, and Liverpool might have scored more themselves but for one achingly tight offside decision and near misses from Mo Salah and Roberto Firmino.

Naby Keïta, having broken his duck against Southampton, now took only another four minutes to nab his second for the club, profiting from unselfish work by Firmino and a telling deflection from the unlucky Oliver Torres.

Salah failed to convert a one-on-one with veteran keeper Iker Casillas, but soon Liverpool doubled their lead in style, Firmino tapping home after neat interplay between Jordan Henderson and Trent Alexander-Arnold.

Moussa Marega will long wonder how he didn't score at Anfield, though, sending Porto's two clearest openings of the night straight at Alisson. And though Klopp's men had to settle for a two-goal win when Sadio Mané's effort early in the second half was ruled out for offside, the result was a fair reflection of the play overall.

The *Telegraph*'s Chris Bascombe reflected that the ambition of Conceição's team on the night contributed to their own demise.

"Porto carried the scars of the 5-0 defeat last season and their revenge mission was brave. Their formation was as aspirational as any side visiting Anfield this season, but there is a fine line between ambitious and reckless and for a while they appeared to fall on the wrong side. They were technically sound in midfield and never shy of leaving their defenders exposed.

"It made for an entertaining game, Liverpool facing a rare problem on their own turf in having to monitor numerous attacking threats, powerful runner Moussa Marega especially dangerous.

"Yet the Porto defence was playing such a high line they were virtually on halfway, ensuring the most basic ball over the top would exploit the pace of Salah and Mané. From the opening exchanges it seemed only a matter of time until Liverpool's chances flowed. So it proved."

Virgil van Dijk had made his Champions League debut in the first leg against Porto in 2017/18 and, despite a tough test in handling Marega on this occasion, the Dutchman was satisfied with the result.

"It is [a good scoreline]," he said. "We've kept a clean sheet, scored two good goals and we can definitely build on it. [Marega] is a strong guy and tough to play against but every striker I seem to play against at the moment is pretty good! I'm enjoying these battles."

There were more battles ahead, not least with Marega in the second leg, but with this result banked, attentions began to turn towards a meeting with Chelsea that bore loud resonance from the Reds' most recent title bid five years before. It was also the game that fell closest to the date that needs no explanation to Liverpool fans: 15 April.

On the 30th anniversary of the Hillsborough disaster, Jürgen Klopp and Jordan Henderson led the first-team squad to pay their respects at the Anfield memorial, followed by staff and players from the academy and women's teams. Many fans also gathered at the ground where, at 3.06pm – the same time as the 1989 FA Cup semi-final was stopped – red balloons were released and a moment of reflection was observed.

In the centre of town, a line of 96 lanterns stood at the steps of St George's Hall, where Mayor of Liverpool Joe Anderson and Lord Mayor Councillor Christine Banks laid wreaths on behalf of the people of the city.

The Chelsea match took place on Sunday – the previous day – and was a fixture that even viewed in isolation had the capacity to provoke a powerful cocktail of emotions. The equivalent match in 2014 featured Steven Gerrard's slip that allowed Demba Ba to score for José Mourinho's side and scupper the Red legend's chance to lift the title as Liverpool captain. A few weeks prior to this visit of Maurizio Sarri's Blues, Gerrard admitted the moment was still "an open wound".

"I hope Liverpool win but it won't make my wound feel any different," said Gerrard, now boss of Rangers in the Scottish Premiership. "I don't over-think and drive myself crazy over it but at the same time, I have been honest and open. It was such a big year. It was the trophy that eluded me, so of course I am always going to look back and wish it was different."

Given the opportunity to act in the present, Klopp struck a forward-looking tone in his press conference, stressing the need to make currency of the past: "We want to write our own history," he said. "If we do that, you can only build on the positives of the past and learn from the negatives... But don't try to avoid the mistakes of the past because that always leads in the wrong direction. We have to do it really positively, really front-footed; that's how we did it the whole season and hopefully we can do that on Sunday again."

Before kick-off, a huge mosaic spelling out "30 YEARS" was held up in the lower tier of the Sir Kenny Dalglish Stand, while the whole of the Kop was given over to another one bearing the number 96 and flanked by memorial flames. It was a sad occasion, too, for the friends, family and admirers of Tommy Smith, the granite-hewn defender who won nine major trophies under Bill Shankly. Smith had died earlier in the week, aged 74. The two teams and officials gathered around the centre circle and a minute's silence was held, the only movement in the ground the fluttering of flags in a gentle breeze.

It was a sign of how times have changed at Anfield in the past five years that only one player in Liverpool's current XI started that pivotal Chelsea game in 2013/14, and back then Mo Salah was playing for the Blues.

Now he was Red to the core and offered up possibly his best performance of the season to date in one of its biggest games. His goal – a missile into the top corner from 30 yards – will stand alongside the best long-range efforts of Gerrard, Robbie Fowler or Dalglish himself in the club's shooting gallery.

Michael Owen, who was one of the most lethal finishers in the club's history during his time at Anfield, said: "That goal took my breath away – it was some strike. But then again, my reaction has been "wow" many times when it comes to Salah."

Chelsea found him virtually uncontainable throughout. His repertoire of feints, changes of direction and rapid shifting of the ball in small spaces made him a constant menace and on another afternoon he might have had two or three assists.

Owen believes the dramatic increase in the Egyptian's goal return during his two seasons at Liverpool is down to a combination of factors: coaching influence, desire for self-improvement and competitive hunger.

"[Salah] showed raw pace at Chelsea but the one thing he has added to his game is that cutting edge all top goalscorers need – a ruthless need to finish –

which he has developed over time," he said. "Now you can see he has an obsession to score goals, to be the top goalscorer, to want that Golden Boot every season, and to reach that level an awful lot is in no small part down to Jürgen Klopp.

"I say 'obsession' because that is what the top goalscorers acquire over a period of time. Once they start scoring, they have that sensation that they don't want to stop. They feel scoring becomes the norm. Then they start comparing themselves with other top goalscorers. Throughout my career I did exactly that, as do a lot of sportsmen when they reach the top of their profession. Scoring no longer becomes such a huge experience, nor does winning or scoring because that is a regular experience. So, it almost becomes a fear that somebody else will do it better than you; you want to continue to strive to raise your own standards even though from the outside people may think they've hit the highest points. It's that fear of not being the best any more that drives you, rather than the thrill of winning or scoring as you've done that a hundred times, two hundred times."

Owen cites Lionel Messi and Cristiano Ronaldo as players whose rivalry has driven both to greater heights of goalscoring excellence. "I am convinced [Messi and Ronaldo] would not have reached their highest level, scored so many goals, if they didn't have each other in their lives. One scores a hat-trick, then the other has to score a hat-trick, sand so it goes on. One scores four, the other has to score four. Mo Salah has tasted it, scored a lot of goals, won the Golden Boot, so scoring becomes the norm, an average day's work, an average experience, so he needs to push himself harder, score 25 goals every season then want more. So it doesn't surprise me anymore what he has achieved. In his first season he started off scoring five goals, then it was 10 goals, then 20 as he put together a run in quick succession, he just keep on going, kept on confounding his critics and everyone else.

"He will want to be compared now with the likes of Messi and Ronaldo in terms of goalscoring and to do that he needs to sustain it, as Messi and Ronaldo have consistently over many years kept up their momentum of goals, an incredible period of time for both of them, and they will be the players that Mo Salah will hold up as the examples he needs to keep up his goal ratio and reach that top echelon of great players."

Owen also spoke of the need, from his own experience, to trust yourself when the goals aren't flying in. This was Salah's second goal in 10 games –

so a lean spell by his standards – but by mid-May he'd be taking a share of the Golden Boot.

"If I went two, three or four games without a goal, the fear factor would make me gravitate closer to the goal, getting into positions I would not naturally have gone into, and you learn from experience that that is the wrong approach. The answer is simple: just to continue to do exactly what you have been doing and the goals will return. You have to realise that all goalscorers, even the greatest, go through times when the goals dry up, but usually it doesn't last too long. If you try too hard, or try to change your game and become more selfish, it doesn't work. You have to concentrate on doing what comes naturally."

Against Chelsea, Salah's natural game was helped by Jordan Henderson being pushed forward on his flank. Their combination play, added to the overlapping of Trent Alexander-Arnold, gave Emerson and Ruben Loftus-Cheek constant problems, and often dragged David Luiz away from the centre to deal with the overload.

Against Southampton, Henderson had scored his first goal in 66 games, and was thriving on his more advanced role with Fabinho enforcing behind. The skipper's dink set up Mané's opener as Liverpool roared out of the traps after half-time and were 2-0 up inside eight minutes.

"What did the manager say at half-time? I can't tell you that!" said Henderson, smiling after the final whistle. "I thought there was a period when we blew them away a bit, but then they had a couple of good chances.

"Overall it's a good performance because Chelsea are a good side. I've moved a little bit further forward in the last few weeks, which I've enjoyed. It's really big for us to be in the title race. We've got a few big games coming up, and we're enjoying it."

Earlier in the day, Manchester City had kept their own title bid on track with a 3-1 success at Selhurst Park. They had five to game to play, Liverpool four, and each team was pushing the other to greater heights.

"Parallels with the Chelsea visit that derailed Liverpool's title pursuit in 2014 ran only as far as the scoreline and a slip in possession from Andy Robertson that was frankly irrelevant," wrote *The Guardian*'s Andy Hunter. "Otherwise this was a match that reinforced the strength of Liverpool's resolve in the face of City pressure and the class they possess to turn the most tense affairs in their favour.

"For Maurizio Sarri it was a fourth defeat in four visits to members of the so-called Big Six this season. Chelsea had opportunities to change the complexion of the afternoon through Eden Hazard but their man of the moment failed to match Salah's contribution to an absorbing afternoon."

Meanwhile, over in Portugal, Porto enjoyed a routine away win against Portimonense to stay level on points with league leaders Benfica in their own title chase, before manager Sérgio Conceição turned his attention to a much stickier problem – how to overturn a two-goal deficit in the second leg of their quarter-final tie with the Reds.

"We face a two-goal deficit against a very strong team who are quick on the break," he said in his press conference. "Getting the attacking balance right is fundamental. I like the way Liverpool play. At times they are the best team in the world.

"The technical team will establish the game plan, then it's up to the players to put it into practice," he added. "They are responsible for everything good that has happened so far. There is no greater motivation than to be competing in a quarter-final and to have the chance to produce a historic comeback."

Either way, on matchday the conditions at least spoke of a certain role reversal. Where Porto's fans had enjoyed a day of spring sunshine by the Mersey, Liverpool's travelling army arrived in Oporto to find it belting down with rain.

Conceição made three changes from the XI that started at Anfield and on paper they looked to make the team substantially stronger. Centre-half Pepe and midfield skipper Hector Herrera were both back from suspension, while tricky Algerian winger Yacine Brahimi kept his place from the weekend's league game after scoring.

Jürgen Klopp sprang a surprise by selecting Divock Origi ahead of Roberto Firmino, while Andy Robertson was back from his suspension, Joel Matip replaced Dejan Lovren who had been ill and left out of the squad, and Gini Wijnaldum stepped in for Jordan Henderson. The manager insisted there had been no problem with Firmino to necessitate the switch up front.

"No issue – just respecting the fantastic form Divock Origi is in for weeks or months already, and bringing in fresh legs," said Klopp. "That's all, the same we do in midfield because we expect a very intense game, we expect a hard-fighting Porto side. So we need to be ready for that.

"Of course [Firmino] is ready for that but because he never gives himself a rest, from time to time we have to do it. But it's not a rest actually, it's bringing in [Origi] and having that option: speed and all that stuff. That's what we thought."

And Klopp was also keen to view the tie through Porto's eyes to guard against any suspicion of easing off in light of the 5-0 win in the Dragão a year before.

"If we were 2-0 down and going into the home leg, would we think we were out? No way," he added. "That's exactly what Porto are thinking. They always have a high intense game in the highest intense atmosphere."

This point was borne out. In the first quarter Porto were rampant. Despite the continuing downpour, the home fans were making a tremendous din and the players took with gusto to the task of trying to reel in the Reds' lead. Burly striker Moussa Marega was again a real nuisance, buffeting Matip and Virgil van Dijk, while Brahimi lent a new edge to the attack with his incisive deliveries from the left; and right-back Eder Militão showed his skill and athleticism up and down the right flank. The home side had 13 attempts to Liverpool's zero. All that was missing was a goal.

It appeared certain that Porto would be the first scorers and then on 25 minutes, a key passage of play turned the match around. Herrera latched on to a long ball, having peeled away from van Dijk, and was through with only Alisson to beat. But van Dijk turned on the afterburners and as the Porto skipper shaped to shoot, the Dutchman pinched the ball off his toe. Gini Wijnaldum's subsequent cross-field pass to Andy Robertson was only half cleared, Sadio Mané passed to the Scot on the overlap and then ran into space at the back post, where he eventually was found by Salah. The flag went up for offside as Mané poked home but the assistant's decision was overturned on video evidence. Suddenly Porto needed four and the atmosphere went flat in all but one section high in the grandstand, where the Reds fans were bouncing.

Beyond the hour, Liverpool poured in another three to Porto's one: Salah finished off a lightning break and pinpoint pass from Trent Alexander-Arnold; Militão responded with a header from a corner; Firmino nodded in a Henderson cross; and van Dijk finished the tie off with another header from Mané's near-post flick-on. A date against Barcelona, conquerors of Manchester United the night before, was sealed. Back in Manchester, though, something quite extraordinary was happening in the all-English quarter-final between City and Tottenham.

Spurs took a one-goal lead to the Etihad but with 20 minutes gone of an eccentric first half the aggregate score was 3-3. Sergio Agüero then put City in front, but Fernando Llorente levelled. At 4-4, the visitors were going through on away goals – but there was one dramatic final twist. Raheem Sterling scored in the third minute of stoppage time to seemingly put the Blues through to meet Ajax, but as the stadium celebrated wildly, VAR officials were checking for offside. Agüero was indeed beyond the last defender as Bernardo Silva's deflection reached him and the goal was chalked off. Tottenham were through; City's quadruple dream was over.

Croeso i Gymru. Wherever you cross over into Wales, it's the changing signs that first indicate a place that feels and sounds a little different. At the nearest point, of course, the border is not far from Birkenhead; but it's the best part of a four-hour drive down to the capital, through Monmouth, past the ruins of Raglan Castle on your right, through Newport and the Brynglas Tunnels and then on to Cardiff. On the city's west side, a swing left at Llandaff Cathedral takes you down to the old Ninian Park, where the new stadium sits. On this particular Sunday afternoon it was resplendent in the spring sunshine.

Here matters at the head and foot of the Premier League table were in play. With Huddersfield and Fulham already headed for the Championship, the Bluebirds were fighting to escape the last relegation spot. A 2-0 win the week before against Brighton – the team they were realistically seeking to overhaul – had given Neil Warnock's side hope. They were now only three points behind with four games to play, and with Brighton arguably having the tougher run-in. They still had to face three top-six sides in Tottenham, Arsenal and Man City. Cardiff had two in Liverpool and Man Utd. There wasn't much in it regarding tariff of difficulty.

Warnock accepted the scale of his task against the Reds: "We realise the challenge – they've shown this season that they can beat anyone on a good day," he said. "We've just got to try and give a good account of ourselves for the fans that are going because it's a sell-out – and it probably could've sold out twice more. It's going to be a great day [but] I don't want it to be a lovely occasion [where] we still get battered. We can work all week, but if we freeze and make a mistake early on we may as well go home. They will just pick you off. That's what you get with quality players."

It was put to the Cardiff boss that the last time his team beat the Reds was 1959, in Bill Shankly's first game in charge of Liverpool. "Was it really? Wow. What a man. My favourite manager of all time," said Warnock. "The last time I beat Liverpool was at Crystal Palace a few years ago [so it] depends on which one you look at!"

The pitch was left unwatered, which had the effect of slowing Liverpool's slick passing. It could be argued that it was the same for both sides, were it not for the fact Liverpool had more than 75 per cent of possession. Warnock remarked deadpan after the game that the groundsman "must have thought there was a hosepipe ban".

The plan to stay solid and counter-attack worked for the home side to go into the break on level terms, though Roberto Firmino should have scored when Sadio Mané delicately unpicked the defence on 22 minutes. The Brazilian spooned his shot high and wide.

The breakthrough didn't come until another half-hour had elapsed and Liverpool executed a training-ground move from a corner. Trent Alexander-Arnold's low centre was powered home by Gini Wijnaldum, the shot perfectly middled past Neil Etheridge, who saw only a blur before the net rippled.

Chances came and went, one for each captain. Jordan Henderson sidefooted over from close range and Sean Morrison inexplicably missed an open goal after misjudging the flight of a corner. And Morrison then dragged Salah down in the box to concede a penalty, which James Milner converted.

That was Liverpool's job done, back on top and over to Man City, whose game in hand was scheduled for the following Wednesday, across the city at Old Trafford.

The chances of a favour from Manchester United – a strange sensation in any event – looked increasingly remote as the new era under Ole Gunnar Solskjær unravelled apace. A 4-0 defeat at Everton earlier on the Sunday could have been much worse. Some commentators anticipated a pasting on a par with the 6-1 that City inflicted on their neighbours in 2011 and while nothing so dramatic transpired, United were comfortably second best in losing 2-0.

Both Liverpool and City had now played 35 games and, with City a point ahead, the equation was no different than it had been for weeks but now more baldly expressed. Three games to play – against opponents that both sides would expect to beat. If either blinked, it was probably curtains. If neither did, the title would be City's.

If there was inspiration that City could somehow be overhauled, it came from Liverpool's brilliant Under-18s side, which travelled to Manchester for the Youth Cup final and came away with the trophy after a dramatic penalty shootout. The match was held at the Etihad Campus with Pep Guardiola and Reds sporting director Michael Edwards both in attendance.

The home side were dominant in the first half. Ex-Barcelona youth teamer Adrián Bernabé was at the heart of their best work from his station on the left flank and they went deservedly ahead in first-half stoppage time when his cross was turned in at the near post by Nabil Touaizi, the Moroccan striker formerly of Valencia.

But coach Barry Lewtas's team rallied in the second half and Whiston-born Bobby Duncan – who returned to his hometown club from City's academy in the summer of 2018 – equalised with only four minutes to play. The goal owed much to a mistake from City keeper Louie Moulden, who was deceived by the flight and palmed the ball into his own net.

With no goals in extra time it went to penalties and Reds captain Paul Glatzel fired home the winning kick before being buried under a pile of jubilant teammates. For Liverpool it was a first Youth Cup win since 2007, for City a fourth final defeat in five years, but given the quality on display, both teams clearly have plenty of young talent waiting to break through.

There was further limelight in midweek, of an unusual kind, for Mo Salah as he was invited to the Time 100 Gala in New York, with the magazine recognising him as one of the 100 most influential people in the world. But it was a whirlwind stopover and Mo would be back and available for selection at the weekend.

Huddersfield were the visitors to Anfield, long-since relegated and it seemed an age since former Terriers boss David Wagner and best friend Jürgen Klopp had conducted a supportive and heartfelt post-match interview at the John Smiths Stadium in October.

A couple of important wins had followed that narrow defeat to Liverpool. Of particular note was a 2-0 success away at Wolves in November that lifted Huddersfield as high at 14th in the league. But the December programme was a disaster. Wagner's team simply couldn't find a regular route to goal and by the time of the visit from fellow strugglers Cardiff in January, they were bottom and eight points from safety. A scoreless draw wasn't enough to convince the board and Wagner was dismissed.

Jan Siewert – coach of Borussia Dortmund's reserve team, as Wagner had been – was appointed but couldn't turn the ship around either. Huddersfield remained rooted to the foot of the table from December to May and only Derby County (11 points in 2007-08) and Sunderland (15 in 2005-06) had ever amassed fewer points in a Premier League season.

The German was still in charge as the Terriers pitched up at Anfield, ostensibly preparing for life in the Championship, but also hoping to give their away fans something to cheer about in the last knockings of a difficult campaign.

A picture of the late Tommy Smith adorned the cover of the matchday programme. In light of his sad passing having coincided with the Hillsborough commemoration two weeks previously, the iconic defender was afforded his own tribute and a minute's silence here.

The XI for the home side featured Daniel Sturridge – starting a league game for the first time since December in place of the injured Roberto Firmino – and Dejan Lovren in for Joel Matip, who dropped to the bench. Also in the dugout was Alex Oxlade-Chamberlain, selected in a matchday squad for the first time in just over a year.

"It's that long ago, we had to think about [what to] call him when we wrote the names on the teamsheet," joked Jürgen Klopp. "Alex Oxlade-Chamberlain – there are a lot of options obviously – Alex, Ox, Chambo, whatever! It's really good news that he's back. He has been back for a while [in training] and now today back in the squad, so it's cool – really cool."

Ox had to wait for his chance to shine, but the starters were into their stride from the first whistle. A high-press on defensive midfielder Jon Gorenc Stanković turned the ball over straight from kick-off and Naby Keïta profited to score Liverpool's fastest ever Premier League goal, timed at 15 seconds.

Huddersfield bounced back and showed they weren't about to lie down, with neat touches from wide players Isaac Mbenza and Karlan Grant keeping the Reds backline honest, but when Sadio Mané nodded in Andy Robertson's cross on 22 minutes, it never looked like the Terriers were going to have enough to net two goals. Only twice had they registered more than one goal in a game all season – and Mo Salah's lobbed third in first-half injury time effectively ended the contest.

So Mané and Salah added one more goal apiece to their tallies as they vied with each other and Arsenal's Pierre-Emerick Aubameyang at the top of the Premier League Golden Boot standings.

Jordan Henderson, who provided the assist for Sadio Mané's second goal with a splendid first-time pass over the top of the defence, said: "It was another brilliant performance. Teams that have been relegated can be dangerous because they have nothing to lose and they go out and play, but we got a great start. We scored some fantastic goals and kept a clean sheet so it was a good night."

Full-back Robertson said the team was committed to pressing hard, whoever the opposition and whatever the situation. "We were expected to win, but you have to go and do it," he said. "We were a bit slack for 10 minutes after the first goal but then we were able to lift it again. The gaffer said at half-time that we need to play as if it was 0-0, and Alex Oxlade-Chamberlain coming on gave everyone a lift as well. All we can do is keep putting pressure on City. Usually 91 points can win the league... it's an incredible points tally from both teams. Could we have done much more? I'm not sure we could."

APRIL MATCH REPORTS

FRIDAY 5 APRIL 2019 | PREMIER LEAGUE | ST MARY'S STADIUM | ATTENDANCE: 31,797

SOUTHAMPTON 1
(Long 9)
LIVERPOOL 3
(Keïta 36, Salah 80, Henderson 86)

Naby Keïta scored a first goal for Liverpool against his old boss and Mo Salah broke a club record as the Reds came from behind to notch a vital Premier League win against relegation-threatened Southampton. Jordan Henderson popped up late to register for the first time since September 2017 and make it a thoroughly satisfactory away day on the south coast.

Shane Long – making a first start since February due to Danny Ings's ineligibility against his parent club – scored early for the hosts; and Saints defended tenaciously for long periods against the visitors' threat from wide areas. But they were eventually undone by a piece of individual brilliance from Salah, straight down the middle of the pitch.

Ralph Hasenhüttl's side were still entertaining thoughts of a home win – and at the very least a point – with 10 minutes left as they probed around the Liverpool box from a corner; but a brilliant block from Sadio Mané as James Ward-Prowse shaped to shoot and Henderson's header forward sent Salah running free from inside his own half. Roberto Firmino put in a lung-bursting sprint to lend support but as the home defence backed off, Salah went alone, threading his finish wide of keeper Angus Gunn.

The Egyptian ripped his shirt off in front of the travelling fans, celebrating an end to a sequence of eight games without a goal. Talk of a "drought" had always been relative, mind you – this striker still broke the club record for the fastest to 50 Premier League goals. The 69 games it took Salah to get there were bettered only by Alan Shearer and Ruud van Nistelrooy.

Long's goal came from a cross clipped in by Ryan Bertrand, the former full-back who now enjoyed an advanced role on the left flank. Skipper Pierre-Emile Højbjerg had made a forward run into the box, flipped the ball on with his head and, as it drifted over Andy Robertson, the Irish striker was able to bring it down on his chest and fire past Alisson.

Mané might have equalised on 16 minutes, but his header from Salah's floated cross was too close to Gunn and Keïta could only hook the rebound into the side-netting. But Saints weren't sitting on their lead and Long passed up a great chance for the second goal. Trent Alexander-Arnold's cross was blocked by Nathan Redmond and Bertrand crossed for Long who completely missed his kick, the surprise of which nearly induced an own goal from Virgil van Dijk. The Dutchman shovelled the ball over the bar in less-than-convincing fashion.

As the half wore on, Liverpool started to control possession and now Hasenhüttl's side did begin to defend deeper, the pressure eventually telling 10 minutes before the break. Robertson's cross from the left just evaded Salah, who went down under a challenge from Bertrand, but Alexander-Arnold retrieved the ball at the byline and swung in a delightful return pass to the back stick, where Keïta – who played under Hasenhüttl at RB Leipzig – rose to nod in, via a deflection from the back of Jan Bednarek.

Southampton began the second half strongly and Nathan Redmond could have restored the lead but didn't commit fully to a header from Jan Valery's swinging cross under pressure from Joel Matip. Redmond continued to look Saints' most dangerous outlet, though, running at the defence and winning a succession of corners.

The Reds had appeals for a penalty waved away by referee Paul Tierney after Keïta went over a challenge by Maya Yoshida. Then the Japanese made a telling block from Firmino and when Robertson's pass to an unmarked Salah went awry, the Egyptian looked frustrated and nerves were beginning to fray.

But did we ever really doubt him? Salah's scamper down the centre took Liverpool ahead and when Firmino made good progress down the right five minutes later, he looked up to see substitute Henderson hurtling into the box and pointing to where he wanted the ball delivered. Wish granted by the Brazilian, the skipper poked home to make the game safe.

TEAMS

SOUTHAMPTON

Gunn; Vestergaard (Austin 83), Yoshida, Bednarek; Valery, Højbjerg, Romeu, Bertrand; (Armstrong 83); Ward-Prowse, Redmond; Long (Sims 62)

LIVERPOOL

Alisson; Alexander-Arnold (Milner 59), Matip, van Dijk, Robertson; Wijnaldum (Henderson 59), Fabinho, Keïta (Lovren 88); Salah, Firmino, Mané

MATCH FACTS

- Trent Alexander-Arnold made his 50th Premier League appearance for Liverpool, the fifth-youngest player to achieve the feat after Michael Owen, Raheem Sterling, Robbie Fowler and Steven Gerrard.
- Liverpool had now won 16 points in the league from losing positions – the best in the division; Southampton had lost 23 points from being in front – the worst record.
- As well as Mo Salah, Shane Long reached 50 Premier League goals – the fourth Irishman to do so after Robbie Keane, Niall Quinn and Damien Duff.

THEY SAID

Southampton manager Ralph Hasenhüttl: "We saw a very interesting game today. Our team scored very early so it was a long way to the end to get a point or three. We showed it is not so easy if we have a plan and surprise them and can cause problems against the big teams. They know this, believe in this and the guys showed up. There was a crucial chance for Shane Long for 2-0 and then it would be very interesting, they were struggling at that point."

TUESDAY 9 APRIL 2019 | UEFA CHAMPIONS LEAGUE QUARTER-FINAL | ANFIELD
ATTENDANCE: 52,465

LIVERPOOL 2
(Keïta 5, Firmino 26)
PORTO 0

The Reds took command of their Champions League quarter-final tie with a composed display against Porto, netting twice early on and keeping a clean sheet against the Portuguese champions.

The tie might have looked very different had Porto forward Moussa Marega shown the composure in front of goal that had already brought him six goals in the competition to this stage. A half-chance in the second minute was thumped wide, and twice the Malian fluffed his lines around the half hour with only Alisson to beat. By then, though, the visitors were already two behind.

Jürgen Klopp retained Naby Keïta after his impressive showing against Southampton, with Jordan Henderson also in midfield and Dejan Lovren coming in for his first start since the FA Cup defeat to Wolves in January. James Milner was selected at left-back for the suspended Andy Robertson.

And Keïta was quickly on the scoresheet. Milner switched an excellent pass out left to Sadio Mané, who scooped the ball between two defenders for Roberto Firmino in the box. He laid off to Keïta on the edge and the Guinean's shot looped in off the foot of Oliver Torres. Keeper Iker Casillas, making his 180th appearance in the Champions League – yes, 180th – was marooned as the ball floated into the top corner.

Liverpool pressed and Mo Salah caught hold of a volley that Casillas was able to block, then the Egyptian seized on a loose back pass but his attempt to squeeze the ball round the Spanish stopper rolled just wide.

The second goal was one of masterful simplicity. Henderson shaped to cross, which caused the Porto backline to hesitate on the 18-yard line, hoping to catch Firmino and Mané offside. So they were on their heels as the skipper played in Trent Alexander-Arnold on the overlap and Firmino was in position to tap the right-back's cross into an empty net. "Brilliant play," said Klopp post-match.

Now came the frantic passage of play that might have altered the complexion of the match. Torres sent a superb through-ball to Marega, who had peeled away from centre-half Lovren. Alisson cleared the striker's effort with his foot, but the rebound was swung back in dangerously and though Tiquinho couldn't apply a firm header, Corona's follow-up deflected up off Keïta and needed to be pushed behind by Alisson for a corner. The Porto players sprinted to the referee in protest that the keeper's clearance had been handled on the byline by Alexander-Arnold, but VAR ruled no foul.

That wasn't the end of it, though – Mané cleared the corner at the near post, but right-winger Otavio beat Salah to the second ball and Marega suddenly had the ball at his feet, onside, eight yards out. He scuffed the shot down into the ground and straight at Alisson, when either side of the keeper would have meant a certain goal.

Anfield thought the home side had a third soon after the break, when Mané clipped home Henderson's delicate lift into the area, but the flag went up for offside and VAR confirmed the decision – correct by a matter of inches.

Alisson and Virgil van Dijk nearly reprised their mix-up from Fulham under pressure from Marega but this time the Dutchman was taking no chances and hacked the ball away from danger.

Marega then drew a routine save from Alisson from a tight angle and blazed another shot over, Salah had an effort blocked by his own man Henderson after tenacious work by Keïta; and Mané arced a long-ranger narrowly wide as the Reds looked to put the tie out of Porto's reach. In the final minutes, Salah caught captain Danilo high on the shin guard with a tackle but this was also reviewed on video evidence and no sanction given.

A two-goal cushion to take to Portugal represented a good night's work and clear favourite status for progression to the semi-finals.

TEAMS

LIVERPOOL

Alisson; Alexander-Arnold, Lovren, van Dijk, Milner; Fabinho, Henderson, Keïta; Firmino (Sturridge 82), Salah, Mané (Origi 73)

PORTO

Casillas; Maxi Pereira (Fernando 77), Felipe, Militão, Alex Telles; Corona, Danilo, Oliver (Costa 73), Otávio; Marega, Soares (Brahimi 62)

MATCH FACTS

- Liverpool extended their unbeaten home run across all European competitions to 21 games (W15 D6).
- Since his Champions League debut in September 2017, Alisson had now kept more clean sheets than any other goalkeeper (9 – Roma 5, Liverpool 4, all at home).
- Roberto Firmino had now been directly involved in 12 goals in his 11 Champions League games at Anfield for Liverpool, scoring seven and assisting five.

THEY SAID

Jordan Henderson, on BT Sport: "They're a good team. They had a couple of half-chances but overall I think we've got to be pleased with the [scoreline]. We had some good moments in the game and obviously we can do better. The second half was a bit stop-start and we didn't create that much but 2-0 and a clean sheet is good to take over there."

SUNDAY 14 APRIL 2019 | PREMIER LEAGUE | ANFIELD | ATTENDANCE: 53,279

LIVERPOOL 2
(Mané 51, Salah 53)
CHELSEA 0

A long-range screamer from Mo Salah against his old club was the standout moment as Liverpool maintained their title challenge on an emotional afternoon at Anfield.

Pre-match tributes were paid to the victims of the Hillsborough disaster – the 30th anniversary of which fell the next day – with mosaics in the Sir Kenny Dalglish Stand and the Kop, and a minute's silence was held before kick-off.

Salah seemed inspired by the occasion and was at his twinkling best throughout, eventually bringing the broadest of smiles to Dalglish's face as his left-foot drive scorched past Kepa Arrizabalaga into the Chelsea net seven minutes after the break. King Kenny would have been pretty pleased with that himself. It left Maurizio Sarri's team stunned after Mané's opener just two minutes previously had separated two sides looking well matched at break. Amid certain grumbles at Stamford Bridge about inflexibility of selection, the Blues boss had chosen to start two of his promising English talents in Ruben Loftus-Cheek and Callum Hudson-Odoi. Both had been flourishing in the England set-up in recent times: the former playing a part in the World Cup in Russia; the latter bursting through in the recent wins over the Czechs and Montenegro. Here, Hudson-Odoi played right of an attacking three with Eden Hazard as a false nine and Willian on the left. Loftus-Cheek was alongside Jorginho and N'Golo Kanté as Sarri matched Klopp's 4-3-3 formation.

In Liverpool's midfield, Jordan Henderson was again handed a more forward role – the number 8 to Fabinho's number 6 – with the Brazilian snapping into tackles, one of which, perfectly timed and legal, nevertheless left Hazard hobbling early on.

Salah was the first take to aim as Sadio Mané's cross cleared a crowd in the middle, but the strike was more shin than boot and flew straight at Kepa. Then the Egyptian went down at the byline after a clip on the shin from David Luiz. Replays were inconclusive but most importantly referee Michael Oliver wasn't interested.

Naby Keïta was bright on the left of midfield and had a couple of promising passes cut out, while Hazard shook off his knock to fire straight at Alisson and Willian blazed wide when shooting from a central position on the edge of the box. Henderson had a fierce effort blocked by David Luiz and Mané curled a shot against the stanchion from Salah's pull-back. This was open, entertaining fare.

After the break, Liverpool attacked with purpose and led within six minutes. A one-two between Salah and Firmino fell to Henderson on a looping run outside and the captain stood the ball up to the far post for Mané to head home.

Even better was to follow when Salah accepted Virgil van Dijk's long pass on the right touchline, checked inside Emerson and took a couple of steps before unleashing a thunderbolt into the top-left corner. Anfield went wild.

On the hour, Hazard engineered two great opportunities within a minute to get his team back in the match; but struck the base of the left post with the first after a pass from Emerson and then couldn't beat Alisson with a volley when found by Willian in virtually the same spot.

Klopp's men saw the game out to erase any doubts that they might falter against Chelsea as the class of 2013/14 had at the same stage of the title race five years before. No slips this time – just a purposeful stride along the home straight.

TEAMS

LIVERPOOL

Alisson; Alexander-Arnold, Matip, van Dijk, Robertson; Henderson (Milner 76),
Fabinho, Keïta (Wijnaldum 66); Salah (Shaqiri 89), Firmino, Mané

CHELSEA

Arrizabalaga; Azpilicueta, Rudiger (Christensen 40), Luiz, Emerson; Kanté, Jorginho,
Loftus-Cheek (Barkley 75); Willian, Hazard, Hudson-Odoi (Higuain 56)

MATCH FACTS

- Jürgen Klopp oversaw his 200th Liverpool match in all competitions. His record of 112 wins in that time is bettered only by Kenny Dalglish (118) and Rafa Benitez (115).
- Sadio Mané's 21 goals thus far in all competitions was his best tally for an English club (he scored 23 for Red Bull Salzburg in Austria in 2013/14).
- Coming on from the bench to replace Naby Keïta, Gini Wijnaldum made his 100th league appearance for the Reds.

THEY SAID

Virgil van Dijk: "What happened five years ago didn't matter today. It was a totally different game, totally different circumstances, and we are very happy with the three points. We managed to put Chelsea under pressure and they didn't play their usual game at times, so all credit to us. We just focus on our games, not City. We'll see, we'll see."

WEDNESDAY 17 APRIL 2019 | UEFA CHAMPIONS LEAGUE QUARTER-FINAL | ESTÁDIO DO DRAGÃO
ATTENDANCE: 49,117

PORTO 1
(Militão 68)
LIVERPOOL 4
(Mané 26, Salah 65, Firmino 77, van Dijk 84)
(1-6 aggregate)

Lightning struck again in rainy Portugal as the Reds eased past Porto to record a five-goal aggregate win for a second successive season and set up a semi-final clash with Barcelona, conquerors of Manchester United the night before.

Goals from Sadio Mané and Mo Salah had rendered the result almost academic, before Éder Militão – the highly rated defender on his way to Real Madrid – struck back. But further efforts from substitute Roberto Firmino and Virgil van Dijk completed the rout on a near-perfect evening for Jürgen Klopp's side. The Dragons' fire was thoroughly doused.

But as at Anfield, Porto will have gone away rueing missed opportunities to erode and even erase the visitors' lead at the start of the game. As early as the first minute, right-winger Jesús Corona slipped past challenges from Andy Robertson and van Dijk to bend a shot towards goal that was only inches over.

And as in the first leg, Moussa Marega was in the thick of the action without being able to turn that threat into goals. The striker drew a save from Alisson from an early free kick but was flagged offside, then couldn't get enough on a header from another set piece to hit the target and Pepe was just unable to reach the flick-on.

The battle between Marega and van Dijk was fascinating, with the Dutchman unusually ill-at-ease in the face of Yacine Brahimi's expert deliveries from the left. Marega sent a volley just wide, then mistimed a shot that Alisson was able to collect. It was all Porto. And then Liverpool went ahead.

Having had scant possession or territory, the Reds found a route to goal, started by a challenge from van Dijk in his own box. Gini Wijnaldum swung the ball left and Mané seized on a weak defensive header to find Robertson haring forward into the area. He cut back for Salah, whose scuffed shot was picked up and returned by Wijnaldum, while Mané circled round to the back post and prodded Salah's improvised through-ball past Iker Casillas.

Mané was given offside. But after more than a minute's deliberation from the video officials, the decision came through – he was level and the goal was given.

The mood of the match was altered for good. Straight from the restart Brahimi fired a shot at Alisson after a nutmeg on Robertson from Militão, but having weathered the storm, now Liverpool were cruising.

After the break Hector Herrera sent a header well wide in a rare chance but Liverpool went further ahead after a classic counter-attack. Roberto Firmino had replaced Divock Origi at half-time and as Porto looked to cross from right-hand side, the Brazilian showed his defensive commitment to pinch the ball from Brahimi, who had wandered over from the left and was now wildly out of position.

Firmino found Wijnaldum, who saw Trent Alexander-Arnold in acres of space. The full-back drove into the opposition half and curved a perfect pass through the retreating defence for Salah. The Egyptian slid the ball past Casillas and ran straight to his English teammate to acknowledge the quality of his assist.

Militão headed in shortly after from a Corona corner but the game was up. Firmino added the simplest of thirds from fellow substitute Jordan Henderson's cross and van Dijk was all alone to head in a Mané flick from James Milner's corner.

262

APRIL

TEAMS

PORTO

Casillas; Militão, Felipe, Pepe, Alex Telles; Corona (Fernando 78), Danilo, Herrera; Otávio (Soares 45), Marega, Brahimi (Costa 81)

LIVERPOOL

Alisson; Alexander-Arnold (Gomes 66), Matip, van Dijk, Robertson (Henderson 71); Fabinho, Wijnaldum, Milner; Mané, Salah, Origi (Firmino 45)

MATCH FACTS

- Jürgen Klopp had now won all 10 of the two-legged ties he had overseen as Liverpool boss – and 17 out of 21 as a manager.
- Porto's Moussa Marega had 10 shots across the quarter-final without scoring. He'd previously scored in six straight Champions League matches.
- Liverpool's front three of Mané, Salah and Firmino were now all level with Ian Rush on 14 European Cup goals, behind only Steven Gerrard (21).

THEY SAID

Porto manager Sérgio Conceição: "Liverpool only had four shots on goal and scored four goals, which demonstrates the quality of their team. [Every] time our opponents entered our penalty area, it was a goal. Our Champions League was fantastic [though], we cannot forget the campaign. Liverpool is a very strong team."

SUNDAY 21 APRIL 2019 | PREMIER LEAGUE | CARDIFF CITY STADIUM | ATTENDANCE: 33,082

CARDIFF CITY 0
LIVERPOOL 2
(Wijnaldum 57, Milner 81 pen)

A record crowd for a club match at the Cardiff City Stadium turned out on a sun-baked Sunday afternoon in the Welsh capital, but it was the visitors who took the spoils from a hard-fought battle with much at stake.

A thumping strike from Gini Wijnaldum and another nerveless penalty from James Milner – both in the second half – saw the Reds past dogged resistance from Neil Warnock's side, who sat deep but had chances of their own, notably an open-goal miss from captain Sean Morrison at 1-0 that left the Cardiff fans wide-eyed in disbelief.

Jürgen Klopp made three changes to the starting XI in Oporto: Roberto Firmino, Jordan Henderson and Naby Keïta came in for Divock Origi, James Milner and Fabinho, with the only issue to be settled as to whether Henderson would remain pushed forward as in recent games, or sit deeper in the presence of Keïta. In the event they both played slightly ahead of Wijnaldum as Liverpool pushed Cardiff back while enjoying 76 per cent of possession.

On a dry and sluggish surface, the Reds began the sharper but the first chance fell to Blues right-winger Junior Hoilett. Nathaniel Mendez-Laing teased his way past Trent Alexander-Arnold on the left and crossed to the far post, where Hoilett brought the ball down on his chest but Andy Robertson was just in time to recover and block the shot.

An uncharacteristic miss from Firmino followed after neat build-up play from Mo Salah and Sadio Mané. With the goal gaping, Firmino lifted over. Mané then snuck in front of Morrison at the near post but couldn't divert Alexander-Arnold's cross on to the target.

The heat in the unshaded portion of the stadium was intense and both teams took on water as the Cardiff physios attended to striker Oumar Niasse, then Salah drew a fine save from Neil Etheridge, the Blues keeper spreading himself to block a near-post finish with his left boot.

Just before the break, Niasse tested Alisson's reflexes with a volley on the turn after Victor Camarasa scuffed his shot into the ground. The Reds keeper reacted smartly to tip over and keep the game goalless.

Liverpool increased the tempo and both Mané and Alexander-Arnold sent efforts over the bar before the breakthrough came in the 56th minute. Alexander-Arnold skimmed a low corner towards the penalty spot and Wijnaldum met it with the sweetest of contacts to bury the chance past Etheridge.

The Reds were now looking to finish the job and Jordan Henderson had a glorious opportunity to make it two when played in Mané but he, too, got under the ball and sent it into the stand.

Cardiff should have made Liverpool pay. When Alisson failed to reach an inswinging corner under pressure from Aron Gunnarsson, Morrison looked to have the simplest of tasks to nod into an empty net. But he misjudged the flight and the ball hit his back to bounce clear.

The afternoon worsened for the Blues skipper with 10 minutes left. He grappled Salah to the ground and referee Martin Atkinson pointed to the spot. Substitute Milner – brought on for fellow sub Fabinho after the Brazilian sustained a head injury – made no mistake with the spot kick, then hobbled off exaggeratedly in front of the Liverpool fans. "Virgil gives me plenty of stick for being an old man," said the evergreen midfielder, 33. "So that one was for him."

TEAMS

CARDIFF CITY
Etheridge; Peltier, Morrison, Manga, Bennett; Gunnarsson; Hoilett (Murphy 83), Camarasa, Ralls (Bacuna 78), Mendez-Laing; Niasse (Zohore 66)

LIVERPOOL
Alisson; Alexander-Arnold (Gomez 85), Matip, Van Dijk, Robertson; Henderson, Wijnaldum; Keïta (Fabinho 71 (Milner 75)); Salah, Firmino, Mané.

MATCH FACTS

- Liverpool had scored more goals from corners than any other side in the Premier League this season (13), while had Cardiff conceded the most (12).
- The Reds had now scored at least once in the last 10 minutes of eight of the last 11 fixtures.
- Liverpool's total of 88 points exceeded their best for a Premier League season, with three games left to play.

THEY SAID

Simon Hughes, *The Independent*: "Liverpool had to wait for the key moment to arrive here but this is now a team used to being patient, one which does not always have its own way from the beginning and has learned to trust itself by earning lots of victories the hard way. This was a belligerent team performance which delivered a result earned by the standard of the collective rather than any individual."

LIVERPOOL 5
(Keïta 1, Mané 23, 66, Salah 45+1, 83)
HUDDERSFIELD TOWN 0

Naby Keïta scored Liverpool's fastest goal in the Premier League as the Reds swept past relegated Huddersfield Town to keep up the title pace with the finish in sight. The Guinean took just 15 seconds to open the scoring before a brace apiece for Sadio Mané and Mo Salah ensured a comfortable victory under the Friday night lights at Anfield.

Beyond the result, the headline news for Jürgen Klopp's side was the return to action (after 367 days) of Alex Oxlade-Chamberlain, who was afforded a huge ovation from the crowd when introduced from the bench on 73 minutes.

The Terriers endured the worst possible start. From kick-off the ball went back to keeper Jonas Lössl, who passed to holding midfielder Jon Gorenc Stanković, but the Slovenian dwelt on the ball and was robbed by Keïta, who gratefully accepted a return from Salah and rolled a finish in off the far post.

However, the visitors quickly recovered their composure and only a couple of minutes after his error, Stanković found space in the box and had a shot blocked by Dejan Lovren. Right-winger Isaac Mbenza, meanwhile, carved out a couple of dangerous situations without troubling Alisson.

Slowly, though, the home side began to turn the screw. Virgil van Dijk headed narrowly over from a Trent Alexander-Arnold corner and was then emboldened to gallop forward, play the ball out to Andy Robertson and trot into the box. Big Virg wasn't needed though, as Robertson arrowed a cross on to the head of Mané, who gave Lössl no chance.

Another pinpoint delivery, this time from Alexander-Arnold, set up a third in first-half stoppage time. The right-back threaded a delicious pass over the top to Salah, who dinked the ball over the advancing keeper.

Huddersfield's Juninho Bacuna was at the centre of the action early in the second period, with one Lovren clearance hitting him and nearly presenting a goal to Karlan Grant, then the busy Dutchman had a goal disallowed for offside, as did Daniel Sturridge at the other end. A minute later, Bacuna warmed Alisson's palms with a sturdy drive from outside the area.

Mo Salah nearly scored a wonder-goal after cheekily lifting the ball over Terence Kongolo's head and firing in an early shot from 25 yards that streaked past Lössl's near post. But Mané's second arrived in short order – a well-directed header across goal from Jordan Henderson's cross.

Oxlade-Chamberlain was denied the perfect return by Lössl, who blocked Ox's shot with his leg after a mazy run brought Anfield to its feet in expectation. And Mané could have had a hat-trick of headers but smacked the post from substitute Xherdan Shaqiri's centre.

Finally, the Swiss released Robertson inside his opposing full-back and Salah had a tap-in for his second and Liverpool's fifth.

TEAMS

LIVERPOOL

Alisson; Alexander-Arnold (Gomez 88), Lovren, van Dijk, Robertson; Henderson, Keïta, Wijnaldum (Shaqiri 73); Salah, Sturridge (Oxlade-Chamberlain 73), Mané

HUDDERSFIELD TOWN

Lössl; Smith, Kongolo, Schindler, Durm; Stanković (Pritchard 81); Mbenza (Kachunga 87), Bacuna, Hogg, Grant; Mounie (Lowe 65)

MATCH FACTS

- Mo Salah made his 100th appearance for Liverpool, Virgil van Dijk made his 50th.
- The 77-point gap between Huddersfield and Liverpool was the widest between top and bottom in the table since the Premier League was formed.
- Alisson's clean sheet equalled the club record of 20 in a Premier League season – set by Pepe Reina in 2005/06 and 2008/09.

THEY SAID

Alex Oxlade-Chamberlain: "I can't tell you how good it feels to be back. Thank you to everyone who helped me get back on the pitch, all of the staff at the club and my teammates, too. Also a big thank you to you, the fans, for supporting me in some of my darkest times as a player. The reception I got tonight is something I'll remember for life."

PREMIER LEAGUE TABLE AT END OF APRIL 2019

Pos	Team	Pld	W	D	L	GF	GA	GD	Pts
1	Manchester City	36	30	2	4	90	22	68	92
2	Liverpool	36	28	7	1	84	20	64	91
3	Tottenham Hotspur	36	23	1	12	65	36	29	70
4	Chelsea	36	20	8	8	60	39	21	68
5	Arsenal	36	20	6	10	69	49	20	66
6	Manchester United	36	19	8	9	64	51	13	65
7	Wolverhampton Wanderers	36	15	9	12	46	44	2	54
8	Leicester City	36	15	6	15	51	47	4	51
9	Everton	36	14	8	14	50	44	6	50
10	Watford	36	14	8	14	51	52	-1	50
11	West Ham United	36	13	7	16	45	54	-9	46
12	Crystal Palace	36	12	7	17	43	48	-5	43
13	Newcastle United	36	11	9	16	36	45	-9	42
14	AFC Bournemouth	36	12	6	18	52	65	-13	42
15	Burnley	36	11	7	18	44	63	-19	40
16	Southampton	36	9	11	16	44	61	-17	38
17	Brighton & Hove Albion	36	9	8	19	33	55	-22	35
18	Cardiff City	36	9	4	23	30	66	-36	31
19	Fulham	36	7	5	24	34	76	-42	26
20	Huddersfield Town	36	3	5	28	20	74	-54	14

UEFA CHAMPIONS LEAGUE QUARTER-FINAL FIRST LEGS

Tuesday 9 April

Liverpool 2 Porto 0

Tottenham 1 Manchester City 0

Wednesday 10 April

Ajax 1 Juventus 1

Manchester United 0 Barcelona 1

UEFA CHAMPIONS LEAGUE QUARTER-FINAL SECOND LEGS

Tuesday 16 April

Barcelona 3 Manchester United 0

(4-0 aggregate)

Juventus 1 Ajax 2

(2-3 aggregate)

Wednesday 17 April

Manchester City 4 Tottenham 3

(4-4 aggregate, Tottenham win on away goals)

Porto 1 Liverpool 4

(1-6 aggregate)

CHAPTER TEN

—

MAY

"IT SHOULD BE IMPOSSIBLE,
BUT BECAUSE IT'S YOU, WE HAVE A CHANCE"

When French football writer Gabriel Hanot watched the early editions of the European Champions' Cup competition that he founded, he was unlikely to have imagined that, over time, Liverpool FC would be England's most garlanded representatives in the competition.

Back then, the box office in English football belonged to Matt Busby's Manchester United and Stan Cullis's Wolverhampton Wanderers – each three times winners of the First Division championship during the 1950s. Cullis even declared his side "champions of the world" after their success in a trial run of "floodlit friendlies" against Continental opposition.

One such match pitted Wolves against Honvéd, the champions of Hungary and home to a number of the players who had recently humbled England 6-3 and 7-1 in two international matches and reached the final of the 1954 World Cup in Switzerland. Ferenc Puskás, Sándor Kocsis, József Bozsik and Zoltán Czibor all played at Molineux, where boggy conditions hampered their passing and Wolves, playing it long, ran out 3-2 winners.

Hanot, who attended the game, was less interested in the clash of styles than the febrile atmosphere at an evening game under floodlights, a comparatively recent innovation that allowed for matches to be held midweek. Through his experience of the European club game, he also believed Real Madrid and AC Milan to be superior to Cullis's side and even Honvéd. There was only one way to prove it – a formalised international competition between nations' leading clubs – and UEFA, eventually, agreed.

The weekend before Puskás and co played in the Black Country, in December 1954, Liverpool were being hammered 9-1 by Birmingham City at nearby St Andrews. The Saturday after, Don Welsh's side would go to Doncaster and get turned over 4-1. Having been relegated from the First Division the season before, the Reds were 15th in the second tier. This was the club quite literally at its lowest ebb.

We all know what happened next. By the end of the decade Bill Shankly was in charge and the long climb to the top had begun. Gabriel Hanot never saw Liverpool win the European Cup; he died in 1968. But he would doubtless have approved of the style in which first Shankly's then Bob Paisley's teams took to the European game in the 1970s and beyond. And he would have relished a clash between the Reds and Barcelona.

Sixty-three years after the first edition of tournament, Barcelona coach Ernesto Valverde's comments about the Liverpool of 2019 might have been equally applicable to Honvéd or the new competition's winners for the first five seasons, the peerless Real Madrid of Alfredo Di Stéfano and Franciso Gento.

"They're very strong, extraordinary up front, they press and play with a very high rhythm and pace," said Valverde. "You can't make any mistakes, you can't switch off: they're a team that have a surge and in 15 minutes they try to steamroller you. And they often succeed."

"It's not so much physical as psychological. You have to be concentrated, ready for when it happens. You have to have an answer for that, a response to their capacity to push you back towards your goal. You have to be able to overcome that pressure they put on you."

Mind you, the Catalans had some pretty nifty attackers of their own, whose qualities were well known on Merseyside. Between them, the South American pair of Philippe Coutinho and Luis Suarez made 334 appearances for the Reds, netting 136 times, and they would be joined up front by one Lionel Messi, five times winner of the *Ballon d'Or*, winner of 34 major trophies and scorer of an astonishing 598 goals for Barça.

At 31, Messi was still at the peak of his powers. A few weeks before this tie he delivered a chipped finish as part of a hat-trick away at Real Betis that drew a standing ovation from the entire stadium and disbelieving laughter from his teammates. However good you thought he was, Messi just kept nudging the bar higher.

So here was the test for Jürgen Klopp and his side at Camp Nou: contain the world's best player without taking your eye off Barça's other significant threats and retain enough of the ball to be able to implement your own attacking plan.

"It's not only about Messi," said Klopp. "We should concentrate on him in a lot of moments but if you only do that, there are 10 [other] world-class players [who will] decide the game easily.

"So many people come to Barcelona, have a plan and an idea, let's do this and that... and get a proper knock! But there are a few that have caused them real problems. We saw the games against Real Sociedad and Levante [narrow wins for Barcelona in the last two league matches]. They both did really well. But the better the opponent, the higher the stakes, the more they [raise their game]. Now they are champions and they can completely focus on the Champions League. I'm really looking forward to it but it will be a tough, tough job."

That job was made even tougher by a combination of misfortune for the Reds and sheer brilliance from the Barça attack that Liverpool reeling at the halfway stage of the tie.

Lionel Messi reached 600 goals for his club with a wonderful swerving free kick that burst into the top corner from 35 yards out to complete a 3-0 win put the Catalans firmly in pole position. And it could have been worse still if Ousmane Dembélé had not spurned a glorious chance to make it four with the last kick of the match.

Liverpool played well, though, their efforts unreflected in the scoreline. Klopp called it their "best away performance in two years" and his side created numerous chances, especially during a second half in which they were largely dominant.

The defence put in a monumental shift against the pace and movement of Messi, Suarez and co. Joe Gomez recovered well from an uncertain start under pressure from Coutinho and Jordi Alba – understandable after so long out of the team – while Andy Robertson was everywhere, using his seemingly inexhaustible engine to appear just when Liverpool needed a block or interception. Virgil van Dijk, named PFA Player of the Year earlier in the week, offered his usual composure and game management but perhaps the most eye-catching effort of all came from Joel Matip, who was restored to the starting XI in place of Dejan Lovren and delivered perhaps his best performance yet for the Reds.

John Scales – a League Cup winner with Liverpool at centre-half in 1995 – was hugely impressed by Matip's showing at Camp Nou. "Van Dijk has been lauded as a world-class defender and rightly so – in the past 12 months I haven't seen anyone better, but Matip, who rarely gets much of a mention, has also been outstanding," he said.

"When you look at his performance in the Nou Camp, even though the team lost, you could see a player that had grown in confidence and stature. So often he was the right player in the right place.

"Matip has grown as the season has gone on, his confidence in particular, and it's been the consistency and sheer brilliance of van Dijk that has stabilised the defence [and] allowed Matip especially to progress. The result is a solid back four, right from the goalkeeper – who is also world class – to every one of the back four.

Scales recognised from his own career the importance of taking your chance when selected, especially in such a high-performing team. "When

I played, there were times when I would dread being injured because you knew you might not get a chance to step back in, that someone else would take your place. For Matip, his chance came when Joe Gomez was injured, and now you can see his tangible benefit to the team.

"Too often players come and go without having a proper chance to show their talents. Matip's form has reached a new level and much of that has to do with the quality of the rest of the back four and the keeper. Of course, it's not just to do with those around you – the formidable unit – he also has had to step up to the plate, which he has done, showing a great deal of intelligence in his play."

Such were the positives to take from a difficult night in Europe. It looked a near-impossible task but Klopp stressed the pride he felt in his team's performance under the most challenging of examinations.

"I'm not sure if we deserved a lot more than we got," he said post-match. "We played a really good football game but at the end they scored three and we didn't score, so that's easy to accept.

"[But] against a side like this, playing this kind of football, I was completely happy. We played between the lines... we were in the box, we had really good chances and caused them a lot of problems.

Klopp added that most people would just look at the result but that as a manager he could use the performance to the players' advantage.

"We played, we controlled the game in moments, we let them run, we had to defend, we created – not chances constantly, because that's not possible, but moments to make a proper chance," he said.

"That's good and that's what you have to do. You have to create by yourself and that's what we did. In the end, nobody is really interested – probably only football nerds will think about it – because it was about the result and we lost 3-0. [But] I can work really well with this game; I will use [it] to show the boys what is possible. It was a brave performance that was very passionate, very lively, creative and direct."

One intriguing twist in the run-in of the 2018/19 league championship was the potential influence on proceedings of former Liverpool managers who were now distributed elsewhere around the top flight. Roy Hodgson's Crystal Palace had already done the Reds an almighty favour back in December by beating Man City at the Etihad, and Newcastle under Rafael Benitez had taken all three points against Pep's men in January at St James's Park. Now both Rafa and Brendan Rodgers would both have a say in the destination of the title deeds in the penultimate round of fixtures.

City would face Rodgers' Leicester City on Monday 6 May, but first Liverpool travelled to meet Newcastle United on the Saturday.

Rafa faced inevitable questions about the temptation to help his former side win the title, in the face of which he remained studiously even-handed.

"My relationship with the city, Liverpool, the fans, is there," he said. "I was there six years; I have good memories. Jürgen Klopp will be doing his best for his fans. We will have 50,000 fans in our stadium and I think everyone will understand we will be professional to do our best. I have friends in the Liverpool camp, I have friends also in Manchester City camp. I have a good relationship with Guardiola and Klopp, so I didn't want to talk with anyone from either side this week. Whatever happens, Liverpool are one of the best teams in the world. We were lucky to stop City at home so we will see what happens against Liverpool. But if they play at their best then it will be difficult for us."

On the evidence of the contest that transpired, there was absolutely no question of Newcastle taking it easy. The match lurched to and fro, with Newcastle equalising twice before the vital contribution of substitute Divock Origi with five minutes of normal time remaining swung it decisively in Liverpool's favour. The Belgian rose to flick Xherdan Shaqiri's free kick past Martin Dubravka to make it 3-2 and keep the title race alive.

Origi scored seven goals in 2018/19 (four to this point but his most vital contributions were to come shortly), which doesn't sound all that impressive until you realise – according to stats website transfermarkt.com – that he achieved that tally in just 673 minutes on the pitch. Or in other words 96 minutes per goal – a better ratio by far than first-choice forwards Mo Salah (161 mins per goal), Sadio Mané (162), or Roberto Firmino (209). When Liverpool really, *really* needed a goal – against Everton, Newcastle, Barcelona, Tottenham – Origi delivered.

A buoyant James Pearce of the *Liverpool Echo* sent his report back from Tyneside: "It was a thrilling, torturous night in the North East. Rafa Benitez had vowed that there would be no favours for his old club and he was true to his word as a resurgent Newcastle pushed Liverpool all the way. The sense of tension was unbearable during a nerve-shredding finale but the Reds got over the line. Once again, when their backs were against the wall, they found a way to win under immense pressure. The character they have shown all season has been breathtaking."

Yet the winning goalscorer might not have been on the pitch at all had Mo Salah not been stretchered off with a head injury after a collision with Dúbravka in the 68th minute, which led to a lengthy delay and eventually to the dismaying news that the Egyptian would be unavailable to take on Barcelona in the Champions League semi-final second leg.

"Mo got the hip of the goalie in his head," Klopp said. "The doctor had to make a decision – and the decision was [to take him] off the pitch and we accept that of course. When we came in, he was sitting in the dressing room and watching the game, or had watched the game. He was then fine but of course we have to wait."

Klopp had little more than a day to prepare his team for the biggest test since his arrival in 2015. Mo Salah was out with concussion, Roberto Firmino was sidelined still with groin trouble and somehow Klopp had to find a way for his team to score at least three times against Barcelona and ensure they didn't manage an away goal.

"There's hope [because] it's football. We are far from giving up," said Klopp. "We give it a try and because of the character of the boys. Two of the world's best strikers are not available tomorrow night and we have to score four goals to go through after 90 minutes. It doesn't make life easier but as long as we have 11 players on the pitch then we will try it and everybody knows that. That's what we want to show, nothing else – just to celebrate the Champions League campaign and give it, either way, a proper finish or another go. That's pretty much the plan. Just try it and if we can do it then wonderful. If not, then fail in the most beautiful way."

Few outside Liverpool genuinely believed the tie could be turned around but Barcelona did have form for susceptibility under pressure in Europe, most recently when losing 3-0 to Roma in the 2017/18 quarter-final second leg and going out on away goals. Even the mighty Barça could be rattled. But it would require all the Reds' reserves of commitment, stamina and nerve to pull it off.

Trent Alexander-Arnold was on the bench in the first leg but the attacking dimension to the full-back's game meant he was a certain pick for Anfield. He spoke to the club website the day before the match to explain just what it would take to succeed.

"We've got to give it everything and if that means leaving ourselves vulnerable at the back then so be it," said Trent. "We back ourselves to be able to defend in two-v-one situations and being outnumbered, but it's all worth the risk really: we've got to take that risk to get the reward.

And he also noted that while odds were against an upset, Liverpool still had one invaluable weapon in their armoury: Anfield.

"I'd say it's probably one of a handful of stadiums where people never write things off because it's just got that history of special nights and special results happening. So I'm sure everyone has that little bit in the back of their mind that anything is possible and we'll be able to pull off something special. We know it's going to be really tough, we know it's a real uphill battle, but anything is possible."

Trent, as much as anyone else, was instrumental in turning an improbable outcome into reality and two pieces of play – in the build-up to Liverpool's second and fourth goals – sum up the extraordinary tenacity, nerve and skill that make the 20-year-old one of the most exciting prospects in world football.

For the first, after a loose pass inside, he was determined to win the ball back and robbed Jordi Alba near the right touchline. He drove forward, looking once, twice, to establish a picture of the movement in and around the area. Seeing Gini Wijnaldum hurtling forward, he fizzed a cross into his path and Dutchman stroked the ball in.

The second was an audacious moment of improvisation that is already part of Liverpool's European Cup folklore. When the third goal went in, the body language of the Barcelona players was telling. Even in their fluorescent kit, the Catalans' wattage was starting to dim. And when Alexander-Arnold won a corner in the 77th minute, the visitors' defensive organisation was unhurried as the players turned their backs and sauntered into position. Too bad. The full-back and his teammate Origi were alert to the possibilities. In a blink the ball was in the net and the Reds were ahead in the tie.

There was another aspect to the goal – and one that wasn't merely off the cuff. Liverpool's technical staff had spotted that Barcelona were sometimes distracted before restarts and took a leisurely approach to their organisation at set pieces. The planning was so meticulous that ballboys were given a video presentation showing footage of the quarter-final against Porto and the areas in which they could improve were highlighted. Operations manager Ray Haughan and Carl Lancaster, a coaching mentor at the academy, instructed them to return balls to Liverpool players as quickly as possible. In the key moment, Oakley Cannonier, a 14-year-old from Liverpool's Academy, hurried a replacement ball to Alexander-Arnold and within seconds it was past Barça keeper Marc-André ter Stegen. 4-0.

It spoke of a team effort that ran right through the club – that everyone involved played their part. Wijnaldum admitted that he had been "really angry" to be relegated to the bench after playing so well in an advanced role in the first leg; but he took advantage of Andy Robertson's injury to summon a match-winning performance in the second half with two goals in two minutes.

"The impact he had, even though [it was] for a short period coming off the bench, was nothing short of impressive. You need to be explosive in midfield and he was just that."

So said Steve McMahon, the combative midfielder who scored 50 times for the Reds in winning three league titles and two FA Cups. For McMahon, Wijnaldum's effort against Barça was the defining midfield performance of the season.

"It's easy to pick a performance that gives the impression of being impressive due to the [lower] level of opponent. For Wijnaldum, this was so impressive because of the importance of the occasion and the skill level of Barcelona.

"I prefer him when he is going forward. When there are three in central midfield, I like to see at least one of the players getting ahead of the strikers from time to time, getting in the box and scoring. And in the last few weeks of the season I noticed a marked improvement in that aspect of the midfield's play."

Klopp had frequently praised his players' mental strength during these final weeks and this effort of will topped the lot.

"What the boys did – this mix, again, of big heart and football skills – is unbelievable," he said. "If you have chances, you have to score because otherwise you get punished. Tonight we scored, in different ways. I said it so often now, the thing that made it really possible – and I said to the boys before the game, 'I don't think it's possible but because it's you, I think we have a chance' – is because they are really mentality giants.

"It's unbelievable after the season we played, the games we had, the injuries we have now in this moment. If you go out there and ask who bet a penny on us, I don't think you'll find a lot of people. And then going out there and putting a performance like this on the pitch... I'm really proud to be the manager of this team. What they did tonight is so special and I will remember it forever."

The German had made it to a third Champions League final as a manager and would face Tottenham, who engineered a "great escape" of their own against Ajax the following night. In fact, Spurs' progress through to the final was part of a broader, competition-wide triumph against the odds. Consider where they were after three games of the group stage in this season's tournament: one point from a draw with PSV left Mauricio Pochettino's side five points behind Inter Milan and eight behind group leaders Barcelona.

"[Our chances of qualifying] are nearly over," said the Argentinian. "We'll see what happens now in the game between Barcelona and Inter Milan but with only one point after three games, it will be so difficult."

Home wins over Inter and PSV gave Spurs hope of catching Inter, but they needed to match or better the Italians' result on Matchday 6 to progress. If Inter beat PSV at home, Tottenham would need to win in the Nou Camp. But they didn't. Inter drew, Lucas Moura popped up with an 85th-minute equaliser in Spain; and Spurs, somehow, had successfully negotiated passage from Group B.

They saw off Borussia Dortmund in the round of 16 with a commanding performance across two legs. But then they endured the drama of the quarter-final with Manchester City and VAR in stoppage time, and were 3-0 down on aggregate, away in Amsterdam, with 45 minutes of the tie left. At which point the Brazilian Moura again rode to the rescue. A second-half hat-trick including a 96th-minute winner broke Ajax hearts and sent the Lilywhites to Madrid for an all-English final, a fixture few would have predicted at any point until it actually happened.

In the days after Liverpool's semi-final, the players reflected on their experience. Andy Robertson said the influence of Anfield as a 12th man could not be overstated.

"All of the decisive moments [in the first leg] had gone against us, and we knew that with Anfield behind us, that momentum could be reversed," he said in a column for The Players' Tribune website. "If I was a sympathetic type, I'd probably feel sorry for opposition players coming to Anfield on European nights. What they're up against is almost unfair. That intoxicating mix of history, passion and unshakable belief is a hell of an advantage to have, and that's why Liverpool have beaten the odds on many occasions, and that's why our supporters turn up convinced that the seemingly impossible is possible.

"We knew that we had a chance when we were in the dressing room waiting to run out. We knew that the manager believed in us because he had told us. We knew that the supporters believed in us because we could hear them. My God, we could hear them. And, probably most important of all, we knew that we believed in ourselves and in each other. That's why when Divock scored in the seventh minute, I didn't just believe. I knew. I knew what was coming – what Anfield was going to create. I hope that doesn't sound disrespectful in any way, because I couldn't have more respect for Barcelona, but on that night it wasn't about them. It was about us. We were fired up by the fans and our hunger was on another level."

Virgil van Dijk highlighted the togetherness throughout the club. "It is the connection we have with the fans that helps us through tough, tough moments, through tough games," he said. None more so than the improbable task against Barça.

"I could not sleep much [the night before the match] – maybe two hours. It was totally crazy," he said, in a later interview from the pre-final training base in Marbella. "From the moment we arrived at the stadium you had the feeling it could be something special. When Divock Origi scored that early goal you could feel the belief. Everything was perfect that night. It wasn't like we had luck. We totally deserved it because anyone would say a team 3-0 down against Barcelona is not going to do it. Messi's going to score – and if they scored one it was almost impossible. But we did it. It was nuts. You can't really describe it."

Goalkeeper Alisson said it was "a story that I'll be telling my children and my grandchildren".

"Now that I'm playing here, I've experienced the amazing things that we have achieved in this Champions League, qualifying for the final in the way that we did, returning from a difficult defeat that many thought was impossible," the Brazilian told the *Liverpool Echo*. "It was achievable through God's blessing, the work that we put in and a lot of dedication, plus the support from the fans on the night, which was incredible. Anything can change a series of events, in one second or one minute. But without a doubt, [my] save against Napoli was pretty much the last touch of the ball, and that save could be counted as a goal, I say. But of course, my teammates played their part as well and that's what makes it so special, to be part of that group and to be able to help them. They are such incredible players."

Jürgen Klopp had the final word on a night that no Liverpool fan will ever forget.

"I was so proud to be a part of a historic night," he told *The Telegraph*. "It was not just the result but the performance. In the game I was full of energy and then [you get] through the press work and you get a little [tired]. When I got home my boys were in and were on fire. I went through the messages I got; it was a game where the football world showed respect. I had a feeling everyone had tried to get my number and wrote me a message. I read a few of them and went to bed. I've seen a lot of games and it was one of the best I ever saw for different reasons. I don't feel pride a lot of times in my life [but this] was so special."

The final was three weeks away but first there was a league championship to decide. The press were calling it 'Judgement Day' – the denouement to arguably the greatest Premier League title race – and the maths were simple: beat City's result against Brighton and the Reds would be lift the trophy for the first time in 29 years. But that required Pep's team to falter, when they had shown little inclination to do so. Vincent Kompany's long-range belter against Leicester on Monday night ensured City kept their noses in front and if successful at the Amex it would represent a 14th straight league win for the reigning champions.

Liverpool hosted Wolves and the day dawned clear and bright on Merseyside. Fans went about their matchday rituals still believing – the last few days had proven that with time left to play, anything was possible. As the crowds began to build around Anfield there was a festival atmosphere in the sunshine and a huge throng greeted the arrival of the Reds' team bus with a chorus of "Allez, allez, allez".

Pitchside, Sir Kenny exchanged pleasantries with John Barnes and Adam Lallana, while Gary Gillespie – a three-time title winner at Anfield in central defence – gave his thoughts on the game ahead for LFCTV.

"It think the players will be nervous," said Gillespie. "We've talked about the build-up when there were five or six games to go and that there shouldn't have been any nerves but it's come down this – a must win – and pray the Brighton do us a favour!

"Any sport that you play, there's always the possibility of an upset, which it would be if Brighton were to get a result against Man City. I was here in 1989 and who would have thought Arsenal could win 2-0 after the form that we had been in and the quality of the side we had? And Jürgen Klopp made that point before the Barcelona match – it was highly unlikely that we were going to win 4-0, but we did."

Overlooking the concourse another former player and club pundit, Jason McAteer, said he believed the momentum from the Reds' last two results could help the team against Wolves.

"It would have been so different if we'd drawn at Newcastle, seen City win [at Leicester] and then gone out of the Champions League," he said. "Coming here today it would all have been an anti-climax and I don't think the lads would have got the credit they deserve for the season they've given us. It's been absolutely phenomenal, the rollercoaster we've been on. And I'm so glad they've taken it to the final day of the season. There's still a buzz about the place – there's still that belief.

"But you've got to give Manchester City credit as well. If they win today, they'll have amassed 198 points in two seasons. To get even close to that side is brilliant. We should be proud of the players – they've answered every question: bouncing back from results that haven't gone their way in Europe, losing key players at crucial times. When the odds are stacked against us we come back time and time again. It epitomises not just the players but the football club, what the fans mean to us and how we all muck in and produce results together."

That sense of the collective was also Jordan Henderson's focus pre-match. "We have great belief in each other no matter who plays or who comes on," said the skipper. "What we've always said is that we'll keep going right to the end, no matter what happens and we've done that again. [There are] big moments every week and we have kept this race going right to the last game. Whoever gets it will deserve it. We couldn't have done any more and we have given everything. We've competed right to the very end."

The match itself was a strange affair, understandably so with much of the focus being drawn towards events at the Amex Stadium. For 21 minutes – between Sadio Mané's opener and Aymeric Laporte's second for Man City – Liverpool were top of the 'as it stands' table and on course to win the league. In such a heady atmosphere of expectation and hope, false rumours about goals could sweep around the stadium in seconds and it was easy to forget Wolves weren't just there to make up the numbers. This was a team that finished seventh in their first season back in the top flight and took five points apiece from Manchester United, Arsenal and Chelsea. And they also knocked Liverpool out of the FA Cup en route to the semi-finals. Manager Nuno Espirito Santo led a highly capable team of spirit and guile.

The men from Molineux dominated much of the game in between Mané's goals, with right wing-back Matt Doherty hitting the crossbar just before half-time and setting up several promising opportunities in the second half. Chances passed with the lead still intact – Raul Jimenez dragged a shot wide and Alisson saved from Diogo Jota – but meanwhile City were piling the pressure on Brighton and converting their opportunities. Mané made the points safe at Anfield with 10 minutes left but by then the Blues were 4-1 up and cruising to the title. The support never wavered but after a 38-match journey, the race was over.

After full-time, there were individual prizes to hand out. The Golden Glove to Alisson for his 21 clean sheets; the Golden Boot shared between Mo Salah and Sadio Mané on 22 goals (Arsenal's Pierre-Emerick Aubameyang, who played under Klopp at Dortmund, received his own version at Burnley's Turf Moor). The U18s had already been presented to the crowd at half-time with their Youth Cup trophy.

The players and families embarked on a lap of honour around the stadium, the biggest cheer reserved for Mo Salah's young daughter, who scored gently at the Kop end.

Jürgen Klopp spoke of his sadness in the moment of defeat but also of his immense pride in his team's achievements. "I'm disappointed and sad that we didn't do it, because I think the boys deserved it, but it's easy to accept against a side that has a point more," he said. "But I'm happy about so many things – it just doesn't feel like that in this moment."

"If I would start telling you all the positive things I could say about this team, we could sit here and go until an hour before the Champions League final starts. That's the truth. I can read all the stats… all the numbers. It's just really exceptional. If you could get an award for the biggest development jump I can remember, then the boys would get that. We have made a big step. And there is more to come."

"Whatever happens, we are what we are because we have come together and we have all played a part. This is Liverpool now: a powerful collective who looks to live in the moment and embrace the joy of it."

In a near-empty Anfield, Trent Alexander-Arnold remained in his kit, firing in crosses for his family and friends as if they were in the local park. Playing still, just for the love of the game.

MAY MATCH REPORTS

WEDNESDAY 1 MAY 2019 | UEFA CHAMPIONS LEAGUE SEMI-FINAL
CAMP NOU | ATTENDANCE: 98,299

BARCELONA 3
(Suarez 26, Messi 75, 82)
LIVERPOOL 0

Lionel Messi reached the milestone of 600 goals for Barcelona as his brace helped the Catalans take control of their semi-final against Liverpool. But the scoreline flattered the home side, who were kept in check for long spells by the visitors and might easily have conceded one or two away goals.

Jürgen Klopp's side were left to rue those missed opportunities – one for Sadio Mané in the first half and one each for James Milner and Mo Salah in the second – and to marvel at the dead-ball skill of Barça's Argentinian maestro, whose stunning free kick from 35 yards to make it 3-0 added yet another highlight to his remarkable showreel.

The Reds boss sprang some surprises in his selection, with four changes from the side that started against Huddersfield. While it was not unexpected that Joel Matip would return in place of Dejan Lovren and Fabinho and James Milner would come into midfield, the inclusion of Joe Gomez at right-back for his first start since December raised a few eyebrows, as did the deployment of Gini Wijnaldum as a 'false nine' in place of Roberto Firmino, the Brazilian deemed fit enough only for the bench.

A giant mosaic in the stadium spelled out the message: "Ready to color Europe". Liverpool fans bellowed "Allez, allez, allez" to lift the players as they walked out. The Champions League anthem was only just audible.

It didn't take long for the match to burst into life. In the third minute, Ivan Rakitic played a neat one-two with Philippe Coutinho and only a well-timed intervention from Matip prevented the Croatian from giving fellow midfielder Arturo Vidal a tap-in.

A minute later Liverpool had strong claims for a penalty when Andy Robertson's long ball forward was nodded into the path of Sadio Mané by Wijnaldum. Mané went down after a nudge in the back from Gerard Piqué but referee Björn Kuipers waved play on.

Rakitic then sought out Jordi Alba down the left, the left-back filling the space vacated by Gomez, who had tracked Coutinho inside. Alba's cross found Messi near the penalty spot but a brilliant diving challenge from Andy Robertson prevented any shot and Milner was able to clear. Mo Salah picked up the ball and went on a mazy run but the move broke down on the edge of the Barça box.

Messi went straight up the other end with a typical scurrying dribble to set up a chance for Coutinho, but Alisson gathered with ease. This was pacy, end-to-end entertainment.

On 25 minutes, Barcelona made the breakthrough. Naby Keïta had just gone off with a groin problem to be replaced by Jordan Henderson, when Vidal hit a fine crossfield pass to Coutinho, who touched it back to Alba. The full-back slid the ball past Henderson and behind the Liverpool backline, where Luis Suarez had made a darting run between the centre-halves. The Uruguayan nipped a finish over Alisson at the near post.

The hosts continued to threaten from their left-flank and Fabinho had to be alert to stop Messi after a combination between Suarez and Alba, but Liverpool might have levelled when Sadio Mané raced in behind the Barça defence on to Jordan Henderson's through-ball. The striker was stretching, though, and couldn't direct his effort on target.

The Reds came out with purpose in the second half and Barcelona's Marc Andre ter Stegen was much the busier of the two goalkeepers. Straight after the break, Milner tested him with a curling shot from the left edge of the area, then Salah brought a better save from the German with a low fizzer from the other side. Milner then strode on to a Salah cross – giving Wiljnaldum a shout to leave it – and his drive had plenty of heft but flew straight into ter Stegen's midriff.

Though Klopp's side appeared to be turning the tie back their way, the threat of Messi was ever-present and with 15 minutes left he added a second, albeit helped by a big slice of luck. Messi's run through the middle was stopped by a tackle from Fabinho but the ball ran on to Sergi Roberto in the box. Andy Robertson made another challenge but this one fell to Suarez. He bundled the ball towards the goal with his thigh and it clattered back off the crossbar to Messi, who chested down and walked it into the empty net.

Barça's third was a much simpler affair and magnificent in its execution. Fabinho stopped another Messi run with a bodycheck and earned a yellow card but the cost would be much greater. From a central position, 35 yards from goal, Messi whipped his kick around the wall and into the top-left corner past a flying Alisson. The stadium roared its approval.

Liverpool nearly hit back immediately as substitute Firmino had a shot cleared off the line and Salah whacked the rebound off the right-hand post. Nothing was going Liverpool's way. Until, that is, the final seconds of the match when a Mo Salah corner was headed clear and Barça suddenly had three-on-two with Ousmane Dembélé, Pique and Messi streaking upfield. Dembélé only had Alisson to beat to effectively kill off the tie but fluffed his shot into the keeper's arms. How important a miss that might prove to be, we'd only find out at Anfield.

TEAMS

LIVERPOOL
Alisson; Gomez, Matip, van Dijk, Robertson; Milner (Origi 85), Fabinho, Keïta (Henderson 24); Mané, Wijnaldum (Firmino 79), Salah

BARCELONA
Ter Stegen; Alba, Lenglet, Pique, Roberto; Vidal, Busquets, Rakitic; Suarez (Dembélé 90+3), Messi, Coutinho (Semedo 60)

MATCH FACTS

- Liverpool had more possession (52%), completed more passes (547) and had more touches in the box (42) than any of Barcelona's other opponents in 2018/19.
- Messi's 600th Barcelona goal came 14 years to the day since his first, against Albacete in May 2005.
- Barcelona's unbeaten run at home in the Champions League had now reached 32 (won 29, drawn 3).

THEY SAID

Virgil van Dijk: "That [free kick] shows where Messi is as a player. When he is at his best, there is nothing you can do to stop him. I am glad I don't play in Spain and have to face him every season. Even when we were attacking, it is always difficult, as you know he is in the corner waiting to attack. He is the best player in the world and the extra level he has shown over the years proves this."

SATURDAY 4 MAY 2019 | PREMIER LEAGUE | ST JAMES'S PARK
ATTENDANCE: 52,206

NEWCASTLE 2
(Atsu 20, Rondon 54)
LIVERPOOL 3
(van Dijk 13, Salah 28, Origi 86)

Liverpool ensured the Premier League title race would go to the final day through another late escape as Divock Origi's header sealed the win at St James's Park. Joy at the win was tempered, though, by a head injury sustained by Mo Salah that would prevent him from playing against Barcelona four days hence.

Origi was brought on as a substitute after Salah had collided with Newcastle keeper Martin Dubravka's hip and the Egyptian was visibly distressed as he was taken off on a stretcher, surrounded by medical staff.

Earlier the Reds had twice been pegged back by their hosts as Rafa Benitez's side showed plenty of appetite for the battle, despite their comfortable position in mid-table.

Virgil van Dijk opened the scoring when Trent Alexander-Arnold swung in a corner from the right and the Dutchman found himself all alone to head home powerfully. But the lead lasted only seven minutes when Matt Ritchie screwed a shot across goal, Salomon Rondon looked certain to finish but the ball struck Alexander-Arnold's arm and Christian Atsu fired in the rebound.

Ayose Perez then hit the bar with a volley after deft chest control but Liverpool went back in front after an equally clever piece of skill from Daniel Sturridge. The striker appeared to be in a cul-de-sac by the corner flag with two defenders in attendance, but a backheel nutmeg allowed Alexander-Arnold to cross for Salah who swept home first time.

Mané was denied a goal by Dubravka after being put through by Salah and after the break Rondon levelled again with a firm drive into the corner after the ball pinged around the box following a Ki Sung-yueng corner.

The Reds strained for a winner but much momentum was dragged out of the game by the long stoppage for treatment to Salah and it took until the 85th minute for the dam finally to burst. Fellow substitute Shaqiri curled a free kick on to Origi's head and into the net via a deflection from Jamal Lascelles.

Eight minutes of stoppage time were agonising for the travelling fans but the game was seen out and the onus back on Manchester City to win their Monday-night clash with Leicester.

TEAMS

NEWCASTLE

Dubravka; Dummett, Schär (Muto 90+1), Lascelles, Manquillo; Hayden, Atsu, Ki, Ritchie; Perez, Rondon

LIVERPOOL

Alisson; Alexander-Arnold, Lovren (Milner 83), van Dijk, Robertson; Henderson, Fabinho, Wijnaldum (Shaqiri 66); Salah (Origi 73), Sturridge, Mané

MATCH FACTS

- Liverpool had now scored 98 goals against Newcastle in the Premier League era – more than against any other team
- Never before in a Premier League season had two defenders reached double figures for assists. Trent Alexander-Arnold and Andy Robertson were now both on 11.
- Liverpool had scored the most headed goals (18) in the Premier League this season.

THEY SAID

Trent Alexander-Arnold: "We always knew it was going to be a tough place to come. We wanted to show we had the mentality to bounce back after the defeat during the week. We do have a strong mentality because we have scored a lot of late winners and equalisers."

TUESDAY 7 MAY 2019 | UEFA CHAMPIONS LEAGUE SEMI-FINAL | ANFIELD | ATTENDANCE: 55,212

LIVERPOOL 4

(Origi 7, 79, Wijnaldum 54, 56)

BARCELONA 0

(4-3 aggregate)

The Reds produced one of the greatest comebacks in the history of football to secure a place in the Champions League final for a second successive season, overturning a three-goal defeat from the first leg against Spanish champions Barcelona on an unforgettable evening at Anfield.

There have been some extraordinary European nights under the lights in this great stadium over the years – Olympiakos 2004, Chelsea 2005, Borussia Dortmund 2016 are three that spring readily to mind – but nothing like this.

It was the combination of adverse circumstances that made it so special: the size of the deficit, the lack of an away goal, the quality of the opposition and the loss of key personnel all built a pre-match narrative in which it was scarcely believable that Liverpool might prevail. And yet they did. Lionel Messi – who always scores – didn't. Divock Origi and Gini Wijnaldum bagged a pair each and Jürgen Klopp's side, incredibly, were through.

The loss of Mo Salah and Roberto Firmino necessitated a reshuffle upfront with Origi playing the central role, flanked by Sadio Mané and Xherdan Shaqiri, who had been a key player in the first half of the season, but hadn't started a game since January. Fabinho, James Milner and Jordan Henderson made up the midfield three, while Trent Alexander-Arnold was back in after his omission from the first leg, alongside Joel Matip, Virgil van Dijk and Andy Robertson at the back.

Having already won the Spanish *La Liga* title before their weekend date with Celta Vigo, Barça coach Ernesto Valverde rested his entire starting XI. They were unchanged from the first leg.

It was cool and cloudy as the crowd built inside the stadium, with the big-eared trophy on display at the foot of the main stand as the assembled broadcast press conducted their pre-match duties. Salah appeared wearing a black T-shirt with giant lettering and a simple message: 'NEVER GIVE UP'.

By the time the teams emerged the atmosphere in the stadium was rocking. Jürgen Klopp looked up at the main stand and smiled, patted the club crest and then embraced assistant Pepijn Lijnders. The German looked around Anfield, his game-face firmly on.

An early goal was vital for the home side to build momentum and Klopp's side came flying out of the traps. Two early corners came to nothing but then Mané anticipated a loose defensive header by Jordi Alba and slipped a pass inside to Jordan Henderson. The Englishman's shot was saved by Marc Andre ter Stegen but the ball rolled out to Origi who tapped it home. Lift-off.

The level of emotion around the ground was such that a large part of the task now was to maintain composure and build on a good start. Fabinho went in the book for a decent-looking tackle on Luis Suarez, having earlier set the tone with a crunching – and also legal – challenge on Lionel Messi as the Argentinian scuttled menacingly towards goal. Mané went down in the Barça box under pressure from Sergi Roberto but referee Cuneyt Cakir ruled no penalty. In his technical area, Klopp waved elaborate semaphore instructions to his players.

Now the visitors pressed for an all-important away goal. Alisson tipped over a clipped first-time effort from Messi, Alba looked to play Messi in when he might have tested the keeper himself, and the Reds stopper made another fine save from Philippe Coutinho, palming the ball wide of the advancing Suarez.

With half an hour played, Henderson was hurt in a collision with centre-half Clement Lenglet. Wijnaldum prepared for action but the skipper returned gingerly to the fray. Then Robertson also went down, after a kick backwards from Suarez while the Scot was chasing down the Uruguayan. Robbo played on until half-time – the scoreline still 1-0 after another important stop by Alisson from Alba in stoppage time – but Klopp withdrew him at the break and Wijnaldum, this time, was on.

If the Dutchman had been itching for a piece of the action while sitting on the bench, he didn't take long to exert his influence. Six minutes into the second period, a determined Alexander-Arnold won the ball back from Alba after losing possession and steered a low pass square across the area. It was almost an identical situation to the first leg, when Wijnaldum let the ball between his legs for Milner to hit. He wasn't letting this one go. His side-foot finish crept under ter Stegen's arm and in at the Kop end.

Just 122 seconds later it was 3-0 – Wijnaldum again. Origi overhit a cross from the right but it was picked up by Shaqiri, who exchanged passes with Milner. The Swiss swung in a cross and Wijnaldum rose above the rooted defence to head it past a stranded ter Stegen. Utter pandemonium ensued in the stands.

The tie was level with 35 minutes to play and still there was the ever-looming threat of Messi. Liverpool's defence had dealt with him effectively to this point but as he'd proved in the first leg, the little genius needs only a sniff of a chance. There was a collective lurch of stomachs in recognition of this when Barça won a free kick almost precisely the same distance from goal from where Messi had delivered into the top corner the week before. This time he struck the wall to widespread relief around Anfield and groans from the exasperated visiting supporters.

The tie was eventually decided by an inspirational bit of quick thinking from Alexander-Arnold. The full-back won a corner, then showed nerve beyond his years to catch the whole Barcelona defence napping. He placed the ball in the quadrant and began to walk off as Shaqiri trotted over to take the kick, then quickly turned and fired in a low cross towards Origi with Barça's backs turned. The striker angled his finish past a startled ter Stegen and Gerard Pique and ran off to celebrate with teammates and substitutes in front of a delirious Kop.

The contrast in body language could not have been more stark. Barça's players looked crestfallen, Liverpool's wide-eyed and buoyant. After five minutes of injury-time, James Milner had the ball between his feet in the corner and referee Cakir blew the final whistle. The Reds had done it.

Henderson collapsed to the ground, Wijnaldum fell to his knees. While other players hugged and celebrated, Messi and his teammates trudged off looking dazed.

The whole Liverpool squad and staff formed a line to sing YNWA in unison in front of the Kop in a scene of togetherness awash with tears from players and fans alike. This was more than a performance, more than a match. A miracle on Merseyside.

TEAMS

LIVERPOOL
Alisson; Alexander-Arnold, Matip, van Dijk, Robertson (Wijnaldum 45); Milner, Fabinho, Henderson; Mané, Shaqiri (Sturridge 90), Origi (Gomez 85)

BARCELONA
Ter Stegen; Roberto, Pique, Lenglet, Alba; Busquets, Rakitic (Malcom 80), Vidal; Messi, Coutinho (Semedo 60), Suarez

MATCH FACTS

- Liverpool had now hosted 19 European semi-finals, winning 15, drawing three and losing only one.
- Jürgen Klopp's side had led at half-time in 26 games in 2018/19 and won every one.
- Barcelona suffered their heaviest defeat against an English side.

THEY SAID

Gini Wijnaldum: "Unbelievable. After the game in Spain we were confident we could score four and win 4-0. People outside doubted us and thought we couldn't do it. But once again we showed everything is possible in football. I was really angry that the manager put me on the bench. I just tried to help my team, I'm happy I could do that with two goals. [The manager] told us [after the first leg that] the tie was totally winnable. He said we should have every belief we could still win."

SUNDAY 12 MAY 2019 | PREMIER LEAGUE | ANFIELD | ATTENDANCE: 53,331

LIVERPOOL 2
(Mané 17, 81)
WOLVERHAMPTON WANDERERS 0

Manchester City retained the Premier League title on the final day of the season, but they were pushed every step of the way by Liverpool, whose defeat of Wolves meant City had needed to win each of their final 14 league games of the campaign to prevail by a single point.

Sadio Mané's brace of goals ensured a share of the Golden Boot prize with Mo Salah and Arsenal's Pierre-Emerick Aubameyang but ultimately there was disappointment at Anfield as the Reds' titanic effort went unrewarded and another season passed without English domestic football's biggest prize. Jürgen Klopp's men lost only one game, were unbeaten at home, and the total of 97 points would have won every other Premier League except the last two.

Wolves pitched up on Merseyside after an impressive campaign of their own – the promoted side's seventh-place finish was a best result in the top flight since 1980, when they had Andy Gray playing up front, Reds legend Emlyn Hughes was captain and they were capable of beating European champions Nottingham Forest to win the League Cup. As they'd proven throughout the campaign, and particularly against the Big Six, this was an exceptionally talented team. A home win for Liverpool was by no means a certainty.

The din around the stadium before and after kick-off was thunderous. The Reds began on the front foot and earned a couple of promising positions. Mo Salah was just crowded out in the box, Virgil van Dijk found Trent Alexander-Arnold with a searching cross-field pass but the full-back's touch was heavy, and Divock Origi fired a shot towards goal that was collected by Wolves keeper Rui Patricio.

The visitors were sitting deep and on 16 minutes, the Reds went ahead. Jordan Henderson played a cute reverse pass to Alexander-Arnold and his cross, via a slight deflection, was thumped in by Mané. As it stood, Liverpool were top but there was a long, long way to go.

Everywhere in the stadium phones were on and some fans had radio commentary playing in earpieces, as they kept their eyes on the action at Anfield and their ears tuned for news from the South Coast. Andy Robertson drilled a shot towards goal that was pushed firmly away by Rui Patricio. Cheers went up as rumours – at first incorrect – of a Brighton goal swept around. But then it was confirmed: Glenn Murray had opened the scoring for the Seagulls. It couldn't happen, could it?

Hopes that City might subside under pressure were quickly doused as Sergio Agüero levelled. And now, where Wolves had been subdued and happy to sit back, now they began to attack with purpose and the Reds suddenly looked shaky. Whatever was happening elsewhere, it wouldn't matter if Liverpool didn't win here.

Mo Salah smacked a volley high into the Kop, but the best chance before the break fell to Matt Doherty, who was on the end of a brilliant, sweeping counterattack and beat Alisson but saw his effort cannon off the crossbar. Meantime, City had gone ahead through Aymeric Laporte and with both contenders leading at half-time, nothing much had changed.

Irish right-back Doherty continued to be Wolves' most productive outlet in the second half, continually getting forward to stretch the Red defence. Raul Jimenez should have hit the target but screwed a shot wide, then the Mexican dummied neatly to present a chance for Diogo Jota but Alisson was quickly out to block. Divock Origi had volleyed over at the other end but the home side's lead looked increasingly fragile.

Now, though, the game appeared to be up. Riyad Mahrez made it 3-1 to City with a long-ranger and Pep's men weren't going to blow a two-goal lead with the finish line in sight. Then it was 4-1, Ilkay Gundogan sealing the deal.

All that remained was the battle for individual accolades: a clean sheet (the 21st of the league campaign) would give Alisson the golden glove; a goal from Mo Salah the golden boot outright. But the last home goal season came, fittingly, from Liverpool's most prolific attacker over the course of the run-in, Sadio Mané. The Senegalese nodded home yet another assist from Alexander-Arnold to match Salah on 22 goals, and for the full-back to break the record for defensive assists with 12. Alex Oxlade-Chamberlain came on to another rousing reception. Next season would hopefully bring better luck for the England international.

Pride and passion poured from the stands at the end as players and their families gave a lap of honour. The title had been tantalisingly close – near enough for a replica trophy to be stationed at Anfield in case City faltered – but even a club-record tally of 97 points was one short.

TEAMS

LIVERPOOL
Alisson; Alexander-Arnold, Matip, van Dijk, Robertson (Gomez 84); Fabinho, Henderson, Wijnaldum (Oxlade-Chamberlain 88); Salah, Mané, Origi (Milner 64)

WOLVERHAMPTON WANDERERS
Patricio; Bennett, Coady, Boly; Doherty (Traore 80), Neves, Dendoncker, Moutinho (Gibbs-White 84), Jonny (Vinagre 84); Jimenez, Jota

MATCH FACTS

• Mo Salah and Virgil van Dijk became the first outfield Liverpool players since Martin Skrtel in 2010/11 to feature in every match of a Premier League season. Alisson Becker was also ever-present in the league.
• The Reds went unbeaten at home for a second successive league season for the first time since 1979/80.
• Sadio Mané (21 goals) was the first player to score more than 20 goals in a single Premier League campaign without any coming from the penalty spot since Luis Suarez (31) and Daniel Sturridge (21) did so, also for the Reds, in 2013/14.

THEY SAID

Liverpool captain Jordan Henderson: "No regrets. We have been outstanding all season and left everything out on the pitch. We have lost one game. People might talk about the draws but we tried everything to win those games. We gave everything over the whole season. City are a fantastic side and you take your hat off to them. Next season we give everything to win it."

PREMIER LEAGUE TABLE AT END OF 2018/19 SEASON

Pos	Team	Pld	W	D	L	GF	GA	GD	Pts
1	Manchester City	38	32	2	4	95	23	72	98
2	Liverpool	38	30	7	1	89	22	67	97
3	Chelsea	38	21	9	8	63	39	24	72
4	Tottenham Hotspur	38	23	2	13	67	39	28	71
5	Arsenal	38	21	7	10	73	51	22	70
6	Manchester United	38	19	9	10	65	54	11	66
7	Wolverhampton Wanderers	38	16	9	13	47	46	1	57
8	Everton	38	15	9	14	54	46	8	54
9	Leicester City	38	15	7	16	51	48	3	52
10	West Ham United	38	15	7	16	52	55	-3	52
11	Watford	38	14	8	16	52	59	-7	50
12	Crystal Palace	38	14	7	17	51	53	-2	49
13	Newcastle United	38	12	9	17	42	48	-6	45
14	AFC Bournemouth	38	13	6	19	56	70	-14	45
15	Burnley	38	11	7	20	45	68	-23	40
16	Southampton	38	9	12	17	45	65	-20	39
17	Brighton & Hove Albion	38	9	9	20	35	60	-25	36
18	Cardiff City	38	10	4	24	34	69	-35	34
19	Fulham	38	7	5	26	34	81	-47	26
20	Huddersfield Town	38	3	7	28	22	76	-54	16

UEFA CHAMPIONS LEAGUE SEMI-FINALS

Tuesday 30 April
Tottenham Hotspur 0 Ajax 1

Wednesday 1 May
Barcelona 3 Liverpool 0

Tuesday 7 May
Liverpool 4 Barcelona 0
(4-3 aggregate)

Wednesday 8 May
Ajax 2 Tottenham Hotspur 3
(3-3 aggregate, Tottenham win on away goals)

CHAPTER ELEVEN

—

JUNE

"WE'VE CONQUERED ALL OF EUROPE,
WE'RE NEVER GONNA STOP"

On the first evening of May, as Lionel Messi's free kick ripped past Alisson into the Nou Camp net and seconds later Mo Salah smacked the woodwork at the other end, it was hard to make a case that this book would need an 11th chapter. Yet here we are, recounting the tale of Liverpool's only fixture, to date, ever played in June.

After the energy-sapping rigours of the league run-in and emotionally draining experience of the semi-final against Barça, Klopp gave the players five days off. Following the final league game against Wolves, the squad took part in light recovery sessions at Melwood, then enjoyed short holidays before reconvening for warm-weather training in Marbella, away from all the hype. The manager had taken his squad there before last season's final against Real and prior to the tie against Bayern. Klopp described it as "two proper weeks as a pre-season".

Naby Keïta travelled with the squad, but there was no intention to rush him back from his adductor injury – he would end up being the only injury absentee from those who might make the starting XI, with Klopp optimistic that Firmino would make it after his own struggles with a groin problem.

The three-week gap between fixtures persuaded Klopp that, in addition to the usual short-sided games that players enjoy in training, something more was required to keep his side in tune. To that end, the club arranged a practice match behind closed doors against Benfica B, the Portuguese side's reserve team that plays in their home league's second tier. It was later reported that the two teams' coaches collaborated to set up Benfica's team as closely as possible in terms of personnel and tactics to that of final opponents Tottenham.

Andy Robertson noted that Spurs usually raised their game against Liverpool and that he expected the final to be no different. "They always seem to give us a good game," he said, "and last season they got the upper hand on us [winning 4-1 at Wembley]. This season we turned that around a wee bit. But at Anfield we were quite lucky, they had a few big chances. We were going for the title, so we had to win it and we got a bit of luck right at the end. But Tottenham are a fantastic team with an unbelievable manager and they have quality the whole way through their squad. Every game we've played has been competitive and we expect that – and I'm sure so will they."

Jürgen Klopp knew the experience of defeat in Kiev would be a huge motivational factor for his players and wanted to use it however he could.

"[The defeat in the final] had a big influence on us," he said. "I remember that situation when we stood in the queue at Kiev in our tracksuits on the way home. Heads down, very frustrated, everyone very disappointed. You weren't allowed to be angry. There were a lot of different emotions. But the plan was: we'll come again. We'll be there again. Now we are.

"Each team who lost a final will think about putting it right. We have the chance to do that. That was the kick-start for the development of this team. This team doesn't compare to the team last year. These boys want to be there. It's not like [we think] 'Oh, it's coming up' and we get scared. We are a completely different team to last year."

Klopp admitted that the long gap between games wasn't ideal, but that the players' commitment had been exemplary. "The best moment for the final would've been five minutes after we beat Barcelona," he said. "[But] the mood in the team is brilliant. The work rate and attitude. The best piece of character of this team is the constant readiness for development."

One ex-Red with a unique viewpoint on the final was Craig Johnston, the South African-born Aussie midfielder who won 10 major trophies – including the European Cup – in his time at Anfield.

Johnston grew up in Newcastle, New South Wales as a Tottenham fan, ended up playing for Liverpool for seven seasons, then spent 18 years as the partner of Vivienne Lewis, the Liverpool-supporting daughter of billionaire Joe Lewis, who owns Spurs. Still with us?

Craig explains further.

"We had a place in London and would go to most of Tottenham's home games at White Hart Lane," he said. "Vivienne was a big Liverpool fan, as was her brother Charlie, long before the family bought Spurs. The funny thing is, Vivienne even applied for a job in the office at Anfield. I was an old Tottenham Hotspur fan before I joined Liverpool. That's probably why we all got on so well."

Johnston credited Joe Lewis with returning Tottenham "to the top tier". He said: "I was there when he bought the club [in 2001]. I have seen him apply the same laser focus as he does to his trading and catering empires and other business activities. Joe doesn't get the credit he deserves for Tottenham's revival as a European giant. And don't forget there has been a complete stadium rebuild in the background. This kind of major upheaval has crippled other teams. Joe has a unique way of looking critically at things. He is obsessed with detail and quality. It was fascinating living with the Lewises for almost 20 years."

Despite "a real soft spot for Spurs", Craig wanted Liverpool to win. "They so deserve to win something after such a magnificent season and their loss in the Champions League final last year. [And Liverpool] is in my blood because I lived in that fabulous city for 10 years. But this is not a done deal by any stretch.

"Beware the underdogs from North London," he warned. "The team that gets the mindset right will win."

In the days leading up to the final, stories abounded of fans' efforts via planes, trains and automobiles to reach Madrid. Tens of thousands more than could possibly be accommodated in the stadium poured into the city, and on matchday a wave of red gathered in the fanzone at Plaza Salvador Dalí, in the shadow (what shade there was on a baking Madrid afternoon) of the giant, Stonehenge-like 'Dolmen de Dalí' monument. The fans were whipped into a frenzy, as they had been for much of the season at Boss events (organised by adopted club troubadour Jamie Webster, renowned for his repertoire of terrace anthems). Elsewhere, a giant replica of the trophy towered over Plaza Oriente and in Plaza Mayor, there were drums, elaborate costumes, freestylers and an artificial pitch hosting matches featuring football legends and amputee, blind and celebral palsy football. The final festival was in full swing.

Meanwhile, the Liverpool's players had gone in the other direction, back from Marbella to make final preparations at Melwood before heading to Spain again on the Friday afternoon. Klopp was joined for press duties by his full-backs Trent Alexander-Arnold and Andy Robertson and the first question asked was about how hot it was in Madrid. The temperature was forecast to be tipping 30 degrees centigrade (even at 9pm local time) for kick-off.

"It's the same for both teams," said Robertson, calmly. "We are both from England so we are used to cooler temperatures. Once the game gets started both have to deal with the same situation. We have prepared for it. We've obviously just landed and we know how hot it is, but it's something we've played in before. We cannot change it."

Alexander-Arnold added: "The sign of a good side is being able to adapt to different circumstances and situations during games."

Xabi Alonso – scorer of Liverpool's equalising goal in the 2005

Champions League final and a winner again with Real nine years later in 2014 – spoke from Madrid about the opportunity for greatness now within reach of these players.

"Once you are able to be even a small part of Liverpool's history, you can be proud of yourself and wherever you go in the world, there will be a Liverpool fan who will be proud of what you achieved," he said. "And to have been able to deliver in that moment for them is something that will stay [with you] forever and hopefully they can be a part of the bigger history of Liverpool."

Alonso's goal came, of course, as he put in the rebound from a penalty, saved by AC Milan's Dida, on the way to a winning shoot-out. Over the course of the Reds' history in European Cup and Champions League finals, spot kicks were a recurrent theme. Alan Kennedy took the last, match-winning penalty in 1984 against Roma in their home stadium, and a couple of days before the final he recalled the scene after extra time.

"Why Joe Fagan picked me, I'll never know!" Alan laughed. "I wondered why he thought I'd be good at them. We'd had a pre-season tournament in Holland, where Alan Hansen and I both took penalties. We both missed. We were terrible!

"From our side there was total confusion. Joe looked at me and – this is absolutely true – said 'Are you okay?'. That was all he said. 'Yeah, I'm okay,' I replied. But I couldn't work it out. I went over to Ronnie Moran and said, 'Joe kept on asking me if I was okay. What does he mean?' 'He wants you to take a penalty,' Ronnie said. 'F****** hell, Ronnie,' I said, 'I wasn't agreeing to that!'

"When I stepped up, I was nervous as hell. The ref said, 'next please', and I started walking to the edge of the penalty box. I thought my legs would fold, I couldn't feel them. It was horrible, scary, and I thought to myself: 'Why I am I here, what am I doing here?' I didn't think of the consequences if I missed or if I scored. I dared not think about it. I just thought that I needed to hit the target. If the keeper made a save – or whatever happened – then well done, keeper, but I must just hit the target.

"Then it got worse. Should I blast it, should I hit it straight, should I place it, should I go left, should I go right? They say you need to make your mind up long before you even walk up to the ball. I was all over the place. I looked back quickly at the lads – they were all praying. I knew what was going through their minds: 'He's just a full-back, doesn't score many goals, he's going to miss.' I remember I needed to take five steps, not five yards, just five steps to get to the ball, I worked that out. I also told myself, 'Come on, you can do it. Whatever happens in the next second, hit that target.' I hit it to the goalkeeper's right, having opened my body, and it went into the corner.

"It meant so much winning that trophy, there were millions watching me, the flashbulbs were going behind the goal as it was the final one. But I had never before been put under so much pressure."

Now a penalty would again prove to be the key moment of a Liverpool final in Europe; this time not as the last act of the drama, but as the opening scene.

JUNE MATCH REPORT

SATURDAY 1 JUNE 2019 | UEFA CHAMPIONS LEAGUE FINAL | ESTADIO WANDA METROPOLITANO | ATTENDANCE: 63,272

TOTTENHAM HOTSPUR 0
LIVERPOOL 2
(Salah pen 2, Origi 87)

A few stops east of the centre of town, on Ligero 7 of the Madrid Metro, sits Estadio Wanda Metropolitano, a curvy, crimp-roofed oval; home to Atlético Madrid and the venue for the final match of an epic season for Liverpool FC.

The sun was dipping as the stands began to fill but the heat was still intense as the opening ceremony commenced with American band Imagine Dragons playing a short set. Flames and fireworks shot into the air next to choreographed drummers in lines spreading out from the stage across the covered playing surface. The band's song "Thunder" – featuring the refrain "never give up on your dreams" – was appropriate, given where both finalists were at various points of their respective semi-finals. Thousands of fans donned "Never Give Up" T-shirts after Mo Salah wore one to watch the Barça second leg.

The players walked out past the trophy and a silver-clad string quartet, playing the Champions League anthem on electric violins, viola and cello. They struck up the riff from the White Stripes' "Seven Nation Army" as the pitch was rapidly cleared of its coverings and both team photos were taken in front of banks of the international press.

The preliminaries were nearly over but before kick-off there was a sad note to proceedings as players and officials gathered around the centre circle and a minute's applause commemorated the life of José Antonio Reyes, whose death in a car crash had been announced on matchday. The 35-year-old former Spanish international was best known on these shores for his three years at Arsenal, but he began and ended his top-level career at Sevilla and played more than 100 times for final hosts Atlético Madrid when their home was across town at the Vicente Calderón.

The news from the starting line-ups was that Harry Kane was selected to start for Tottenham, 53 days after his injury in the quarter-final against Manchester City, with semi-final hero Lucas Moura dropping to the bench. Harry Winks was passed fit for his first game since that same quarter-final first leg and was selected ahead of Eric Dier and Victor Wanyama in midfield.

For Liverpool, James Milner missed out in midfield, with skipper Jordan Henderson, Fabinho, and Gini Wijnaldum making up the midfield three. Roberto Firmino – absent since limping out of the first leg against Barcelona – would lead the line. The Liverpool end was a sea of red banners, the last pre-match "YNWA" sung with as much gusto as any all season.

The whistle blew and, 22 seconds after kick-off, before the crowd had even had time to settle in their seats, the evening's defining moment had already occurred. There had only been a few exchanges of aerial ping-pong: Virgil van Dijk won a header on halfway, Wiljnaldum touched on to Henderson and the Englishman released Sadio Mané with a first-time ball over the top. As Mané weighed his options on the corner of the box, Moussa Sissoko tracked back and raised his right arm as if to direct Kieran Trippier to show Mané down the line. Mané tried to clip the ball into the centre but it struck Sissoko's chest and outstretched arm – and referee Damir Skomina pointed straight to the penalty spot. VAR confirmed the award.

Mo Salah assumed spot-kick duties and thumped it down the middle as Spurs keeper Hugo Lloris dived to his left. The red half of the stadium erupted; the white half was stunned. Liverpool had a crucial early lead and, after that... well, the kindest thing would be to say that it wasn't exactly a classic.

Perhaps it was the heat, or the magnitude of the occasion, or the fact that carefully laid plans for the early part of the match were – for both sides – ripped up within a few seconds. But the match simply failed to ignite.

Son Heung-Min showed some neat footwork early on but as the ball broke to Sissoko from Joel Matip's tackle, the Frenchman belted it high into the Liverpool fans from 25 yards out.

Liverpool's best outlet was Mané, who was stretching the play and looking to latch on to deliveries from deep. Such a pass from Matip set up an attacking platform with 16 minutes played, from which Liverpool worked the ball to Trent Alexander-Arnold, in space on the right. The full-back took a couple of touches and unleashed a shot that skimmed just past the far post.

Mané also linked with Wijnadum on the left flank and the Dutchman touched a pass back to Andy Robertson. One of his trademarked whipped crosses was well defended by Danny Rose as Mo Salah closed in at the back post.

Liverpool's best effort before the break came from Robertson after a searching pass from Matip set him running towards goal. The Scot's powerful drive was on target but central and Lloris was able to touch it over the bar. From the resultant corner, Salah sent a difficult volley high into the Spurs fans.

It was the start of a brief period of pressure from the Reds, but too often the delivery from corners failed to clear the first defender.

With a couple of minutes to play before half-time, good work by Rose released Dele Alli for a three-on-three break but Alli's pass into Son was loose and easily collected by Alisson. Then, in stoppage time, the usually accurate Eriksen sent a shot wildly off-target from the edge of the area, rather summing up a disjointed 45 minutes.

Early in second half Spurs' Trippier skirted the touchline with a pass to find the run of Son who returned the ball to the advancing full-back. His looping cross found Dele Alli, whose header at the far post was mistimed and cleared. Harry Kane then pulled down a 60-yard pass from Lloris unchallenged and was able to drive into the Liverpool area; but his square ball across evaded Son and ran out for a throw.

Eight minutes into the second period, Wijnaldum clipped a pass into Salah, who was faced up against Jan Vertonghen but the defender blocked the Egyptian's solo effort. However, Salah showed tenacity to win the ball back and it was worked to Andy Robertson, whose cross nearly found Mané – but was collected well by Loris at the feet of the striker.

At the other end, Dele Alli found space in behind from a brilliant pass over the top from Christian Eriksen but his shot was blocked by Trent Alexander-Arnold and tidied to Matip by Jordan Henderson.

Around the hour, Firmino was replaced by Divock Origi and Wijnaldum by James Milner, the latter having a good chance on 68 minutes as Mané strode away from Christian Eriksen. Salah touched the ball into the path of Milner on the edge of the box but the Englishman's left-footed effort slid just wide of the right-hand post with Lloris beaten.

Spurs engineered a dangerous break when Son's flick around the corner was returned by Kane, but Alli's subsequent attempt to bend the ball into the far corner spun harmlessly into Alisson's gloves. Then Alli headed over after a crossfield pass from Kane, found Trippier on the right – but the referee had, anyway, given a foul for a push on Matip.

With 79 minutes played, Tottenham's best chance to take the match further came and went. Son took aim from range and drew a good save to Alisson's right. The ball was worked back by Danny Rose to the feet of Lucas Moura – who had replaced Harry Winks. Could it be Moura again to the rescue with a late goal? No. Alisson was extended again, this time to his left, but the chance was snuffed out.

Four minutes on, a moment of danger as Milner clipped Rose on the edge of – but clearly outside – the area. The free kick was well struck by Eriksen, maybe just going wide or heading for the post, but Alisson applied two firm palms to push it clear. The resultant corner missed everyone in the centre, was flicked goalwards by Moura and Son headed it over from a yard out. The flag went up as Son was offside.

Tottenham had finally raised their game and were pushing hard for an equaliser but, with four minutes of normal time remaining, the Reds found a vital second goal – and breathing space at last.

Andy Robertson curled in a dangerous pass looking for Salah, which was put behind by Danny Rose off his shoulder. Milner's corner was flicked out by Son to Virgil van Dijk, whose shot was blocked by Eric Dier. The ball looped up and Dier tried to head out but another challenge from van Dijk meant it dropped to Joel Matip, who played short to Origi. With one touch to set, the Belgian swept his finish into the far corner.

"Allez, allez, allez" rang out around the stadium as Spurs now attacked with increasing desperation. Danny Rose struck a shot towards Alisson that was saved comfortably, a good effort from Son was tipped wide by the keeper and then Kane shot straight at the Brazilian. Now it was "YNWA" before a chorus of whistles urging the end of the match.

At the end, the substitutes and staff sprinted on to the pitch, while players collapsed to the turf, exhausted by 90 minutes of stifling heat and emotional effort. The stands seethed with celebrating Reds. Liverpool had done it again – for a sixth time, champions of Europe.

TEAMS

TOTTENHAM HOTSPUR

Lloris; Trippier, Alderweireld, Vertonghen, Rose; Winks (Moura 66), Sissoko (Dier 74); Eriksen, Alli (Llorente 81), Son; Kane

LIVERPOOL

Alisson; Alexander-Arnold, Matip, Van Dijk, Robertson; Fabinho (Origi 58), Henderson, Wijnaldum (Milner 62); Salah, Firmino, Mané (Gomez 90)

MATCH FACTS

- With 35.4% possession, Liverpool became the first side to win the Champions League final with less of the ball than the opposition since Inter Milan beat Bayern Munich in 2010.
- Mo Salah's opener was the second-fastest goal in a Champions League final (1 min 48 secs), only behind Paolo Maldini (50 secs) for AC Milan versus Liverpool in 2005.
- Divock Origi scored with all three of his shots in the Champions League this season.

THEY SAID

Tottenham manager Mauricio Pochettino: "[The early penalty] is a circumstance that you cannot manage and it's difficult to prepare [for]. You never believe that you are going to be 1-0 down after one minute. It changed the dynamic emotionally in the game so it was very tough psychologically. But you learn, you live the experience, as Liverpool did last year. I'm so pleased to manage this group of players. But I want to congratulate Liverpool as I think they had a fantastic season."

Jürgen Klopp: "I'm so happy for our boys, I'm so happy for all these [fans] and I'm so happy for my family [who] suffer every year when we go to a final in the last game of the season and we lose. So they deserve it more than anyone as they are so supportive. Did you ever see a team like this, fighting with absolutely no fuel in the tank anymore? And then a goalkeeper who makes difficult things look easy. It'll be the best night of my life."

The celebrations went on. A beaming Steven Gerrard exchanged handshakes with friends in the crowd. Jordan Henderson found his father Brian and the pair embraced, the emotion pouring out of the club captain and his dad.

"It's just very emotional," said Brian. "The tears come. You start shaking. You grab your wife, you grab your daughter-in-law, you grab anybody that's around you... just so, so happy."

Jürgen Klopp hugged every player he could find and Mauricio Pochettino made a point after commiserating with his own players to shake each of Liverpool's by the hand. A classy touch from a fine manager.

Ian Rush brought out the trophy, newly engraved and now with a pair of red ribbons adorning its ears. The players accepted their medals from UEFA president Aleksander Čeferin, with Liverpool owner John W Henry looking on proudly from the podium. And finally – the ultimate moment of celebration. Henderson lifted the pot from its stand, strolled across to his waiting teammates, turned towards them for a brief moment then back to face the crowd. The captain thrust the trophy high above his head in shower of sparks and a blizzard of confetti.

The players went over to join the fans as Queen's "We Are the Champions" rang out from the stadium speakers, the entire Red end singing along. A group led by Fabinho and Roberto Firmino grabbed Klopp and the whole team raised him above their shoulders, giving the manager the bumps to the delight of the supporters, who cheered every lift into the air. The manager then conducted his own set of cheers. These were magical moments for all those lucky enough to get a ticket.

Once back the dressing room, the players danced, sang and posed with the trophy, taking selfies with their medals and delighting in every minute of the experience.

Back in the centre of town, the scenes were no less intense. Flags were waved and scarves were twirled as tens of thousands reacted to the victory.

And back home in Liverpool, fans poured out of the pubs to celebrate in the streets. Wherever Reds fans were in the world, it promised to be a *very* long night.

It was estimated that as many as 100,000 Reds had made the trip to Madrid, and now more than five times as many as that lined the streets of the city for the homecoming trophy parade the following day.

The players flew back from Madrid with their precious cargo in the morning and then a convoy of vehicles – the main team bus at its centre – made its way along Queen's Drive, along Rocky Lane and through West Derby, along Leeds Street and sweeping down to the waterfront to finish at The Strand.

At first it was followed by a small throng, eager to savour every moment, then the crowds built and built along the route. Jürgen Klopp had his legs dangling off the back corner of the main team bus, sipping a beer, smiling and waving to the assembled fans. Some players wore tops with a gold number "6" and "Champions of Europe" written on the back. And soon every vantage point available was being adopted: parents' shoulders, roofs of shops, bus stops – anywhere would do for a glimpse of the returning heroes.

"It's amazing, it's something special," said Virgil van Dijk, as he passed banks of supporters on the kerbside. "You have to really experience it. It's unbelievable what it does to the city and obviously to the club as well. I'm very proud to be sitting on this coach and hopefully we can have more days like this. I think there's still more to come but it's already been past my expectations. I'm just taking everything in and enjoying every bit of it with all of these fans."

Alisson wandered over and gave the Dutchman a beardy peck on the cheek. Divock Origi – a hero in both semi-final and final victories – shook his head in disbelief at the number of fans who had turned out to welcome the team home.

"You don't realise how many people are passionate in this city about the club. I knew it was a lot but this has surprised me," he said, as red ticker-tape flew through the air. "I've scored important goals [before], in World Cup qualifiers and [games] like that. But scoring in a Champions League final is special. It's hard to describe."

Scarves were being waved, songs sung again and red smoke from flares drifted on the breeze. At the front of the bus, Trent Alexander-Arnold hugged the European Cup close. "Just a normal lad from Liverpool," as he noted on social media, "whose dreams came true."

The air was crackling as the Liver Building hove into view, with fans shinning up lampposts, standing on top of traffic lights. Rockets and red smoke flew from one of the towers of the building itself. Thousands upon thousands of people stood on The Strand – 30, 40, 50 deep. Jordan Henderson dangled the Cup precariously off the front of the bus, almost close enough for those below to touch.

Jürgen Klopp gave his final thoughts from the top of the bus, reflecting on how important his and his team's achievement was for the Red half of the city.

"It's so overwhelming what the people are doing," he said. "When you have a direct eye contact and you see how much it means to them that's touching, to be honest. It's brilliant.

You see in their eyes how much it means. It's unbelievable. Crazy."

Then the heroes were gone. The bus edged past the designated end of the route, then sped back to Melwood, and fans dispersed smiling, the sun slowly beginning to set beyond the Mersey. There would be more challenges to face, more mountains to climb, but on this early summer Sunday, the feeling was one only of intense satisfaction. The Reds – unarguably, inescapably – were back. Allez, allez, allez.

AFTERWORD

BY IAN RUSH

When I think back to my time as a player for Liverpool, to win any trophy was welcome. But it was the norm for Liverpool in those glory days. Times change and while I feel this win was long overdue, I also believe it will spur this team to go on and achieve more. They'll have the taste for it now.

Back in the 1970s and '80s, there were no individuals at the club and we played as a team both on and off the pitch under managers who didn't take second place as an option. It wasn't just about the players; it was about the entire club from the management to the staff to the tea ladies. We were a family and everyone played their part.

When people say we now have a team that can be as successful as we were the 1980s, I will agree that the potential is definitely there on the pitch, and because I work as club ambassador I see first-hand how the manager, chairman Peter Moore and all the backroom staff have helped us go from strength to strength over the past couple of seasons.

Jürgen Klopp has now firmly cemented his place on the world stage as one of the best managers in a highly competitive era. As a tactician and man-manager, he is second to none in my opinion; and his aura is infectious.

Liverpool's fan base is the heartbeat of the club's success – the supporters have been incredible this season and they have the power to help the players to achieve more and more.

Most of all, Liverpool FC is back where it belongs – at the top of European football. Players want to play for this club now; Liverpool are a team that most aspire to join. I really believe that the current team can achieve great things and I look forward to being a part of it.

YNWA.

Ian Rush, Liverpool FC ambassador and executive board member

AFTERWORD

BY JORDAN HENDERSON

To all of you Reds. Winning the Champions League against Spurs was a fitting way to end what's been an exhilarating, emotional and hugely successful season for Liverpool Football Club.

It is an enormous honour and a privilege to be captain of this great club. Lifting the trophy in Madrid alongside my team-mates to bring the European Cup back to Anfield for the sixth time was one of the greatest moments of both my life and my career. The memories from not just that night, but the entire journey to get there, will stay with us all forever.

A club of this history and magnitude should be challenging for major honours year in year out, and we hope and believe that this is just the start. We are all hungry for more.

We should look back at our Premier League campaign with great pride too. To have achieved 97 points and to only lose one league game in the entire season was a phenomenal achievement by the team. Of course, we were bitterly disappointed to narrowly miss out on the title by just a single point, but we will use the huge number of positives from the campaign to fuel us for the new season ahead. We will be doing all we can to reward our fans by going one better next season.

There is something uniquely special about our club and the support that you give us at Anfield that is not replicated anywhere else. On behalf of all of the playing squad, I'd like to take this opportunity to thank you, our fans, for always believing in us and supporting us. We are very lucky to have the best fans in the world here at Liverpool, and your support really does make the difference.

I hope you all enjoy your summer break. See you in August.

YNWA.

Jordan Henderson, Liverpool FC captain